The Vacation

A 2026 Michigan Notable Book

The Vacation

A Teenage Migrant Farmworker's Experience
Picking Cherries in Michigan

Robert "Carlos" Fuentes

Illustrated by Kristen Wasil
2025

The Vacation: A Teenage Migrant Farmworker's Experience Picking Cherries in Michigan
by Robert "Carlos" Fuentes
Copyright © 2025 by Robert Fuentes

Published by Robert Carlos Fuentes. For additional information, contact Carlos Fuentes at carlosfuentesmsu@gmail.com.

First edition 2025

ISBN: 979-8-9985029-0-3 (paperback)
ISBN: 979-8-9985029-1-0 (ebook)
ISBN: 979-8-9985029-2-7 (hardcover)

LCCN: 2025909148

Cover design by Julia Bolash. juliabolash@gmail.com

This story is dedicated to the farmers and migrant farmworkers of America. Your relentless labor, often performed without recognition, sustains our nation. The fruits of your toil nourish our tables and enrich our lives. Thank you for your unwavering dedication and your vital role in our communities.

"Living with fear stops us from taking risks,
and if you don't go out on the branch,
you're never going to get the best fruit."
Sarah Parish

TABLE OF CONTENTS

TABLE OF ILLUSTRATIONS

ACKNOWLEDGMENTS

This story would not have been possible without the unwavering support and encouragement of many remarkable individuals. I am deeply grateful to the following people for their invaluable contributions to the creation of this book:

A special thanks to my wife, Beatrice, for her patience with all the papers and materials related to the story that cluttered our home during my writing process.

I also want to express my gratitude to my sons, Noel and Andreas, for their enthusiasm and for motivating me to share my story with the world.

Thank you to Luis Alonzo Garcia for helping me refine and clarify the core message I wanted to convey.

I want to express my gratitude to Bryan Whitledge, who encouraged me from the start and helped ignite my passion for writing my story.

A heartfelt thank you to Eli Fuentes, Ester Ramos, Honda Joe Fuentes, Joe "Decky" Moreno Jr., Abel Rodriguez, Abran Fuentes, and Theodore Larry Esch for their insightful assistance and unwavering support throughout the writing process. A special thanks to Sandy Hinchcliff, whose encouragement inspired me to write this story in the first place. I would like to thank Nora Vasquez-Kowich for the vital information she provided.

I am also grateful to Julius W. Kolaric for sharing the rich history of Leelanau County cherry farmers and allowing me to experience the harvest firsthand in his orchards. Thank you to Marcelino and Leticia Tapia for their warm hospitality each summer during the cherry harvest.

Thanks to Gilberto Varela Martinez for historical information on Tejano music.

A special thank you to Chris Alpers for providing a tour of his workers as they harvested cherries and for his genuine interest in my story.

My sincere thanks to Dr. Rick Paulsen for providing valuable insights that refined my narrative.

Thanks to Julia Bolash for the book cover design. A big thank you to Kristen Wasil for her illustrations.

Thank you to Dr. Ruben Martinez and Rachael Elisa Moreno for reviewing my book.

Finally, I would like to express my appreciation to Julie Taylor at the Michigan State University Libraries for her genuine interest in my book, as well as for her expert guidance and assistance in preparing it for publication.

INTRODUCTION

For generations, the cherry orchards of Leelanau County, Michigan, have depended on the hands of migrant farmworkers. Families traveled north each summer, following the harvest, their labor ensuring that the trees gave up their delicious fruit. These workers, primarily from Texas and Mexico, built a seasonal community among the rows of cherry trees, their presence as much a part of the landscape as the orchards themselves.

Then came the machines. With the arrival of the cherry shaker, the backbreaking tradition of handpicking cherries gave way to mechanized efficiency. In a matter of years, the thousands of workers who had once filled the orchards, their laughter and voices rising with the rustling leaves, were no longer needed. A way of life was disappearing.

CHAPTER ONE

LEADING UP TO CHERRYLAND

MONDAY, 21 JULY 1969

"Bob, please get Junior; we have something to tell you," Mom says as I walk into the house. I find Junior in the garage, working on his bicycle. A few minutes later, Junior and I head to the kitchen, where Mom and Dad sit at the table enjoying coffee and sweet rolls. We wonder what news they have for us. As Dad sips his coffee, he tells us we're going on a vacation to Lake Leelanau, Michigan. I'm surprised because we've never gone on a vacation before. Some kids in our neighborhood take vacations at their family cabins, most located north of Clare, Michigan. He tells us on our vacation, we will camp in a tent, go to the beach, have picnics and barbecues, and enjoy the great outdoors. However, he also tells us we'll spend all day picking cherries from eight to five, Monday through Friday, plus a few hours on Saturday morning. Dad adds that we'll get paid for picking; the more we pick, the more money we can make. Junior is furious when he learns what our "vacation" will be. For him, picking cherries is not a vacation at all. He doesn't want anything to do with it. My perspective is the opposite of Junior's. I'm excited to find out what we're going to do.

All my life, from time to time, I've heard my parents and relatives talk about "la cherry dulce." La cherry dulce means the sweet cherry. When I hear them mention la cherry dulce in conversations, they are always laughing. Even with my limited Spanish, I know they are talking about the fun times and experiences they had picking cherries in Lake Leelanau, Michigan. I am so excited that we're going to "la cherry dulce!"

There are many reasons why I want to go, even if it means picking cherries. It will be fun hanging out with Junior, and since he's had many girlfriends, he can teach me a thing or two.

Another reason I want to go is that I'll be around some other Fuentes relatives I really like and who are already there. One of them is our favorite cousin, Decky, from Archbold, Ohio. He and his family are already up north picking cherries and will be there for two more weeks. Junior and I always stay at Decky's house when we visit our Fuentes relatives in northern Ohio. It's always a blast with Decky. Dad's sister, Aunt Chacha, her husband, Uncle Ruben Acevedo, and their kids—my cousins Raquel, Polaco, Abel, Rebeca, Tonina, and Cheque—will also be there. I look forward to seeing Grandpa and Grandma Fuentes. Mom says they're coming up later in the week. Grandpa will hold Sunday church services at the Ted Esch Farm, as he has done many times in previous years.

I'll have a chance to learn more Spanish. I'll be with relatives who speak Spanish as their first language, and I've always admired their ability to do so. I'm very proud of my Mexican heritage and want to be able to speak Spanish. Hopefully, I'll learn more and won't feel too embarrassed to make mistakes while speaking Spanish in front of others.

I'm excited about all the delicious Mexican food Mom, Grandma, and my aunts will make, as well as their sweet lemon iced tea.

The thought of being in the beautiful Lake Michigan and Lake Leelanau area excites me. You have the majestic Lake Michigan, with its immense beauty and sandy beaches. After every workday, we'll go to Lake Leelanau to swim and have fun.

I want to go because I love cherries. This part of Michigan is full of cherry orchards. I call this area Cherryland; you won't find cherry orchards around Alma. I can never get enough of cherries; here's my chance to eat as many as I want.

I also love being on farms, especially cherry farms. Being around the tractors, barns, open fields, and orchards attracts me.

There's also a chance for new adventures and experiences. I'm excited to break away from the same old routine and try something new. Alma sometimes feels dull, and getting away is always nice.

It'll be a relief to take a break from helping Dad "clean the places." Cleaning the places means assisting Dad with his commercial floor cleaning business. He has business cards that say "Joseph's Janitorial Service 517-463-2967." On the weekends, Junior and I help Dad clean a few churches, several offices, and car dealerships. Some of Dad's friends, Tony Randazzo and Joe Hernandez, will be cleaning while we're away.

How can I say this vacation will be boring? I don't care that I have to pick cherries; I actually enjoy picking cherries. I'm all in!

FRIDAY, 25 JULY 1969

The day before we leave, we are all busy getting everything we need together for our trip to Lake Leelanau. Mom is doing her best to get us kids involved in doing whatever we can to get things ready.

Before I start the chores that Mom and Dad have for me, I walk over to Jim Janesak's house to see if he is already up. Jim is one of my best friends. It's around nine in the morning, and I'm excited to start the day. There is so much to do before we leave tomorrow. The grass is still wet from the evening dew. I hear the cooing of a mourning dove in a tree not far from me, and the sky is full of blue with clouds here and there. It will be another gorgeous and hot July day in Michigan. This is much better than the seven months of endless gray and cold skies we get yearly in Michigan.

On my way to Jim's house, I spot a blackcap bush in the little woods between our house and walk to it. The small woods have several blackcap locations, and I know them all. As I approach the berry bush, I am careful not to disturb the giant yellow spiders with their psychedelic-looking bodies. They make enormous spider webs at night, and I'm always amazed by how many new ones appear in the woods the following morning. I've had nightmares over these dangerous-looking spiders, although I don't know how poisonous they are, if at all. I pick a few berries. The plump blackcaps still have the morning dew on them. In my mouth go the ripe and plump berries. The sweet and savory black juice gushes through my mouth, sending sweet, savory delight to my palate. These berries are one of the highlights of my Michigan summers. Mom introduced me to the joys and benefits of foraging for naturally growing fruits that are found wild in Michigan during the summer.

Over the years, we've had a lot of fun in the woods. We've held army battles, cowboy-and-Indian fights, and played hide-and-seek (even at night). Junior, Jim, and I have camped in the woods several times. We are always careful to watch out for the spiders and their webs. The thought of running into one of these spider webs, especially at night when you can't see them, gives me the chills. We don't want them around since we are always in the woods doing something. They freak us out.

Continuing my walk, I hear our dog, Bruno. He's heading to the backyard to do his daily poop, I guess. On the other side of the street, I see Mr. and Mrs. Burt pulling weeds from their half-acre garden. They have a green thumb. Year after year, their garden produces an abundance of tomatoes, green beans, lettuce, radishes, sweet corn, watermelon, melon, cabbage, carrots, and more. They are too busy to see me, so I don't wave at them. In the background is the constant sound of pneumatic tools ferociously undoing the big tire lug nuts on semi-trucks and trailers from the Alma Tire Service. Once the lug nuts are off, you hear a worker hitting the rim with a sledgehammer to remove the tire. It typically begins at six in the morning and can last until nine at night. We are so used to the sound. This is one of the places we help Dad clean.

As I approach Jim's house, I see his dog, Lucky, inside the screened-in front porch. He spots me walking on the sidewalk and begins to bark loudly. His teeth display a mean and vicious look, even though he knows who I am. I always call him "Lucks to the Booms." Jim's mom, Betty, answers the door, and I greet her with a good morning. She lets Jim know I'm at the door. Facing the stairwell from the living room, Betty yells for Jim. I assume he's in his bedroom upstairs. I prefer to wait for him outside to avoid the stale tobacco air that permeates Jim's house. Betty always has a lit cigarette in her mouth, so the house never gets a chance to air out. You can be inside for only a few minutes and walk out with all your clothes smelling of tobacco smoke.

A few minutes later, Jim joins me outside. Since we live so close, we frequently see each other throughout the day. He's like another brother to Junior and me. I tell him we are going on a vacation. He's surprised and laughs when I say to him that part of the vacation is picking cherries. We decide to bike around the neighborhood after Junior and I mow the lawn.

I head home and see our cat, Quieta Girl, coming out of the woods and onto our west-side lawn. Was she in a romantic mood last night or on the hunt for catching prey? She's a fine huntress. Her specialties are mice and birds. She loves to walk around the yard, parading her latest catch with the dead victim dangling from her tightly closed mouth with a face that says, "Look what I caught!"

To prepare for the vacation, we all have different responsibilities. Mom will be busy buying food at the IGA Supermarket for our trip, preparing meals, washing, cleaning, and packing clothes for Dad, Timmy, and Tito, as well as a hundred other things for our vacation. Sandy will help Mom around the house with whatever she can do. Timmy will be out of the way playing in the sandbox. Tito will also be out of the way as he hangs out with his imaginary friend, Suitcase, and with Chuck Janesak, Tito's best friend and Jim's younger brother. Dad will clean, wash, and wax the truck, top off the fuel tank, check the oil, and ensure all systems are ready. Dad takes pride in having clean, rust-free, and well-maintained vehicles. We've never had a new car, but the cars Dad buys are always reliable and nice-looking. Junior and I are responsible for mowing the lawn and packing our things.

Everything will have to fit in the back of our pickup truck. The pickup has a cap for the back. We'll have to fit in a lot of the food we are going to need, as well as cooking and eating utensils, work clothes and casual clothes, toiletries, a large water container, laundry supplies, bedding, a substantial three-room tent that we are borrowing from the Royal Rangers, Dad's guitar and amplifier, as well as other miscellaneous items, and finally us kids! It will be a tight fit, but it doesn't matter; we're going on a vacation!

After cutting the lawn, packing all my stuff for our trip, and having lunch, I ride my bike to Jim's house to start our bike ride. We ride around the neighborhood, racing down the streets and checking out what's happening. The wind cools us down and provides relief from the July heat. Our bike ride is nothing special. Jim and I don't have to do anything special to have fun; we just enjoy hanging out together. On Eastward Street, we see Crazy Cat with his younger brother and sister in his front yard. Further down, we pass the Benavidez house and see Mrs. Benavidez on the front porch talking to her son, Mundo, in Spanish. We wave. On Grover Avenue, we turn right and ride on Sunset Lane, where we see Mike Covington in his baseball uniform, getting ready to get into a car. We wave at him. He is always playing some sport. He's the best athlete in our neighborhood.

Back on Grover Avenue, we pass by the neighborhood store, Watson's, as we bike southward out of town toward the Cornwell Farm at the city limit. From there, the road is no longer paved. All around us are neatly planted fields of corn, soybeans, and navy beans. We ride just beyond the railroad tracks and then turn back into town.

Coming up to Watson's Store, we turn right and ride on Rosedale Street and pass the Potter home. I think of their son, Wesley Roy Potter, who was recently killed in action in Vietnam. He was only nineteen years old. Since first grade, kids thought she had cooties. We pass by Mrs. Zelinski's house. She was our sixth-grade teacher at Republic School. Shortly beyond, we see Dave Gamboa at his house and say hello. We continue biking down almost every street in our neighborhood: Dean, Pleasant, Elmwood, Linwood, Grove, Eastward, Williamette, and Bostwick. The petroleum smell of Total Refinery hits our nostrils as we bike down Elmwood (the eastern boundary of our neighborhood). It's hard for me to get out of my mind that tomorrow we leave for our "vacation."

Later in the afternoon, I ride my bike to Luis Garcia's house to say goodbye to him. Luis is my other best friend. I remind him that we leave tomorrow for Lake Leelanau to pick cherries for a week and maybe two. He laughs at me and says I'm just going up there for fun and not work. A spurt of laughter erupts in my mind as I think about Dad saying we are going on a vacation. I don't tell Luis my thoughts. He says I have no idea what it is like to do migrant work and to live the migrant life. He tells me it is hard, dirty, thankless, and physically strenuous work. His family is still partly in the migrant farmworker stream. All Mexican American families in our neighborhood were from Texas and came to Michigan as migrant farmworkers. Luis tells me that he and his family have already done two weeks of hoeing at some local fields and will soon be heading up north to pick cherries at a farm on Old Mission Peninsula.

He hurt my feelings because even though my experience won't be like someone who does this work for a living, I will still have an understanding, even if it is brief. I'm grateful that my parents could leave the hard life of migrant farmworkers and find full-time yearly work so that we don't have to follow the crops and constantly move around.

Luis and I have grown up very differently. Luis' family recently moved to our neighborhood from Waco, Texas. In Texas, he grew up in an area where many Mexican Americans speak Spanish and live within their Mexican subculture. I grew up in Michigan and, for the most part, integrated reasonably well into mainstream American culture, where you don't hear much Spanish.

Mom and Dad didn't teach us Spanish when we were growing up. Sometimes, I'm mad, disappointed, and frustrated that I didn't get the opportunity to learn it. I missed out on being involved in and understanding a lot of the conversations that were in Spanish, which I heard growing up. Spanish is spoken every day at Luis' home.

It's nighttime. Junior and I talk to each other while lying in our beds. He has on his transistor radio tuned into the Wolfman Jack Show. Wolfman Jack has a fantastic radio persona, making his program fun and energetic to listen to. We listen to songs like Neil Diamond's "Sweet Caroline," which came out a few months ago in May. This is one of my favorite songs. Another song I like a lot is "Baby I Love You" by Andy Kim. So many great songs are out this summer. We quit talking whenever a song we both like comes on. Already, the Wolfman has played another of our favorite songs, "Sugar Sugar" by the Archies. I look forward to seeing Decky and having dialogues about Wolfman Jack and the current hit music. I can't wait to hear what Decky's favorite songs are.

We can never play rock and roll music in front of Mom and Dad. Dad calls this type of music "devil music." Our church, the Assembly of God, is against rock and roll music. We've heard many sermons on how listening to rock and roll is a sin. We will go to hell for listening to it. This condemnation doesn't stop Junior and me from tuning into rock stations on the radio. We never saw it as a sin. I love the music for its energetic rhythms, beats, and melodies. As a young teenager, my hormones are flying, and I am finally starting to admit that I like girls openly. The music appeals to my teenage experience.

Wolfman Jack just played "Good Morning Star Shine" by Oliver. I've never liked that song. We need to keep the music volume down since Tito, who's ten years old, went to sleep at 9 pm, and it's now 10:30 pm.

How pleasant it will be to escape the constant sounds I hear in our neighborhood. There's the continuous low-level hissing from the steam and petroleum exhaust stacks at Total Refinery, just three blocks from our house. It will be nice to get away from the sound of trains switching boxcars all day and night for the Lobdell Emery factory, located just one block north of us. I look forward to escaping the loud noises from the factory's heavy machine presses that shape metal to create car grills and other products for Ford Motor Company. I also want to avoid the frequent freight trains that pass by, day and night, blowing their horns to give fair and ample warning of their approach to the intersection with main street Alma. I'm so used to these sounds—they don't bother me; however, I look forward to a change.

I will miss Bruno, but I know he'll be in good hands. Joe Hernandez will stay at our house and take care of Bruno. Joe is okay with dogs and gets along with Bruno just fine. Bruno would like to go with us, although he would be in the way of many of our plans. He's Junior's dog. Bruno obeys Junior the most and is a faithful dog.

If Bruno weren't such an alpha dog, there could be a chance of him going with us. Anytime Bruno sees a dog, he runs to the dog and does the usual butt smell ritual. Bruno usually tries to start a fight with another male dog. Bruno, an Australian sheepdog, is so protective of us, especially Junior. Bruno jumped out of our car several times when he saw a dog and started fighting. I guess he thought the dog was threatening us.

Junior is writing a letter to Cindy Pace, his girlfriend. Cindy is at Lost Valley Church Camp, located outside of Gaylord, Michigan, and will be there for the entire week. They started dating almost as soon as the Pace family came to our church. Cindy is the daughter of our new pastor, Thomas Pace, whom we call Brother Pace. Instead of calling Christian adults Mr. and Mrs., we refer to them as brother and sister. Cindy replaced Junior's long-standing girlfriend, Janine Ferguson. I never thought they would break up, as she's been Junior's girlfriend since elementary school.

Junior has had girlfriends since first grade. The first was Franny, and he would go to her house for playdates. In fourth grade, a neighbor girl named Carol Leonard became his girlfriend. Later, Janine and Cindy came along.

Only a few years ago did I publicly admit that I like girls. Debbie Harrison was the first girl I wanted to be my girlfriend. However, I lost out to Jim. She liked Jim more than me. I don't think they did much together. Last year, I liked Marsha Richards. She was in seventh grade. We wrote many notes and held hands, but never kissed.

Because of Junior's experiences with girls, I think he'll be able to teach me a lot about attracting a pretty girl and making her my girlfriend. Maybe we will meet some cute girls on our vacation.

I'll miss Jim while we're gone. We always find something fun to do. In the summertime, we bike around the neighborhood, town, Conservation Park in Alma, or the Alma College campus. We usually get an excellent physical workout. We're always looking for and ready for anything that sounds adventurous, and we always find a way to have fun.

I slow the thought train riding fast in my mind to listen to The Temptations perform their hit song, "Can't Get Next to You." Wolfman is playing a lot of Motown music. It's so driving; not the thing I need right now. I know I should get a good night's sleep to be as fresh and ready as possible for tomorrow.

I think about our cat, Quieta Girl. I know she will be just fine. She comes around to her food and water bowls whenever she is ready to eat or drink. Quieta Girl is a calico cat and our most memorable pet cat. She typically has litters of between four and six kittens each. She's quite the neighborhood lover. Junior and I used to tease her and give her a hard time. Consequently, she didn't trust us. I've asked her for forgiveness, and now we get along just fine.

My mind is fading in and out, and although I love the song that Wolfman is playing, I find myself falling asleep.

SATURDAY, 26 JULY 1969

The day has arrived for us to leave for our vacation! It's another typical July morning in Mid-Michigan, with a blue sky that will gradually become hazy and reach 80 degrees as the day progresses. It promises to be a good day for traveling. Mom tends to be quicker than Dad at getting things moving, which annoys him. Mom is frustrated that Dad isn't moving faster. Even though most of the packing was finished last night, it's still taking us a couple of hours to prepare everything. Bruno can sense that something important is happening and wants to be involved. He's following Junior wherever he goes. There are countless trips from the house to the back of the truck with items for the journey. Junior and I help by moving some of the larger items, like all the bedding gear, towels, bags, suitcases filled with clothes, the tent, lawn chairs, Dad's guitar, and a guitar amplifier. Dad is at the truck, carefully arranging all the items we bring out.

Little by little, and after a few tense moments sprinkled here and there, we are all packed up and ready to go. The back of our 1965 International Harvester light green D-1100 half-ton pickup has everything we need for the trip. The truck looks brand new after Dad waxed it. It will be a reasonably tight fit once Junior, Sandy, Tito, and I arrange ourselves in the back. The cap has windows on the sides and one on the front and back. Timmy will be sitting in the front with Mom and Dad.

Dad and Mom are in the kitchen and give Junior and me each $5.00 to spend on whatever we want. Mom also gives us two quarters to buy penny candies for the kids. Dad and Joe are having coffee and rolls while Dad gives Joe the final instructions on how to clean the places while we are gone. Since Joe will be staying at the house, Dad and Mom tell him everything he needs to know about the house and where things are located.

Within seconds of getting our money, Junior and I jump on our bikes and head out to Shirley and Peters Store at the intersection of Republic and Superior Streets to buy candy and things for our trip. We leave the store with big red hot cinnamon jawbreakers, Baby Ruth, Hershey's, and Maple Bun candy bars, and baseball card packs with bubble gum inside. We buy Tootsie Pops, Squirrels, and Jolly Rancher penny candies for Timmy, Sandy, and Tito.

Later, Junior and I quickly ride to Paul's Pharmacy and pick up the most recent *Superman* and *Thor* action-hero comic books. This will make for some quick and easy reading on the trip. Hopefully, Decky brought his comic books up north. He always has a lot of them. On our way back to the house, we see Jim by the pickup truck checking things out.

It's finally time to go. We say our final goodbyes to Joe and Jim. Everybody begins to climb into the truck. Bruno's tail wags vigorously; he is anxious and feels left out of our plans. Dad is looking cool with his dark sunglasses on. To the side of him is his red plaid thermos filled with piping hot coffee for the journey. We pull out of the driveway that has Dad's 1959 white-colored Chrysler Imperial and the red 1962 Ford Econoline van that Dad uses for his commercial cleaning business.

As Dad backs out of the driveway and drives down Dean Street, Mom taps on the cab window and says she is ready to pray for our safe travels. We all bow our heads and close our eyes. As soon as Dad gets on Republic Street, we are suddenly interrupted by Bruno barking as he runs down the street, chasing us. Dad returns to the house so Junior can jump out and put Bruno inside.

Off we go. What a super feeling it is to leave Alma. Dad drives eastbound on Superior Street while Mom continues her prayer for our journey. Quickly, we pass by Lobdell Emery Manufacturing and leave behind the 24-hour clanking of the machine presses. The sound soon leaves our ears, followed by the loud sounds and smell of Total Refinery.

Shortly after leaving Alma, we pass by Debbie Deline's house. Junior and I attended kindergarten and part of first grade with her and her older sister at Bailey Elementary School. The school is in the country, a mile outside Alma. We still see each other at school.

We pass Shirley Road, where we lived until 1961. Many Mexican American families live here. Mexican Americans in the Alma area call this place La Curva (The Curve). This is what I've always known it as, not by Shirley Road. My friends Paul Ortiz, Lee Fabela, and Henry Vasquez live here. The entire area used to belong to Henry's grandfather, Enrique Vasquez. Enrique is a farmer and is the one who brought Grandpa Fuentes and his family, who lived in Texas, to Michigan to work in his fields. Part of La Curva, where our former house is, was an open space used by migrant farmworkers as a place where they could stay while they worked in the fields.

Grandpa Ramon built our little, unadorned cinder block house at 5748 Shirley Road in the early 1950s for his brother Sisto Ramon. Later, we moved into the tiny house, which became the parsonage for the nearby Spanish Pentecostal Church after we moved out. I just found out that Grandpa Ramon and Uncle Arnulfo Martinez built the church.

We are now on the freeway, heading for Lake Leelanau! We begin to fine-tune our personal spaces in the back of the pickup. Junior is behind the driver's side, just behind the tire by the side window. I'm on the opposite side. Sandy and Tito are in the middle area. Within a minute, we pass Harrison Lake, between Alma and St. Louis. It's a former gravel pit converted to a picnic area and beach. This is where I got baptized last summer. I can still see Brother Pace dipping me in the lake. We pass by Phil Coston's produce market. Mr. Coston is one of our neighbors. We also pass by the Detroiter Mobile Home plant, which has a large parking lot with finished trailer homes.

Since this is a Saturday morning in the summer, many pickup trucks with mounted campers are pulling trailers or boats. There are so many nice-looking cars on the road, too.

Mother Nature has been generous, providing Michigan farmers with an excellent agricultural year. We pass hundreds of fields of corn that appear very healthy. The corn looks very good for this time of year. I love the smell of cornfields in the summer after the sun goes down. The other fields also appear healthy. The bushy green sugar beet plants and soybeans appear full and thriving. The navy bean fields look good, too.

Dad slowly passes an army convoy that is probably heading to Camp Grayling. In the back of the truck, we all wave at the soldiers sitting in the front seats of the military vehicles. They wave back.

Mom taps on the rear window, smiling, to see how we are all doing. We give her a thumbs-up.

I'm trying to get as comfortable as I can. We still have two hours to go before we arrive. A slight smell of exhaust comes into the back, so Junior and I open the side windows. The sound of the engine and truck is slightly loud, but it's okay because I'm excited about being on the road.

The ride is much more enjoyable now that we are around Clare. A billboard just south of Clare that's been there since I can remember reads, "Gateway to the North – Clare, Michigan." I've always believed this to be true. The landscape changes from flat agricultural land to rolling hills draped with forests of hardwood and softwood trees. We begin to see small ponds and small lakes. The soil becomes sandy. The farms disappear and are replaced by forests full of campsites, hiking trails, and other leisure facilities.

Junior and I are excited about all the cool cars we see on the road. This is the decade of muscle cars—fast and sexy. We give a thumbs-up to all the cool cars that pass by, and in return, the drivers usually give us a thumbs-up and a big smile. Junior doesn't like to give his thumbs-up to anything other than a Chrysler, Plymouth, or Dodge; in other words, it has to be Mopar. I'm sure it's because Dad grew us up on Mopar Chrysler vehicles. I'm different. I'm a Mopar fan, but I give a thumbs-up if I see another car I like. For example, I love the Pontiac GTO, especially the 1968 and 1969 models. A few have passed us, and I gave all of them a thumbs-up. So far, we've seen a few Oldsmobile 442s, many Ford Mustangs, Pontiac Firebirds, Chevrolet Malibus, Camaros, Novas, Corvettes, Dodge Chargers, Super Bees, and many other fantastic, fast muscle cars.

As we pass the exit for Wilson State Park near Harrison, Michigan, I immediately think of the time Junior and I went camping there with the Royal Rangers. It was a fun time, but it could have turned into a disaster. I was on my way to the lake when I decided to take a shortcut and started running downhill off the pathway to reach it. I was in a dangerous situation as my speed increased down the steep slope. I couldn't slow down. I was out of control. I ran over bushes and came too close to branches and trees. I thought there was no way to avoid getting a broken leg, a fractured skull, or broken ribs. Panic began to set in. I quickly started saying a prayer for help. I finally regained control as I approached the flat bottom. It was a terrifying experience.

The Royal Ranger program is similar to the Boy Scout program. It's for boys in the Assembly of God Church. Jerry Crawford is the Royal Ranger Commander for our church. He was a sergeant in the US Army and does an excellent job teaching us boys about leadership, discipline, camaraderie, how to live a Christian life, the value of being a good citizen, enjoying the outdoors, camping, camp lore, land navigation using a compass, and much more.

We continue to wave hello to people passing and give thumbs-ups to the cool cars. We don't wave at mean-looking people.

Junior releases a silent, but deadly (SBD) fart. The odor quickly spreads through the enclosed area. I look at him. He looks like he's trying to keep a straight face. He's guilty, and I say it to him. Sandy and Tito are finding it very stinky as well. Junior is laughing and enjoying the little fun he's having on us.

Dad slowly passes a semi-truck. I gaze at the large black tires. I count 42 tires. Dad is taking his time passing it. I don't like being this close to big trucks on the highway.

From a distance, I notice a motorcycle quickly gaining speed toward us. Riding a high-handlebar bike is a tanned male in his mid-twenties with long, silky black hair flowing wildly beneath his helmet. He looks so hip and cool. We wave and give him a thumbs-up as he passes by. In return, he gives us a big, warm, confident smile.

I notice that his motorcycle license plate is from Nicaragua! I'm amazed by how far he has traveled. This adventurous-looking person inspires me with the wild idea of riding a motorcycle from Michigan to the southern tip of South America.

Sandy and Tito are starting to annoy each other. I knew it would happen. At least Timmy isn't in the back; he always finds a way to rile up Tito and Sandy.

Passing to the west of Houghton Lake, I can see slight glimpses of the immense lake. The freeway cuts through a boggy and marshy area that was once part of the lake when it was bigger.

We pass signs for Higgins Lake North and Higgins Lake South state parks. I think of all the people camping at these two popular state parks, and I know many are having fun.

Dad gets off at the rest area south of the Grayling exit for lunch. All of us kids spread out and explore the area. Mom finds a picnic table near the pine tree with the ninety-degree branch. Junior and I go to the tree to inspect it. Mom makes a quick lunch of bologna and cheese sandwiches, Lay's potato chips, Frito-

Lay corn chips, and a pop (soft drink) for us. Dad is enjoying a cup of hot coffee from his mug. After a half-hour stop, we are back on the freeway.

Just south of Grayling, our highway, US-27, merges with I-75. The road becomes much more congested with other vehicles from Detroit, Flint, Saginaw, Midland, and Bay City, and other places.

Dad gets off at the Grayling exit. Grayling has always been a place of interest for Junior and me. As usual, we pass by the American Legion and notice the static display of an F-80 Shooting Star fighter jet, marked by its six 50-caliber machine gun holes in the nose and its large wing tanks. F-80s are warbirds from the Korean Conflict (1950-1953). What combat did this jet participate in? It's been here since my childhood.

Grayling is busy with tourists and military personnel everywhere. People are in canoes on the AuSable River, and the restaurants are full of hungry customers. Junior and I notice the cute, pretty girls standing in line at the ice cream store close to the M-72 westbound turn. We pass canoe and livery stores, as well as the famous Fred Bear Archery Store.

In a few minutes, we come to the intersection for Camp Grayling. Military trucks get off M-72 for Camp Grayling.

Camp Grayling is a Michigan National Guard training facility used by the Army and Air Force National Guard and Reserve units. Summers are busy at Camp Grayling as military personnel are busy during their annual two-week training. National Guard and Reserve soldiers are everywhere in their military vehicles. Dad calls them the playboys. He says they only want to get away from their homes, get away from their wives, and have fun playing army. There are thousands of soldiers and airmen here. We see several convoys coming from or going to Camp Grayling.

Military traffic quickly lessens as we continue westbound for Traverse City.

The drive to Kalkaska is boring, so I nap as best I can. As I close my eyes, I think of how I have been interested in military things since early childhood. I think of all the plastic toy soldiers and toy guns I've had, all the army movies I've seen, and all the Revolutionary War, Civil War, and World War II history books I have read. Memories of playing army in the woods with Jim, Junior, and other boys in our neighborhood come to mind. I wonder what it would be like to be in the military. Would I like it? What would I want to do? Slowly, I doze off into sleep. I wake up as we make the turn for downtown Kalkaska. The town has always looked so boring to me.

Less than 20 miles before we get to Acme, Michigan, the road takes us through the lovely forest and hilly landscapes of the Pere Marquette State Forest. Many signs indicate campgrounds, public access points for fishing, firewood for sale, and other tourist attractions. We pass by signs for Elk and Torch Lakes.

We pass several large flatbed stake trucks, their backs covered with army green canvas. They have Texas license plates, so I presume they are migrant farmworkers from Texas who are here to pick cherries.

A few miles before Acme, I see some roadside stands selling cherries. The cherries look incredibly delicious, and my mouth is watering. I can't wait to go to the orchard, pick as many as I want, and eat them.

We finally make it to the Traverse City area! There are many people here, and the traffic becomes denser. Migrant farmworker stake trucks and cars with Texas plates are sprinkled throughout the thick traffic. It starts at Acme, Michigan, where the M-72 highway bends southwest and joins US-31. This is where the trip begins to get exciting. All of us in the back of the pickup are excited to see all the activity we are approaching. We can now see the sparkling and inviting freshwater of the Grand Traverse Bay East Arm! There are motorboats and sailboats in the water. There are skiers behind motorboats. We pass hotels, motels, and restaurants.

Closer to Traverse City, we pass some gorgeous-looking beachfront houses. Several have pink plastic flamingoes in front. Some houses have concrete statues of short black men in a servant's uniform, holding a lantern at the entrance to their driveways. These cement garden ornament statues are found wherever I've been in Michigan and Ohio. We're all pointing to houses we like.

We pass Traverse City State Park, which is full of campers of all types. People are sitting on lawn chairs around their campsites. Some campers wear bathing suits and hold beach items as they walk to the state park beach on the shore of the lovely Grand Traverse Bay.

We're excited to see all this energy in Traverse City. Our eyes constantly move to take in all the activity around us. Children ride banana bikes in the park; moms walk around with their young children, and some push strollers. The sidewalk is busy with roller skaters, joggers, and walkers. My head turns left and right as I see pretty girls everywhere.

Beyond the state park is the intersection with M-37, which leads to Old Mission Peninsula. This is where my friend Luis Garcia and his family will be this coming week to pick cherries. There's so much traffic at the intersection that we wait for three light changes before we get through. During the wait, I notice a nice-looking convertible with its top down blasting out on its radio "Honky Tonk Woman" by the Rolling Stones. Since there are many cherry orchards on Old Mission Peninsula, there are a lot of migrant farmworker trucks and cars going or coming from the peninsula.

We pass by the Giant Department Store. We have one in Alma. The parking lot is full. Some vehicles have Texas plates.

We pass by Clinch Park and see the miniature city display of Traverse City, along with the marina filled with stylish boats and yachts. The public beach near Clinch Park is crowded with people playing in the water, lounging on the sandy shore, and sunbathing to get their tans. On the opposite side of the park, at a distance, stands the famous ten-story Park Hotel, built in the 1930s.

Dad exits M-72 at the intersection with M-22 heading north. This town is called Greilickville, which is always bustling in the summer. If you continue on M-72, it will lead you to Sleeping Bear Sand Dunes. We've visited the dunes several times over the years. We pass by numerous boat mooring sites and a few restaurants along the west shore of Grand Traverse Bay West Arm. A highlight of the trip is seeing the yacht club. The size of some of these yachts is incredible. I wonder who owns them. What do they do for a living? Where do they live? Where do they sail their yachts?

Several small roadside parks on M-22 are on the shore of the Grand Traverse Bay. All of us in the back are surprised when Dad stops at one of these. Dad and Mom say they want to freshen up and be prepared for our arrival. We all get out and stretch. Dad hangs up a mirror on one of the white birch trees to shave. Close by is his plaid thermos on the picnic table. All of us kids walk down to the small beach. The cool lake water feels so refreshing; however, it's not a good place to swim. The lake floor has too many stones for me to enjoy walking on. However, the place offers a splendid view of the bay. You can see across to Old Mission Peninsula. Junior and I find flat stones and throw them onto the lake's surface, hoping they will skim across the calm water; many do.

Fifteen minutes later, we're back on the road. A few miles before Suttons Bay, we pass by a cherry processing plant and the first farms with cherry orchards. Cherry trees are loaded with dark purple, plump, sweet cherries. Due to the weight of all the cherries, many branches are bent down, and many touch the ground. I see the first migrant farmworker camps farther back and off the highway.

We pass through Suttons Bay, Michigan. It's a small tourist town. Junior and I look at the pretty girls in line at the ice cream shop we pass by. Around a mile north of Suttons Bay is a sign that marks the 45th parallel. At this point, you are the same distance from the North Pole as you are from the Equator.

Leaving Suttons Bay, Dad turns left onto County Road 204, which leads to Lake Leelanau and Leland. The land suddenly becomes hilly, and the road winds. In just a few minutes, we arrive at the outskirts of the village of Lake Leelanau. Dad makes a right turn and continues north on Eagle Highway. We pass several cherry stands along the highway, and barley and corn fields are scattered throughout. The scenery is beautiful as we drive by charming farms with rustic appeal. Some of these farms are nestled against the wooded and sandy hills.

In less than three miles, Dad turns left, westbound on Esch Road. East of Eagle Highway, the road is called Horn Road. The intersection is at the crest of the long hill. The view at the intersection is spectacular. You can see cherry orchards as far as your eyes can see. Three corners of the Eagle Highway and Esch/Horn Road intersection are planted with cherry trees. For the first time on the trip, you know that you are definitely in Cherryland.

Mr. Waterman's house is the second residence on the right side of the road. Dad pulls into the driveway and drives down the long path lined with beautifully fragrant white pine trees. It's a stunning new hexagonal house featuring a spacious veranda on the west side that overlooks Lake Leelanau and Lake Michigan. Dad exits the truck and approaches the house to inform the Waterman family of our arrival and gather any necessary information. He greets Herrick Waterman and his daughter, Anne. Dad has known them both since he was a teenager. Herrick is retired, and Anne is now in charge of operations.

Soon, Dad is back in the pickup, drives westbound down the road, and turns into the next driveway, only a few hundred feet away. Lazy-eyed Susan, daylily, and Queen Anne's lace flowers are everywhere along the road. Slowly, Dad drives down the white gravel stone drive, drawing the attention of a German shepherd dog barking at us. This is our destination: the Waterman Farm. We have arrived!

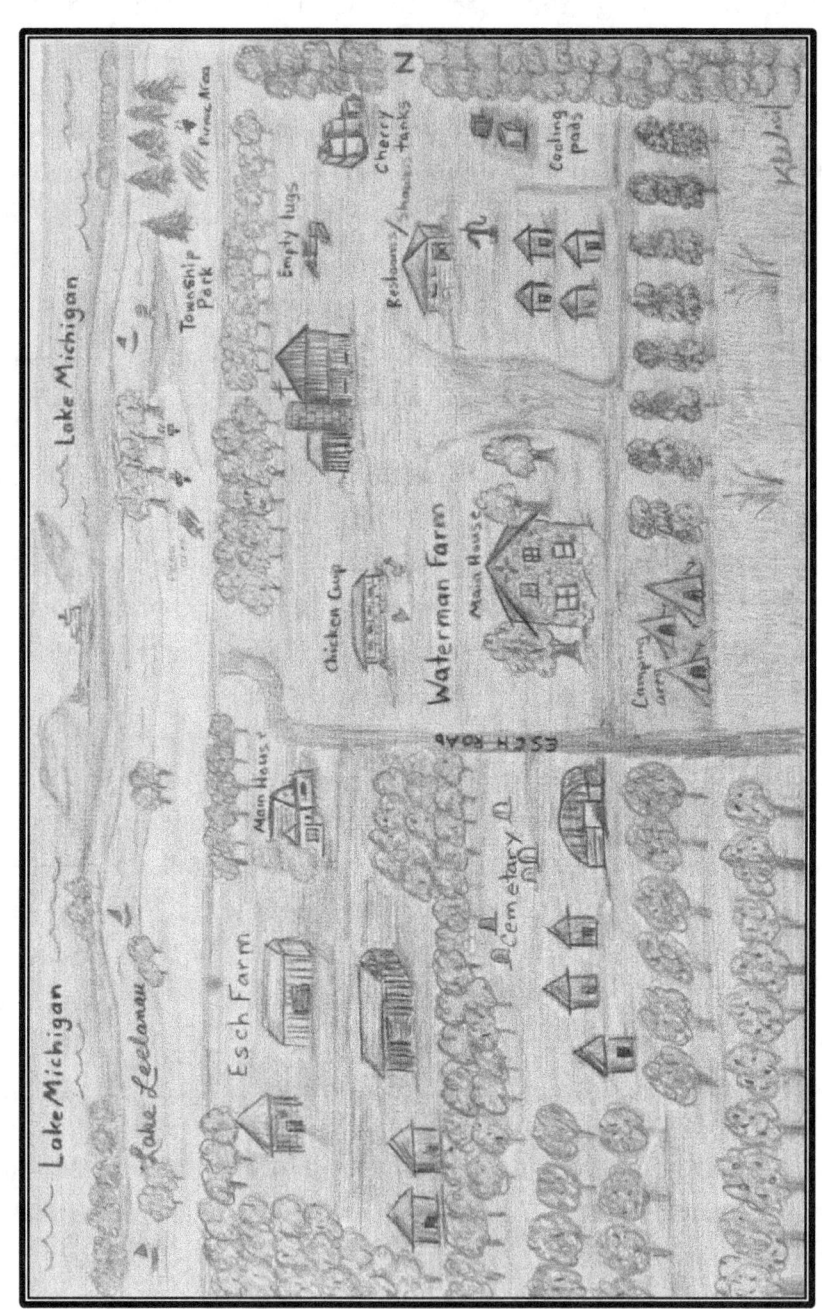

Cherryland Map

22

CHAPTER TWO

CHERRYLAND

SATURDAY, 26 JULY 1969

It's not even 2 pm, and here we are. What a relief to get out of the cramped and noxious-smelling pickup. It feels great to stretch my body. Decky and his family are not around. Someone told Mom and Dad they are in Traverse City shopping and will be back around 4 pm.

The first thing I notice is the pervasive smell of pesticide in the air, which, for some reason, is pleasing to me. I guess it's because it reminds me of coming up here many times as a child. It also reminds me of when Aunt Chacha and her family stop by our house on their way back home after picking cherries for the season. She usually gives us a lug of sweet black cherries and a lug of tart cherries. They always smell of pesticide.

Since I was around four years old, I've loved farms, and it feels fantastic to be back on one. I love the smell of them, the farm equipment and tractors, the old wood barns built from the late 1800s to the 1930s, the planted fields, the orchards, and the animals.

Junior and I hear a truck approaching on the road. Since we have a few minutes before we need to do anything, we walk to the side of the road and see a stake truck with a load of cherries. We refer to stake trucks and semi-trucks as "hawny trucks." We call them hawny trucks because of their engines' loud, powerful sound. We want the driver to honk his horn. With our forearms bent upwards at 90 degrees and our upper arms parallel to the ground, we move our arms up and down with clenched fists. As most kids know, this is the gesture for the driver to honk his horn. The driver smiles at us and honks his horn several times. Junior and I grin at each other and walk back to the pickup.

It doesn't take long for us to notice the mosquitoes. They are everywhere. Everyone puts on Off mosquito repellent. I love the smell of it. I spray it all over my body so these pests won't bother me.

It's time to unpack and start setting up what I call "camp." After the long ride here, I look forward to getting my body moving. Dad chose a spot to put up the tent. It's around 30 feet off the road and on the side of the driveway. Dad chose this spot for the small thicket of trees and bushes that provides us some privacy from the rest of the farm. Dad drives the truck to our tent site. Junior and I find a picnic table on the farm grounds and carry it to our campsite. It's a bit heavy, but it will be helpful at our tent site.

The tent setup goes smoothly because we laid out all the pieces. Tito and Timmy help out. At first, I thought they would only be in the way, but as it turns out, they're okay workers, considering their young age. They bring us whatever we need. They are happy to be a part of putting it up.   We place the tent above the ground tarp that is over sandy, soft ground, and drive the stakes in. Next, we work on putting up vertical and horizontal supports. After the tent is up, we make final adjustments by tightening the ropes.

Junior and I bring in sleeping bags, sheets, blankets, pillows, a blow-up mattress (for Mom and Dad), food items, clothes, and countless other little things. The tent has one large area with two side rooms. Mom and Sandy are inside the tent, ready to set up.

Meanwhile, Dad sips his coffee and works on getting the Coleman gas lantern up and ready at the picnic table.

After Junior and I bring everything to the tent, we head off to fill the Igloo five-gallon water jug. The communal water pump is close to the big barn. We take turns pumping. The water is cold. I drink the refreshing well water from my cupped hand and splash water on my head and face. The black military boots

Uncle Dan Ramon (Mom's brother) gave me are getting splashed, but it doesn't bother me because I'm ready for adventure! Close by are a few ladies washing clothes outside with an electric wringer washer. Mom had one.

Seeing the wringer washer immediately made me think of the day Junior and I decided to play with Mom's washer in the backyard. It was a beautiful summer day, and Mom was inside the house. I was no older than five because we still lived at La Curva. Sandy was in the backyard. Mom had a load of dirty clothes in the washer. Junior and I wanted to see what the rollers on the washing machine would do to Sandy's arm. We put Sandy's arm between the drying rollers as they were rolling. She burst out with screams and cries of shock and pain. Junior and I got scared. Luckily, the rollers stopped moving, but her arm was stuck. We didn't know how to get her arm out. We tried to calm her down, but she kept on crying because of fright and pain. I felt terrible for what we had done. Soon, Mom appears. She is furious at Junior and me. As she scolds us, she gently moves the rollers to remove Sandy's arm. After more scolding, she demands that we apologize to Sandy and says she will tell Dad what we did, and she did. We got a hot and hard spanking from Dad with his leather "Mr. Lee" belt. Even the memory of that spanking brings shivers to my body.

As we fill the water jug, I notice the cherry orchards north of us and only 100 yards away. I wonder if we will pick in this part of the orchard. I can't wait to put some cherries in my mouth.

We fill the Igloo to the top. It's not fun hauling five gallons of water back to the campsite. We pass some children playing. All of them are speaking Spanish. Because of the weight of the water jug, we take a couple of short breaks before arriving at the campsite. Mom thanks us for the water. The campsite is now ready for us to use. There is nothing else Junior and I need to do. We are free at last!

Junior and I waste no time heading out to the orchard to eat all the cherries we desire. I scan the trees around me and choose one of the loaded branches filled with big, juicy black cherries. Into my mouth, they go after a quick brushing off of pesticide. The white powdered pesticide has a sulfur-like smell. The scent reminds me of the flares that railroad workers use when switching trains. Once in a while, Jim, Junior, and I go to the railroad tracks near our house and pick up half-used ones. I like the smell.

I'm in heaven with these cherries. They are so tasty. I start by putting one cherry in my mouth, but soon begin to put three or four at a time. They are so addictive. I can't get enough. I see two big, plump cherries attached and pick them; occasionally, I find cherries like this. I think they bring good luck. I show Junior, and he's somewhat impressed; he's seen them before. He finds a tree and quickly begins to devour the delectable delights. I am overwhelmed by all the cherries that are around me. You can walk for miles and still walk through cherry orchards belonging to different farmers. I pick two more handfuls of cherries to eat later.

Now that our bellies are full and our craving for cherries has been satisfied, we head back to the farm. We spot the pickup belonging to Decky's family, which means Decky is back at the farm! Junior and I quicken our pace as we make our way back to see Decky.

Slightly sweaty and with hands dirty and sticky from the dark purple cherry juice, we shake hands with Decky. He is just as excited to see us as we are to see him. I know we will have a great time with Decky; we always do. Now, we have a week to hang out with him. I tell Decky I'll meet him shortly because I need to wash my hands and the cherries at the pump. I then drop off the cherries and leave them on the picnic table to enjoy later.

Junior and I walk to the building where Decky and his family are staying. Inside the building are Uncle Joe and Aunt Maruca Moreno, Decky's parents. Aunt

Maruca is Dad's twin sister. Her real name is Mary, but we've always called her Aunt Maruca. All of Decky's siblings are there too. Cousin Ester is the oldest at 16 years old. Ana is 13, and Marti is 12. Mom, Dad, and all my siblings are also there. The atmosphere is filled with laughter and animated conversation. I politely greet everyone as I walk in. Mom informs us that dinner will be ready in a couple of hours. We then quickly leave with Decky.

Since this is the first time we kids have stayed at the Waterman Farm, we ask Decky to show us around the farm. Decky's friend, Jaime Gamboa from McAllen, Texas, quickly joins us. The Gamboa family stays in the same building as the Morenos, but in a different housing unit. Jaime is my age.

Decky and Jaime start by taking us to the big wood barn. The barn has three levels: the main floor, the hay loft, and the lower floor. The main floor has an entrance on the north side. It has two enormous wooden doors on a track. The doors are open. A few sparrows fly around inside the barn. It's enormous and has a lot of vacant open space inside. Inside the barn, to the left of the doors, is a pile of cherry-picking harnesses, pails, and orchard ladders. Also on the left are a couple of enclosed rooms. To the side of the rooms is a counter with shelves above and cabinets below. There are bags of unopened pesticides and some that are open on the floor.

Walking on the thick wood planks on the main floor, I quickly pay attention to the cream-colored orchard model Case tractor. The aerodynamic shape of its fenders and skirts protects the driver, the tractor's cab, and engine parts while going through the orchards. This type of protection is mainly needed when the farmer is spraying or pruning the orchards. Sitting on the tractor, my eyes wander around the dashboard, throttle, clutch, choke, brakes, PTO, the sleek lines, and all the other knobs and accessories around me. I'm in love.

At the back of the spacious main floor, there is a pesticide sprayer that connects to a tractor. Dried residue on the sprayer gives off a strong pesticide odor. On the northwest side of the barn's main floor, there are a few rooms. One is filled with unused single metal beds covered in cobwebs and dust. Adjacent to this is a stack of mattresses for the beds. On the south side of the main floor, several living quarters for families are separated by thick green canvas curtains.

The hayloft above us is about a third the size of the main floor. The wooden ladder doesn't look very inviting to climb. We decide not to go up. I rarely turn down a chance to explore a hayloft, but climbing it doesn't look too safe.

We exit the main entrance and walk outside to get to the opposite side of the barn, where the lower floor is located on the south side. Part of the floor is in the ground. The entrance is similar to the main entrance on the north side. A plaque on the side of the entrance says "1928," the year the barn was built. A car with Ohio plates is parked nearby. Some families stay on the lower floor, so we don't go in. The Rodriguez family, from Archbold, Ohio, is staying here. Moises Rodriguez sees us and meets up with us. Decky introduces Junior and me to Moises. He is 14 years old.

On the northeast side, outside the barn, is a tractor with a flatbed trailer hitched to the back. Jumping on the trailer, I notice the cherry juice stains on the floor from the crushed cherries that never made it to market. I can smell that sulfur smell again. I climb up and sit in the cushiony seat of the new John Deere tractor. It feels so good to sit on it.

Near the southeast side of the barn sits an empty chicken coop. A glance inside sparks the idea of turning it into a clubhouse. We see a lot of potential, but the space needs a thorough cleaning. The chicken coop is constructed from fieldstone and measures around sixteen feet by twelve feet with a height of nine feet. There are windows at the top of the walls on all four sides. The west and east walls feature wooden nesting structures for chickens to lay eggs. The coop doesn't seem to have been used recently. We all agree to return later to clean it up and hang out inside.

As soon as we exit the chicken coop, Tito spots us and announces it's time to eat. Walking to Decky's for supper, I notice how many cars are parked at the farm. I realize that many more people are staying here than I previously thought— around 100, I would say. Children are jump roping, kicking balls, running, and skipping; one child cries, while another rides a bike in the driveway. A little boy in a full diaper enjoys a bottle of milk. There are chubby kids with tan skin, skinny ones, pretty ones, and some that others might consider ugly. They all contribute to the lively atmosphere. The smell of tortillas wafts through the air, making me even hungrier.

Dinner is at Decky's living quarters. All of us kids in the Moreno and Fuentes families are taking shifts to eat supper. Even though it's hot inside, I don't mind because the Mexican food smells so inviting. I sit on a cherry lug because all the chairs are being used by those eating.

I look around Decky's home away from home. The building is made of cinder blocks and was constructed in the 1940s. It contains four separate living quarters for farmworkers. The inside looks similar to the Esch Farm places we've stayed at. Above the clean concrete floor, a bare light hangs from the ceiling. A fan on a stand rotates warm air around the room, spreading the pleasing smell of kerosine fuel exhaust and freshly made flour tortillas.

The kitchen area is well-stocked. It has a wooden counter. On the counter sits a metal pan filled with items to be washed, including a cutting board, dishes, and utensils used for preparing beans, rice, chicken, and salsa. There are also dirty glasses and silverware. The "molcajete" (a mortar and pestle made of volcanic rock used to make salsa and guacamole) is beside the pan. Every Mexican American family I know has one of these. An empty pan sits nearby. I assume it will be filled with water to rinse the dishes. Also on the counter is a two-burner kerosene stove. On one burner, a pot of water is beginning to boil, likely for washing dishes. The other burner holds a "comal" (a hot plate used to make tortillas) with a flour tortilla that's almost ready to be taken off. The tortilla has burnt spots, just how I like them.

On a shelf are jalapeños, tomatoes, onions, cumin seeds, cilantro, Morton salt, pepper, Clabber Girl baking powder, and cans of tomato paste. A small open cupboard contains a can of Crisco shortening, a large can of Maxwell House coffee, a five-pound bag of Pioneer sugar, a ten-pound sack of flour, a bag of lemons, and a box of Lipton tea bags. A silver metallic tortilla press hangs on the wall, primarily used for making corn tortillas. We have one back home. Below, on the floor, sits a burlap bag of rice and another bag of pinto beans. Nearby, a large aluminum container holds water, with a metal spoon hooked on the side. Hanging from a nail on the wall is a rope of garlic.

A clothesline in one corner of the room has secadores (dish towels) and bath towels drying. Nearby are a mop and bucket, a bottle of Pine-Sol cleaner, a broom, and a dustpan. A large box of Tide laundry detergent sits near a wooden and metal washboard, along with several piles of sorted dirty clothes that will soon be washed. The piles of dirty clothing smell faintly of pesticide.

A thick army green canvas separates the sleeping area from the other part of the dimly lit room. Inside are bunk beds for Decky and his sisters and a small bed for Aunt Maruca and Uncle Joe. Each family member's belongings are on or near the beds where they sleep.

As we sit at the table before eating, Mom insists that we each take a scripture card from the small wooden container labeled "Pan de Vida" (Bread of Life) in the center of the dining table. Each card, measuring half an inch by three inches, features a verse from the Holy Bible. We typically select one before dinner and read the verse on it. Since the cards are in Spanish, Decky reads Junior's and my cards and translates them into English. We also have both the English and Spanish versions at home.

Now it's our time to eat. Decky, Junior, and I pray and pass around the freshly made flour tortillas, Mexican rice, refried beans, chicken, and salsa. Decky drinks his favorite pop – Coca-Cola – while Junior and I have cherry-flavored Kool-Aid. The food is so delicious. The aromas and flavors of Mexican food make me proud of my culture. The salsa made of garlic, cumin, onion, and jalapeno is spicy and makes the exterior of my nose sweat, just the way I like my salsa! We're enjoying the food and consequently not talking much. Occasionally, I look at the tortilla I'm eating and notice the different figures it makes after I tear off a piece to eat. I see a wolf, a bear, and later a monster. I usually do this when I eat tortillas. It's fun and creative.

With their aprons on, Mom and Aunt Maruca are busy in the kitchen. They talk and laugh a lot. Mom rolls out tortilla masa (dough) balls and puts them on the comal. Aunt Maruca cleans up the kitchen. She wipes the sweat off her brow. I notice her tender and warm eyes. She is one of my favorite aunts. Mom hands us freshly made tortillas off the comal. I can't stop eating these tortillas. I would love to eat more, but my belly is full. After eating, we thank Mom and Aunt Maruca for the excellent meal.

Decky gives us a close look at their new 1968 Ford Ranger F100 pickup. It has a 360 V8 engine with a three-speed manual on the column. The interior and exterior are a medium blue color. It's a ½ ton with an eight-foot bed. The pickup is fantastic; it's among the best-looking pickups I've ever seen. Decky opens the hood and shows us the clean engine and compartment. Jumping into the cab, I breathe in the pleasing smell of the new vehicle. Decky turns on the truck. He quickly tries to find a good station on the AM/FM radio.

Suddenly, I see Ana and Marti walking with a stunning-looking girl. She is gorgeous! Decky and Junior are still talking, but my mind is focused on what I just saw. My heart jumps, and I feel nervous. I ask Decky who the girl is with Ana and Marti. Decky replies, "That's Jaime's younger sister Lety. Why? Do you like her?" The tempo of the vacation just kicked into high gear. My mind is set on meeting her.

After listening to a couple more songs, Ana, Marti, and Lety return, and I notice Lety's long, silky, shiny, dark brown hair. Her soft hair ends in the middle of her back. Her smile captivates me. The smile makes me wonder if her heart is as pretty as she looks. A girl, to me, is not pretty unless she has a caring heart. Ana and Marti wave at us. Lety looks our way. She is smiling and looking right into my eyes! The girls turn the corner and disappear from my sight. My mind tries to process what I have just seen. I'm jolted out of my mesmerized state when I hear Decky ask us if we want a ride in the truck. Junior and I eagerly say yes. Quickly, I run to let Mom know our plan.

"Where do you want to go?" Decky asks. "To the beach!" replies Junior. Sugar Sugar by the Archies is coming through strong on the radio. Decky makes a right turn onto Esch Road and speeds toward the beach. The farms and orchards are whizzing by. I'm not feeling safe. I glance at the speedometer. Decky accelerates to 70 miles per hour. We're coming up to a long curve in the road. He slows it down, but not enough for comfort. At the end of the road, he turns right for the beach. He makes the engine show its strength as he accelerates, going through the gears quickly and making the tires peel out. I'm scared. I ask him to slow down. Dreadful thoughts of a possible accident run through my tense mind. He's a daredevil. With a big, confident grin, he replies, "I've got it all under control. What are you, a pussy?" When we get to the beach, Decky spins the truck around, making donuts in the spacious white stone parking lot.

After several donut turns, we return to the road heading north on County Road 641. Decky, of course, peels out and leaves black marks on the road. I don't mind the peeling out or the donuts; the speed at which he drives terrifies me. He turns right onto Alpers Road, heading east. We zoom by well-kept farms, orchards, and fields. How many times will my life pass by me in my mind? This is the part of my cousin that I don't like. He's too risky at times. The song "96 Tears" by Question

Mark and the Mysterians is playing on the radio. We all love this song. The group is from Bay City and Saginaw, Michigan. At the intersection with Eagle Highway, he turns right to head back to the farm. The view is incredible! There are thousands of cherry trees lined up in orchards. The beauty of the orchards takes my mind off the mental discomfort I'm feeling riding with Decky. Soon, we reach the intersection with Esch Road. Decky makes a right turn. A minute later, we're at the entrance to the farm. I'm so relieved to get out of the pickup. I thank God that nothing terrible happened to us.

After the scary ride, Decky goes around the camp to let the guys our age know they should come to help clean up the chicken coop if they want to hang out. Jaime and Moises come along with a couple of other guys who don't speak much English. We quickly clean up as much as we can to make it tidy and comfortable. Chicken feathers and dried droppings are scattered about on the floor, along with dried insect carcasses. I run back to the tent to get our broom and dustpan. Jaime and Moises gather a bunch of cherry lugs that we'll use for our chairs. Junior and I work together to remove all the cobwebs and spiders with the broom. We then focus on the windows and the floor. The place is full of dust, so we open the doors and windows to air out the chicken coop.

After the cleaning, we sit on the cherry lugs and relax. We discuss baseball, girls, comic books, big-time wrestling, our favorite action heroes, and more. I think I'm going to enjoy hanging out with Jaime and Moises. Although I feel a little nervous around all these new guys, I like this clubhouse idea. It's fun. I didn't think we'd have a clubhouse during our vacation.

It's been a long day. There's a cool nip in the air. The sky is dark and clear, revealing sparkling stars that look like diamonds. Most people are either in bed or indoors at this time. However, some men are gathered at the back of the farm, sitting in lawn chairs, drinking beer, and chatting.

Reflecting on the day as usual, I feel full of life and hope for the possibilities that await us during our vacation. I reflect on how good it is to take risks in overcoming my shyness. I hate being shy. I feel anxious about meeting all these new guys. I know I lose out on opportunities because I'm shy. I think of Lety, this beautiful girl that I would love to get to know. I ask God to give me the courage and the chance to meet her. I'm happy because I'm with my family and we are doing something different together. I'm joyful because I'm around relatives that I care about. I'm happy to be immersed in my Mexican culture. There is so much I want to know about my culture. Knowing my heritage and culture means knowing myself better. I look one more time at the stars, and with a smile, I thank God for this beautiful time here.

Quietly as I can, I unzip the tent zipper and crawl into my space. The wind blows mildly as I lie in my sleeping bag, looking at the tent ceiling. Smiling, I see Lety in my mind's eye. I think that every time I hear Sugar Sugar by the Archies, I will think of Lety. Knowing I should shut out all thoughts, I do my best to drift into that land of sleep.

SUNDAY, 27 JULY 1969

The birds are the first living creatures to wake up, or at least it seems that way. Their sounds start with their movements, followed by chirps, whistles, trills, coos, and screeches. Lying in my sleeping bag, I hear the birds that have nests in the little crop of trees and bushes by our tent. I know I have a couple more hours before I have to get up. The stone below the tent in my sleeping area is annoying. This small stone is where my ankles are when I'm sleeping. The pleasant thoughts of Lety overcome the physical discomfort of this obnoxious stone.

Mom is the first one to get up. She acts as my clock. I know I have at least an hour to get up.

It's time to get up. We have one and a half hours before church starts at the Esch Farm. There's a lot to do before we go. Sitting down at the picnic table to have breakfast, Mom tells me that Grandpa and Grandma Fuentes arrived last night and are staying at the Esch Farm for the weekend as they always do during the cherry harvest. Grandpa works full-time at Scott Port-a-fold in Archbold and can only come on weekends. Mom also reminds me that Sunday School starts at 9:30, followed by the main service.

Shortly after breakfast, I start getting ready for church and head to the bathroom. From a distance, I scan the area ahead of me to see if anybody I know is entering or leaving the female bathroom. I don't want any girls I know around when I use the bathroom. It's because I'm very private about these things. For example, when walking to the bathroom, and if I need it, I hide the roll of toilet paper I carry. I don't want people to know what I'm going to do.

The bathroom looks relatively new and is made of cinder block. The layout is identical for both the female and male sides. There are two sinks with mirrors above them, two toilet stalls, and two shower stalls. A cinder block wall divides the male and female restrooms, although it doesn't reach the ceiling. Upon entering the bathroom, I take in the pleasing aromas of pine boards and plywood. The floor is relatively clean. There's minimal graffiti written in ink or marker on the four-foot by eight-foot plywood panels. In black marker, I notice, "Jose Morelos de Mercedes, Texas 1966." Another reads, "Fabian y Lucinda 1968," with a heart. Another one with initials inside a heart is "ZA + CR." A few others say, "Dios le bendiga, Dios es amor" (God bless you, God is love) and "Elvia, te quiero mucho" (Elvia, I love you a lot).

Because of the bathroom's design, you can hear almost everything on the female side. I don't want anyone I know to find out what I'm doing, and I also don't want to overhear what the girls are up to, especially if Lety or one of my female cousins is using the toilet.

This bathroom is much better than the outhouses we've used in previous years at the Esch Farm. I was always cautious when using these outhouses because of the wolf spiders often found in the corners. They look so terrifying. I typically lined the wooden seat with toilet paper and wouldn't sit for long, worrying there might be a spider underneath the seat ready to bite my butt.

As I sit on the toilet, a couple of daddy longlegs spiders crawl slowly across the concrete floor in front of me. I'm not bothered; I know they don't bite. I've held many in my hands before.

I take a fast shower. The well water is cold and uncomfortable initially, but I get used to it within minutes. After taking a shower, I feel much more awake.

Back at the tent, I put on my black trousers and a light blue long-sleeve shirt. I put the black clip-on tie in my pocket; I will put it on at the last minute before church. Reluctantly, I moisten my hair and apply Brylcreem from the tube. This is a hair styling product specifically designed for men. Dad insists that we use it. Junior and I hate the stuff. It's not what teens use these days. It marks you as old-fashioned. Dad's generation uses it. The male movie stars in the old black-and-white movies used it too. I wouldn't say I like the smell of it either. I also think the oily substance attracts dust and dirt. There's no sense complaining.

The last thing Junior and I do is shine our shoes. We go to an open area carrying our shoes and a can of Amway "Shoe Spray." The label says, "High Gloss Formula - No buffing required." "Once over lightly for a durable, lasting shine!" The stuff is very toxic, and the smell can be overwhelming. Dad and Mom started selling Amway a couple of years ago. Amway sells thousands of products. We never run out of Amway Shoe Spray. I hold my breath and spray my shoes so as not to breathe in the overwhelming fumes. The smell resembles Tester's glue, the type Junior, Decky, and I use for gluing our plastic model cars. Walking back to the tent, we drop off the shoe polish and tell Mom we are walking with Decky to the Esch Farm for church.

It's a short half-mile walk to the Esch Farm. The three of us are fully awake and ready to seize the day. I see an aluminum beer can on the shoulder of the road, slightly hidden by tall weeds, and kick it onto the road. We take turns kicking it until it is too flat and of no use to us. We then amuse ourselves by throwing stones to the sides of the road and throwing them downhill and into the weeds on both sides. It's an easy downhill walk. We pass the Michell Farm on the opposite side of the Waterman Farm. I don't see much activity there, but I wonder if any pretty girls are there. I try to keep my black high-top leather shoes clean, so I only walk on the road. Both sides of Esch Road have cherry orchards. The majority of the orchards are planted with varieties of sweet cherries. We pass by the small East Leland Cemetery. Many former cherry farmers and family members are buried here: Esch, Kahrs, Alpers, Spinniken, and the Waterman families. Others buried here are among the first White people to settle in this area.

There's a lot of activity taking place at the Esch Farm. From a distance, I see Dad and Uncle Joe in the west barn on the main floor, where the service will occur. They are tuning their guitars and getting them ready for the service.

Junior, Decky, and I explore the big red barn across from where the service will be. We walk up the inclined, wide drive that leads to the main entrance. On the left side, walking in (north side), are several living quarters, portioned off from the main floor by a large green army canvas. The canvas provides some privacy for the families staying in the living quarters. Similar to the Waterman barn, there is a hallway on the other side of the canvas with three doors that open to separate living quarters. Aunt Chacha and Uncle Ruben Acevedo are staying in one of these quarters. We scope out the entire barn. The main floor is a vast open space. We are quickly drawn to the tire swing hanging from a support beam. We all take a few swings before exploring the rest of the barn. I love barns, especially old wooden ones like this one. What would an old barn be in Michigan without bird nests made by pigeons, sparrows, and barn swallows? Hundreds of old and new cobwebs are in the corners, high and low, here and there.

I hear the musicians in the other barn playing their guitars and accordion. They are playing short pieces of songs that may be sung during the morning service. After each short song, they check their instruments to see if they are still in tune and make the necessary adjustments.

I figure it's almost time for the service to start. The musicians are done practicing church music, and Dad is playing a secular instrumental song that he loves. I hum along as they play. I've never asked Dad what the song's name is.

A few minutes later, we make our way across the drive to the church service site. People are shuffling in as the musicians start playing again. All the adults are holding big black Holy Bibles and songbooks. Some of the women and girls have tambourines. There are parents with their children. Everyone has a smile on their face and greets each other with handshakes and hugs. The children look immaculate in their church clothes and with their hair in place.

 Grandpa greets everyone at the entrance in his gray suit, white shirt, and slim dark tie. I get in line and say hello to Grandpa. He greets me with his usual firm handshake and a big smile. Grandpa has held church services at the Esch Farm since 1946, when he first came to Lake Leelanau to pick cherries with his family.

Everyone finds a place to sit on one of the benches made of thick wood planks. There is only one pew in the front where Grandma and some other ladies sit. I walk over to Grandma and greet her. Grandma is wearing a purple paisley pattern dress below her ankles and a pair of beige nylons with thick black lines on the back of each leg. She always wears this type of stocking. She gives me a warm smile and says good morning in Spanish. I've never heard her speak any English. The congregation faces outward toward the driveway and the big barn on the other side of the drive. It's held on the main floor where farm implements are stored when the harvest is over. Everybody is in their best, clean clothes, only worn for church. Mom is greeting many people. She knows many of them from past summers picking cherries when she and Dad were teenagers. Dad,

Uncle Joe Moreno, and one of the Rodriguez brothers are playing guitars. Cousin Abel Acevedo is playing accordion. He was never a churchgoer, but I heard he had recently become a Christian. That aside, he is a fantastic accordion player. I never knew he could play until now.

I put on my clip-on tie as I enter the church. It feels tight and uncomfortable.

Grandpa Fuentes cues the musicians and the song leader that it's time to start. The musicians finish playing the stanza they are playing and end the song. Grandpa greets everyone and asks everyone to stand for the opening prayer. All attention is on him except for the baby, who is crying. The mother is doing her best to calm the baby. After the prayer and a few announcements, we are excused to attend our Sunday School class. There are classes for adults, teens, and preteens. The adult class is held in the west barn, where we are now.

As we walk to our teen class, my mind wanders, and I start thinking about some articles in the large box of family photos and memorabilia we have back home. In the box is an announcement in the *Leelanau Enterprise and Tribune* for August 2, 1951. It talks about Grandpa Fuentes conducting church services at the Theodore Esch Orchard in East Leland, Michigan, and how he is here to harvest another year's cherry crop. It goes on to say that the public is invited to attend the services on Sunday, from 10 am to 12 noon, and Sunday night, from 8 pm to 10 pm. The announcement mentions the service is entirely in Spanish and that the hymns are accompanied by a trumpet, two guitars, and an accordion. It continues with how appreciative Grandpa and the congregation are of the business people and cherry growers who donated comfortable benches for them for the church services. The article finishes with a big thank you from Grandpa and the congregation to the Traverse City clubs sponsoring the fiesta planned to take place at the Traverse City fairgrounds.

I think about another article in our photo box from the *Leelanau Enterprise and Tribune*, August 10, 1950, "Mexican Cherry Pickers Attend Church Under the

Trees in East Leland Orchard." The article's writer attended the service and wrote about Grandpa Fuentes conducting church services in Spanish on the front lawn of Theodore Esch's home. It says Theodore Esch would give everyone a hearty welcome at the beginning of the Sunday morning service. The article talks about the 100 cherry pickers in Grandpa's congregation who are picking in East Leland and Lake Leelanau orchards, all the way south to John Grant's farm and north to Herrick Waterman's orchard. It mentions the congregation clapping to the rousing music created by the guitar players, accordion player, and Grandpa's sermon, "Where will you find yourself at the end of the road?" The writer adds that the guitar players are students at the Latin American Bible Institute in Fort Worth, Texas, picking cherries to save up for their tuition and room and board. It talks about how Grandpa could be any country preacher you would find in any Michigan church. The article ends by stating that Grandpa and his congregation will return south later in the week, some to Ohio to pick tomatoes, some to Indiana to work in the beet fields, and some back to their homes in Texas.

Decky, Junior, and I follow our Sunday school teacher. The class is held outside under the shade of some large trees. There is a slight warm breeze in the air. The class is in Spanish. Once everyone is settled, our teacher, Estela Acevedo, begins a small icebreaker and asks everyone to introduce themselves by stating their name and where they are from. I freeze with fear for two reasons. First, I don't like talking in front of groups. Secondly, at times, when I'm around Mexican Americans or Mexicans I don't know, I experience a fear that people will misjudge me for my inability to speak Spanish and perceive that I am trying to be a White person and that I am not proud of my Mexican heritage. I've experienced this many times. This, of course, is so far from the truth. I've always had a desire to know my culture and to be able to speak Spanish. Mom and Dad didn't teach us Spanish because they were told by school officials that children suffer educationally if they speak more than one language. So here I am, unable to speak Spanish. I snap out of this fear and think that whoever is judging me is wrong for not acting in the love and spirit of God, especially if we are in church on a Sunday. Decky ends up helping Junior and me a lot by interpreting for us when needed. Decky is fluent in Spanish. His dad is from Guadalajara, Mexico, and they visit relatives there frequently.

Estela asks the class to take turns reading the Bible scriptures that relate to her lesson. She gives us ample time to look up the scriptures and asks if everyone is ready. Junior and I follow Decky's index finger as he shows us which word is being read. I want to learn how to read Spanish. Maybe someday, Mom can teach me by reading the Spanish Bible when we get home. Since I don't know the specifics of what is being said, my mind wanders a lot. I still love being in this class, though, because I'm around other Pentecostal Mexican Christians my age.

Moises and Abel Rodriguez are in the class with us. Their older brother, Miseal, is the pastor of the Asamblea de Dios (Assembly of God) Church in Archbold. We always pass by the church when we visit our relatives in Ohio. Once in a while, we attend a service at their church. For this reason, I've always referred to their church as the Rodriguez Church.

There are 12 children in the Rodriguez family, with seven being males. They are very handsome and resemble the iconic image of a Mexican man. I can envision them in Mariachi outfits or as charros (Mexican cowboys dressed in elaborate traditional dress). Abel looks like he could be Elvis Presley's brother with his long, thick sideburns. Some of his brothers have thick, well-groomed mustaches.

The Perez girls from Fayette, Ohio, are also in our class: Gloria, Regina, Rosy, Mary, and Stella. They are stunning. They attend the Rodriguez church. The Perez family is staying in the Waterman barn on the lower floor. Moi's older brother Abel and Regina like each other.

My mind goes back and forth, from hearing what the teacher is saying to wandering. I ask Decky occasionally what's being said to get the gist of the

41

lesson. The sounds of cars going by and the birds in the trees around us make it hard to hear Estela. Then, of course, I can't get Lety out of my mind.

I think of my home church, the Assembly of God, in St. Louis, Michigan. It's a small church with around 90 people, primarily White. Our church includes two individuals from Hungary, Brother and Sister Zoter, and one person from Romania, Sister Kocsis. Their English is quite limited. Along with our family, several other Mexican American families also attend. Overall, I enjoy going to our church. Still, I often wish we attended a Spanish-speaking church where I could be surrounded by other Mexican Americans and immersed in my Mexican culture.

Being around Mexican guys and girls my age in this Sunday School class feels so good. My church hardly has any teenagers. A few pretty girls are sitting near me. It would be nice to have a girlfriend who shares the same faith as I do. Apart from church, there's not even one Mexican American girl at junior high school with whom I have any chemistry.

My mind wanders off the class lesson and begins thinking about random things. I'm curious about what Jim Janesak is doing back home. I can't wait to tell Jim about the fun stuff I'm doing here. I wonder if Luis is already on the other side of the Grand Traverse Bay on Old Mission Peninsula. I notice the pretty geraniums in the window boxes of the Esch home and the peony flowers in the well-kept lawn. I see the growth of cedar trees to the side of the house by the garage, where Grandpa and Grandma stay whenever they are around. Overhead, a couple of jets pass high in the sky, leaving their white, cloudy trails behind. I've never flown before, but I would love to one day.

Fifty minutes later, the class is over. We have ten minutes until the church service begins.

We slowly walk back to the west barn, where the morning worship service will be held and where the adult class takes place. I wish I could take off my clip-on tie and unbutton the top button of my shirt. I feel like I have a noose around my neck.

The musicians are playing songs as everyone walks in. Decky, Junior, and I find a place to sit in the back. It's an excellent view of everyone. A few of the ladies are swinging their plastic, made in Japan, fold-up fans back and forth to eke out some coolness in the air around them. Some ladies have tambourines to the side of their Bibles and purses, ready to use once the service begins.

Although there is no script for Pentecostal services, the service usually follows this order: welcome, prayer, songs, offering, testimonies, prayer requests from the congregation, prayer for the requests, the sermon, the altar call, personal prayer at the altar, and the dismissal.

Grandpa gives the musicians a subtle cue that he is ready to start. Soon, the music ends. Grandpa's commanding and seasoned preacher's voice asks everyone to stand for the opening prayer. His rich, resonant voice comes out clearly through his microphone. His prayer is powerful and puts us in the right frame of mind for the service. I adjust my thoughts and get into a state of reverence toward God. There are many amens and hallelujahs from adults around me throughout Grandpa's prayer.

After the prayer and while standing, Grandpa motions for the song leader to come to the pulpit and lead the songs. The song leader directs us to turn to page 30 for those singing from the "*Himnos de Gloria*" (*Hymns of Glory*) songbook. Others brought the other widely used songbook, which you will find at Spanish Pentecostal churches, called "Rayos *de Esperanza*" (*Rays of Hope*). Mom and Dad have both songbooks. A few seconds later, the musicians give us the introduction to "Hay Poder" (There is Power). "Hay Poder" is also titled "Quieres Ser Salvo" (Do You Want to Be Saved?). We sing this song at our church. It's one of my favorites and a popular song sung at Pentecostal churches. The tambourines are in full swing while many of us clap our hands. The musicians are doing a fantastic job of playing these beautiful songs I grew up with and love to hear.

 Pentecostals are not afraid to show strong emotions throughout the service. The music begins to take over my feelings. A couple of tears run down my face; I don't want Decky or Junior to see me with tears. I fight hard to hold back any more tears, and it works. My tears are not of sorrow but of joy in hearing the song sung in Spanish and seeing other people freely express their emotions as they worship. I always get this way at Grandpa's church in Wauseon, Ohio. Decky and Junior don't get as emotional as I do at services.

At Grandpa's church in Ohio, I usually go forward to the altar during the altar call. With the music playing in the background and the congregation still singing, I'd be crying at the altar, acknowledging my sin and asking for forgiveness or guidance from God with whatever problems I had at the time.

We continue standing for the next song, "Dulce Comunion" (Sweet Communion). Pentecostals are used to standing up a lot when singing in church. From young to old, most people sing from their hearts and with gusto. A couple are off-tune, but many good singers drown them out. A couple of older Mexican American ladies are playing tambourines. Their blubbery upper arms are in full swing and in rhythm with their tambourines. Some of the young girls are playing their tambourines as well. They have excellent rhythm and offer much to the music quality. Even though I don't know the Spanish lyrics of the songs, I know them in English. I follow along in the songbook with Decky, who points out where we are. The music portion of the service is my favorite part. I can only clap my hands and sing the few phrases I know of these songs. I do it with enthusiasm; I love being here.

The song leader announces that it's time to collect the offering. The musicians play as people come forward to place money in the small basket situated on the altar before the pulpit.

We sing a couple more songs, and the song leader asks if anyone would like to give a testimony about what God has done for them. Several people get up and share their personal stories about how God has helped them deal with some particular problem they experienced. During the testimonies, the congregation gives many hallelujahs.

After a couple more songs, Grandpa takes over the service. I glance at Junior and see him drawing a 1969 Dodge Charger racing car on a piece of paper. Grandpa begins his sermon. It's on salvation. This is the main sermon at many Pentecostal churches at a Sunday morning service. He weaves together various verses from the Bible that relate to the salvation blueprint. Everyone with a Bible opens it and follows Grandpa through his sermon; the only Bible version used is the "Reina Valera." The version is similar to the King James Version.

I look around to see where everybody is. Grandma is sitting in the pew. It's much better for her back than sitting on a wooden plank with no back support. Mom sits in the front with Tito, Timmy, and Sandy. Aunt Maruca and Aunt Chacha are sitting close together. Uncle Ruben, Aunt Chacha's husband, is not here. I never see him in church, even though he grew up in a Pentecostal family. His family is from the Rio Grande Valley of Texas, also known as the Valley. He's known the Fuentes family since the mid-1940s.

As time passes, some children, including Tito and Timmy, become fidgety. Mom gives them a couple of warnings not to act up, or she will tell Dad.

I don't know precisely what Grandpa is saying as he preaches in Spanish, but I do know the basic salvation outline and scriptures in the Bible related to salvation.

Growing up Pentecostal, I've heard hundreds of salvation sermons. I can't blame the young ones for getting fidgety; they are just being how kids are.

Similar to Sunday School, my mind begins to wander in different directions. I'm thinking about the woods at the south end of the Esch Farm. In previous years, Decky, Junior, and I have walked back to the woods but were too scared to go far inside. We were scared of a possible bear or other wild and ferocious animal that could injure or kill us. We've always thought the woods to be haunted. We'd get the jitters. We thought there might be a ghost or something else scary. I think the main reason for us being scared was that it would start getting dark by the time we were able to explore this distant part of the farm; there was always something else we were doing. When we finished picking cherries and going to the lake to clean up and eat, there would be minimal time to explore the woods. In short, the fear of the dark and being somewhere we didn't know much about kept us away.

I remember a previous year when we stayed at the Esch Farm to pick cherries. We stayed in one of the barns. One night, Sandy needed to use the outhouse to pee. The outhouse was just outside the barn, and Mom took her there. Sandy was about four years old. Next to the outhouse, there was an albino skunk. Sandy thought it looked so pretty and said to Mom, "Look, Mommy, it's a pretty kitty cat!" Mom was terrified when she saw the skunk and immediately ran back to the barn to call Dad. Junior and I heard the commotion and wondered what was happening. We followed Dad to find out. Sandy finished her business in the outhouse while Dad shooed the skunk away to prevent it from spraying them. Junior and I were amazed to see an albino skunk and followed it from a distance for a little while.

My mind returns to the service when I hear loud amens and hallelujahs. It's been over an hour since the service started. Grandpa is beginning the altar call and inviting anybody who wants to accept Jesus as their savior to come forward. We're standing with our heads bowed and eyes closed. The musicians are

46

playing the song "En La Cruz" (At the Cross). Grandpa prays that the Holy Spirit will convict and soften the hearts of those thinking of coming forward to accept Jesus Christ as their savior. He also prays for those who have left the faith but want to return to God. Some adults are praying for those who might want to come forward to the altar. Grandpa continues to speak more softly to those thinking of coming forward. Mom has her eyes closed, and with tears, she is praying. Nobody comes forward for salvation.

Grandpa then opens the altar to those who have something they would like to pray for. Many people come forward. Grandpa asks some older Christian men and women to help him pray for those who have come to the altar. He asks each person their prayer request before he and the other Christian men and women who have come up to help him begin to pray. Grandpa has a small vial of olive oil. He puts a dab on his index finger and presses his finger on the forehead of the person being prayed for. The other helpers join Grandpa by placing their hands on the person's shoulders. The arms of all those who have gone forward for prayer go up. Many have tears flowing down their cheeks. Many shouts of joy are kindled by the hope of God's answer to their specific prayer/s. The church barn is filled with spiritual energy. Grandpa and the helpers go down the line and pray for everyone at the altar this way. Meanwhile, the congregation prays, sings, claps, and plays tambourines. One by one, the people who went forward return to their seats.

Grandpa ends the service. He encourages everyone to stay strong in their faith and closes the service with a prayer. The musicians continue to play as the congregation shuffles out. I take off my tie and unbutton the top button of my shirt. Hallelujah, I can breathe! I see so many cheerful faces. People begin conversing with each other. Mom, being Mom, is talking with as many people as she can. She is so friendly and warm, and people love her. Dad and the other musicians don't want to stop playing. He's in his element when he has a guitar in his lap. The people who attended the service look happy and are now spiritually fed and ready for the day and week. The children are so glad the service is over, so they can continue being kids and move around. Little by little, the place clears out as families leave the barn.

Mom, Dad, and other relatives plan what we will do after church. It's decided that every family will make food for all to share back at the Waterman Farm. There are also plans for a softball game after the meal.

Junior, Decky, cousins Abel and Polaco, and I decide to walk back to the Waterman Farm. Walking toward the road, we notice a porcupine in a cherry tree on the other side. We quickly move toward the tree to get a better look at it. I've never seen one up close. I'm excited to see one. I fear their sharp quills and don't want to disturb them to the point where they release some of them on us. To my horror, Polaco and Abel immediately pick up stones and begin to stone the defenseless creature. I didn't think anybody had plans to kill the animal. I'm asking them politely not to do it. They laugh at me and continue to stone the poor animal. Since being nice didn't do anything to change their minds, I yell at them to stop. Nothing changes their actions. The porcupine moves slowly and gasps for air. A minute later, it falls from the tree. I'm full of disgust. It didn't screech or howl, but I could see the pain in its agonized face. Eventually, the porcupine died. What kind of person would do such a mean act, especially after a church service? I feel sad for the animal and think about how cruel my cousins are. The stoning of the porcupine put me in an unhappy state of mind. This outrageous and cruel act was the only thing on my mind as we walked up the steep incline back to the Waterman Farm.

I can't wait to get out of these dress clothes and shoes and put on my jeans and T-shirt. I'm so hungry, too, and the thought of the stoning of the porcupine still lingers in my mind.

I'm determined to find out who this Lety is. Does she have a boyfriend? Is she friendly? Would she be interested in me? I have so many questions in my mind. I need to figure out how I can meet her. The best way is to ask Marti or Ana, since they always hang out with Lety. By chance, I see them sitting at one of the farm picnic tables. They are making necklaces out of gum wrappers. They see me chewing gum and ask if I have any gum wrappers. I pull out the wrappers in my pocket and offer them a piece of Wrigley's Doublemint chewing gum. I always have a pack in my right front pocket. Without hesitation, I ask them about Lety. "Why do you want to know about her?" asks Ana. "Do you like her?" With a slight blush, I tell them I think she is beautiful and that I'd like to meet her. Both cousins giggle and find it amusing. They tell me that Lety is 13 years old, lives in McAllen, Texas, doesn't have a boyfriend, and is friendly and fun. Hope floods my inner core with possibilities with Lety! I ask Ana and Marti to introduce me to Lety. Ana gives me difficulty by being coy about whether she will help me. She loves playing the hard-to-get role. Finally, they agree to help me.

While walking around the farm, I notice several guys washing and waxing their cars. Decky tells me who the owners are. All the guys live near Archbold, Ohio. Chayo Lerma owns a 1964 maroon Nova with a 327 cubic-inch engine and a four-speed on the floor. Richard Perez has a 1966 turquoise-blue Chevrolet Chevelle. Beto Jaramillo has a 1968 white Plymouth Road Runner with a black vinyl top. Every car is fantastic. Decky tells me that occasionally, they drag race off Eagle Highway.

The softball game I heard about after church starts around 3 pm. I don't know who planned it. Maybe Dad came up with the plan. He loves softball. He made sure we brought the bats, balls, and softball mittens. Anybody can play, but that only applies to guys.

My stomach churns with those nervous butterflies; I don't like this feeling. I get this way whenever I have to play a group sport. I'm not a good athlete. I usually get picked last for a team. I'm incredibly nervous because I'm presuming Lety will watch the game on the sidelines. I don't think this is a good way to impress her. I know Decky and Junior will be playing, so I must. I know it will be a good challenge for me. I don't want to be dominated by the fear of making a fool of myself in front of Lety and others. I want to have fun.

A few minutes before the game starts, I see Lety walking our way with Marti and Ana. I also see all the pretty Perez girls sitting on lawn chairs on the side of the ball field. There are so many cute girls here!

Two captains are chosen. They're taking turns deciding who they want on their team. As expected, I am one of the last to be selected. All the other players appear motivated and eager to show off their athletic prowess. Not me. I feel very nervous. The team captain asks each of us to share our softball skill levels. Based on that, he places me between two good players. I quickly find out that there are many good players. This heightens my already disturbed nervous system. The worst thing I want to happen is to strike out every time I bat. I'm also not a good thrower or catcher. God, please help me. I don't want to let my team down. I'm afraid that in no time, the players will know how bad I am.

Play ball! It's game time. Before I know it, I'm up on deck warming up and swinging the bat. My adrenaline is flowing. The batter hits a ball to right field and gets to second base. I'm feeling the pressure.

"Strike one! Strike two! Strike three! I'm out. I'm only consoled by the fact that the pitcher is outstanding. I'm not the only one who is striking out. I'm getting a vibe from my teammates that they don't have a lot of faith in me to help win the game.

The next batter hits the ball to outer field. Cheers erupt from our fans. In comes our player from second base. The batter gets to third base. I'm excited that we have some good players on my team and a chance of winning the game. Our next player is Abel Rodriguez. He hits a home run! The fans and team let out a roar of excitement. The following two players hit fly balls and are out. Off to the field we go.

The spectators are alive and cheer for their chosen team. I constantly look furtively at Lety to see how engaged she is in watching the game. She appears more interested in talking with the girls than in the game. I feel a slight sense of relief. Maybe she won't notice too much about how bad I am.

I'm finding out who the good players are. The Rodriguez brothers are good players. Our opponents have many good players, too. Dad, Junior, and Decky are good players. Jaime is not bad; better than I am.

Our captain places me in the right field, where only a few batters hit. I'm happy to be here. I don't want a lot of action my way. Whenever the ball does come my way, the first and second base players run to my area to try to get the ball. I'm feeling embarrassed, but what can I do?

After our opponents hit a few runs, we're back at bat. When it's my turn to bat again, I nervously move up to home plate and position myself. Dad yells out to me I'm batting on the wrong side of home plate. He says that since I'm right-handed, I should be on the left side of the plate. I never knew this, and consequently, I never batted from the left. Other players agree with Dad. I'm feeling the added pressure of learning how to stand and where to place my hands in front of everybody. But that pressure quickly dissipates when, to my delight, I hit the ball and make it to first base. Luckily, the hitters after me are good. With their hits, I make it to home plate! At least I have helped the team by counting as a run.

At the end of the six-inning game, our team wins. Now I can relax. I hope we don't have another game during our vacation. One of the good things about the game was getting to know Jaime Gamboa and Moises Rodriguez better. But the best thing about the game was that Lety smiled at me! I forget how many times I looked at her during the game.

We go back to the barn to spend more time exploring. In one of the enclosed rooms, we come across a military chest. Stenciled in white paint on the olive green military chest is "Smith, Conway, USMC, Major," followed by his military identification number. These are the chests that U.S. Marines receive to store their personal items in. I love anything military, so I'm immediately intrigued by what we have encountered. I wonder what is inside the chest. This Major Smith must be a tough and courageous man if he is in the Marines. I wonder if he is still in the military and where he is today.

A plan has been made to go to Lake Leelanau town for ice cream! Decky will drive their pickup. Summers are not complete without ice cream.

In the distance, I see Marti, Ana, and Lety playing with Hula Hoops and having fun. I'm impressed with how good they are. Once they see me, they stop playing with the Hula Hoops and walk my way. Adrenaline rushes through my body, making me feel like I will crumble. Am I really going to meet this gorgeous creature? Dear God, please help me out. I don't want to make a fool of myself. All three girls are smiling. Their long, dark brown, silky hair gently flows in the wind as they walk my way. Ana begins the introduction, "Lety, this is my cousin Bob." I look directly into Lety's eyes with a big smile as Ana says this. Lety responds with a perky, "Hi Bob, nice to meet you. So, you are from Michigan. I think it would be cool to live here. I like the weather, the lakes, and the green forests. Michigan looks like a fun place to live." I respond, "Do you like snow?" Lety replies, "I've never seen snow, but I'd like to make a snowman." Lety asks me if I've ever been to Texas. I reply that I have not, but I would love to go. I'm enjoying her bubbly and energetic personality. She's very animated as she speaks. I'm enjoying and somewhat mesmerized by her pretty hands as she gestures while talking. Her contagious smile makes it easy for me to smile in return. I'm feeling much more at ease. I'm happy that she's not the timid type of person. If so, I would feel uncomfortable asking her all the questions. I'd also be wondering why she was quiet. Is it because she finds me boring, or doesn't like me? Reading Ana and Marti's body language, I can tell they want to do something other than listen to Lety and me talk.

To have more time around Lety, I tell Ana and Marti that I know how to make bracelets and necklaces out of dandelion stalks and that I can show them how to make them. They are interested! I gather several dandelion stalks and show them how to do it. They are impressed. Lety is impressed, too, and likes how they look. We give each other lovely big smiles as I tell her it was nice meeting her.

As we depart, my mind reels with the excitement of meeting Lety. I feel so nervous, with all this adrenaline flowing through my body.

Shortly afterward, we are ready to head to Lake Leelanau for ice cream. It will be even more fun now that Lety is going with us! I have another chance to be around her. Decky and Junior climb into the truck cab. I notice the pickup cap was taken off the back. I get in the back of the pickup with Lety, Ana, and Marti. The girls wear jean shorts, with pretty T-shirts and purses draped across their shoulders. As they climb into the back, I can smell the feminine fragrances of their shampooed hair. They have lip gloss on and look fabulous. I smile on the outside and tremble on the inside. Here's my chance to get to know her; I don't want to blow it.

I move to the cab's rear and hold onto the metal cab as I stand up. I quickly find out how hot the metal is. Thankfully, I have a napkin in my pocket and use it as a barrier for my hands to grip the cab. The girls squat and brace onto the sides of the pickup. Our hair is blowing around as Decky picks up speed. The hot air turns into cool, refreshing air as it hits our faces. A huge smile is on my face. I look back at the girls. They're enjoying themselves and laughing. Lety and I smile at each other. I can't wait to talk with her at the ice cream shop.

Even though it's a short trip to the shop, I'm nervous because of how Decky drives. This fun excursion could quickly end in tragedy. I take my mind off this scary thought and focus on the fun the girls are having with each other.

At the end of Eagle Highway, Decky makes a right turn that takes us into the village of Lake Leelanau. Just beyond the bridge that takes us over the narrow part of Lake Leelanau is NJ's, the store with the ice cream shop inside. NJ's has been here as long as I can remember. It's hard for Decky to find a parking space.

The store is bustling with customers. This is the closest store to buy basic groceries and the only place in town to get ice cream. We jump out of the pickup and fast-walk to the store to get in line for ice cream. Entering the store, we are instantly hit by the chilly air-conditioned air. As I walk to the ice cream line, the wooden plank floor creaks below me. The store is full of tourists, locals, and farm workers buying things; some are in line for ice cream. I order a chocolate/vanilla twist cone. As I wait for my order, I notice some of the items being sold in the store are targeted towards farmworkers, such as magazines in Spanish, Virgin de Guadalupe candles, tortilla presses, washboards, manteca (lard), garlic ropes, and other things related to Mexican culture.

Once everyone has their ice cream, we walk back into the hot July sun. The ice cream tastes so good. I'm having fun hanging out with Junior and Decky, but my mind is also on the girls: Lety, Ana, and Marti. I join them for a while. Lety's nonverbal language shows me she is happy to have me around. I don't stay too long because I can tell that Ana wants to hang out with girls. Lety and I exchange warm, electrifying smiles. I wish we could spend hours together, but we must be back within the hour to get ready for church. A feeling that Lety and I connected burns brightly in my mind.

I suggest a walk to the woods before the evening church service at the Esch Farm to Decky and Junior. We get the clearance from Mom, but we must promise to be at church on time. We agree. Junior and I start getting ready by putting

Brylcreem in our hair, changing clothes, and slipping into our newly glazed dress shoes. The shoes look perfect, but I can't have much fun in them. We bring light jackets, knowing the air will be cooler later in the evening.

Walking down the hill to the Esch Farm, just like this morning on the way to church, I find another aluminum beer can that the three of us kick as we walk to pass the time. After several kicks, it's beyond any use to us. Decky finds another one to kick until it, too, becomes useless. In the far background, we see Lake Leelanau; slightly beyond that, we can see one of Michigan's inner seas, Lake Michigan. The cemetery is quiet and is so well-maintained. We talk about how scary this peaceful cemetery might be when we walk back after the church service, and when it's dark out. Overhead, several vultures fly effortlessly high in the sky, occasionally flapping their wings. Their excellent vision is focused on road kill or other tasty, putrid, and spoiled meat delights. How nice it would be to be able to fly like them. Much farther above are the contrails of large jets flying east to west. We arrive in less than ten minutes.

Entering the first gravel drive entrance, I see a crop of cedar trees and quickly run to one to snip off a piece of a fern. I smash it with my fingernails to get the smell of the cedar. I bring my cupped hand with the cedar pieces to my nose and inhale the pleasing aroma.

People of various ages are outside engaging in different activities. Tejano music is playing from the speakers of a parked car. The singer performs a Mexican yell in the song. I love it! I'm actually practicing mine when no one is around. Decky says it's a song by Little Joe and the Latinaires. Children are everywhere playing. Cousin Cheque has a baby bottle in his mouth. Knowing we don't have much time, we go to the big barn on the east side and take a few turns swinging on the truck tire swing. The sun is coming through the barn's tall, vertical wood planks. The fairly new green and yellow orchard model John Deere tractor is outside the barn with a metal floor flatbed trailer. I jump on the trailer and smash some cherries that didn't reach the processing plant. The trailer is covered with a dry, sticky mixture of cherry juice and gritty sand. The trailer also has skirts to cover the tires for safety reasons. I get off the trailer and sit on the tractor seat. John Deere tractors are my favorite. For a minute, I think of growing up at "La Curva." One of our neighbors, the Luis Arizola family, had a small farm and a new Ford medium-size blue and white tractor with power steering. Hermano Luis (Brother Luis) gave Junior and me a ride several times. I would sit in his lap, and Junior would stand on the side between the big black tire and the seat. We would take turns doing this.

Our attention then focuses on checking out the Esch stake truck. Among other things, Ted Esch uses his hawny truck to take the picked cherries to the Sutton's Bay cherry processing plant. It's a 1958 Chevrolet two-ton flatbed light brown colored stake truck. It has four tires in the back, with one axle and a two-speed transmission, offering six to eight speeds. The front has four headlamps. It's a nice-looking truck. The three of us jump up on the back of the truck. Like the trailer, many cherries are smashed on the wooden flatbed floor. As usual, we all take turns sitting in the driver's seat. The cab sits high, offering a commanding view of my surroundings.

We pass by more hawny trucks belonging to some of the farmworkers here. Most of them have white and black truck plates from Texas that say "Lone Star State," although there are a few with dark black and white colored license plates with "69 Ohio" on the bottom. The trucks that belong to the Catholic families have small statues of La Virgen de Guadalupe, Mexico's Virgin Mother of Jesus, attached to the dashboard. Many people have a Saint Christopher medallion necklace hanging on the rearview mirror. The trucks are spotless and well-maintained. They look so impressive. Some trucks still have thick olive green canvas covering the truck bed. Every time I smell green canvas, it reminds me of these trucks.

We continue our walk.   We pass several clotheslines laden with many work clothes that will soon be taken off, folded, and used for tomorrow's workday and throughout the upcoming week. A beautiful 1957 turquoise Chevrolet Bel Air is parked by one of the barns with Texas plates. Many Mexicans I know refer to this as the Mexican car. We love the car's style. A mother is bathing her two-year-old child in a galvanized steel tub, known as a "bandeja." The poor child is crying and shivering as the mother's hands quickly move about the child's body with a washcloth (toallita) soaked with soap from the bar of Ivory Soap she is using.

Cousins Tonina and Rebeca are waving at us, and a memory of them quickly comes to me. It was a sunny summer afternoon in July. We still lived at La Curva. I was three or four years old. Aunt Chacha, Uncle Ruben Acevedo, and their five children were visiting us. They were coming from Ohio to pick cherries in Lake Leelanau. Dad planned a ball game that took place in our backyard. All the males played. I was the youngest boy playing. I was so nervous when it was my time to bat. I hit the ball but ran to third base instead of first base. Everyone was laughing at me. Dad got so mad at me that he told me to go to my room and stay in my bed. I left the game, running away, feeling embarrassed, angry, and with tears streaming down my face. I went to my bedroom, climbed into my baby crib, and continued to cry huge tears that were mixed with the anger I had toward Dad. What did I know about softball at that age? What will everybody think of me? They all saw what I did. After ten minutes of crying, cousin Rebeca came in and soothed my hurt and angered heart. She spoke gently to me and asked why I was crying. She told me not to worry about anything. Everything will be alright. A few minutes later, cousin Tonina walked in and, seeing her sister calming me down, began to do the same. In no time, I was back in a calm state of mind. They were empathetic and gentle, with a genuine laugh and smile that soothed my distress. Since then, they hold a very special place in my heart. Rebeca is a year older than I, and Tonina is my age. I've always liked them.

Cousin Rachel Acevedo (Aunt Chacha's oldest daughter) sits in a lawn chair in front of the east barn where they are staying. She's reading a Mexican historieta, a small booklet of short stories in comic book form. The historieta is in Spanish and printed in Mexico. Historietas are common in Mexican American communities. There are stories about the Mexican Revolution that took place in the early 1900s. There are novelas (soap operas), stories of courageous caballeros (gentlemen), murder, suspense, love, romance, brave macho men, and more. They're made of cheap pulpy paper, have a lot of illustrations, and are inexpensive to buy. They offer easy reading for those who can read Spanish. I imagine she bought them in Texas and probably bought some at NJ's. I ask Raquel if I can look at one of the historietas piled on the side of her chair. I quickly browse several and get the gist of the stories based on the illustrations; I wish I could read and understand them.

The Esch Farm is alive with activity. In the background, Dad and the other musicians practice songs for tonight's service. A couple of pretty little girls are playing and running outside in pink and powder blue silky, frilly, and lacey dresses. Their long, pretty, soft, dark brown hair flows behind them. They're full of giggles, and their tanned bodies are full of youth and vitality. Their dresses are the kind that many Mexican American little girls wear. Your average White American girl would find these dresses a bit overdone with femininity because of the abundance of frills and ribbons. Excited chatter and laughter come from a group of young boys in front of the other barn where the girls are playing. A lady is throwing out mop water onto the side of the entrance of their dwelling. The smell of Pine-Sol liquid cleaner hits my nostrils. This is mixed with the delightful aroma of freshly made flour tortillas. A farmworker has Mariachi music coming out of his car stereo system.

Cousin Polaco is finishing drying his beautiful 1958 Ford F-100 red-colored short-bed pickup. The truck is very handsome looking with its rear side fenders. Mexican music is playing from his eight-track tape player from inside his truck. On the seat is a stack of Tejano, Ranchero, and Mexican music. I see tapes by Joe Bravo, Freddy Martinez, Flaco Jimenez, Little Joe and the Latinaires, and others. The truck is immaculate. It has baby moon caps accented with shiny black rims. Inside the truck, I see the four-speed stick shift on the floor. A ribbon of small, soft, white cloth balls is decorated at the top of the windshield. A pair of white and black foam dice hangs from the rearview mirror. The steering wheel has a steering wheel spinner knob. I move the stack of historietas and eight-track tapes on the seat and sit down. I can tell from Polaco's eyes that this is his pride and joy. He opens the hood to show us the eight-cylinder engine. The engine compartment is as clean as the rest of the truck. He revs up the engine to give us a demonstration of the powerful engine's sound.

Before church, we decide to walk to the haunted woods. We head down the slightly sandy two-track path southward toward the cherry orchards. I jump on the Case Orchard beige tractor that we pass by. I love it! I love the aerodynamic design of the tractor. Close to the tractor is a messy pile of empty cherry lugs with the names of different orchards and cherry processing plants such as Esch, Red Path, Alpers, Waterman, Traverse City Canning Company, Kahrs, Stimmel, Morgan Canning Company, Kolaric, Elk Rapids Packing Company, Pet Milk Company, F&M, Burnette Farms Packing Company, HY Wendt, Morgan-McCool, Inc., Kroupa, J&S Orchard Company and a few others. Some are new, but most look like they have been used for a few years. Junior and Decky keep walking. I catch up to them. We pass by the other worker dwellings. The Esch Farm has close to 100 adult cherry pickers staying here. The dwellings are constructed of cinder blocks and measure approximately 20 feet by 50 feet, with aluminum sheeted roofs. Another structure, formerly a pig pen, was later converted into a dwelling. The Frank Chapa family stays here.

We leave the farm and start our walk to the woods. We pass through a vacant field, but soon, we are in the orchards. The two-track is stamped with the tire prints of the tractor and trailer used to pick up the filled cherry lugs. We walk in a zigzag fashion in a southwest direction to reach our destination. This is the closest part of the woods to us. As the crow flies, it's around a third of a mile from the farm. Crickets and grasshoppers are everywhere. A cicada bug with its shrill, high-pitched sound is in a tree nearby.

Ted Esch has 80 acres of cherry trees. We pass through six or seven distinct orchards. Some of the orchards have young, small trees that don't have many cherries. Other orchards are mature, with branches hanging slightly down and loaded with cherries. Some orchards have one type of cherry, while others have a variety of cherry types.

We pass through orchards with sweet white cherries, known as Napoleon cherries. This type of cherry is also named Royal Ann or Queen Anne. These cherries have firm bodies with bright yellow, orange, pink, and red hues. They are not as sweet as the dark, sweet cherries, but I like eating them. These cherries are sent to the market to make the famous maraschino cherry. These are processed cherries you find on top of ice cream sundaes and certain desserts. You also find them in cans of fruit cocktail.

Now, we're passing by a Schmidt sweet cherry orchard. These dark, large cherries have mahogany-colored tints. The Schmidt cherry is one of my favorites. The dark juice is so tasty.

On the other side of the Schmidt cherry orchard is a Gold cherry orchard. These firm, medium-sized, golden-yellow sweet cherries are also used to make maraschino cherries. This type of cherry is tasty but not one of my favorites.

Close by us are some Ulster sweet cherry orchards. They look so inviting to eat. This type of cherry is dark in color, with dark red juice and a firm texture. So enjoyable to eat.

We pass by a couple of Montmorency cherry orchards. This bright red tart cherry, with soft skin and juicy tart flesh, is one of my favorites. These cherries are mainly used for cooking and baking. They are also used to make cherry concentrate, cherry juice, jams, and preserves. You usually don't see fresh tart cherries sold in stores. Mom cans this type of cherry to make her incredible cherry pies.

I stop at a tree several times and pick a handful of the best, plumpest cherries I see. I quickly rub off the pesticide and dirt on the cherries with one of the napkins I have in my pocket. The cherries are so delicious and juicy. My hands now have a slight scent of pesticide and are stained with a purplish stain from the juice. I don't mind.

The cherries are superb. The big black ones are my favorite. I also like the Royal Anns with the yellow, orange, and reddish tints, but I love the tarts, too. I love all of them.

I pass several trees I want to climb, but I can't because of my polished shoes. I can't get dirty, and I'm screaming inside to have fun.

We finally reach the end of the orchard, climb over the rusty barbed wire fence, and enter the woods. Ted Esch owns part of the woods. It's hilly and covered with various hardwood trees. Michigan wildlife, such as the porcupine, skunk, opossum, fox, coyote, wild turkey, squirrel, and deer, can be found here. The Esch family hunts here during deer season. We believe there could be a bobcat or other type of wild cat out here, and consequently, we feel somewhat tense and fearful, so we stay fully alert. It's hard to get through the woods and not mess up my shoes because there are no paths we can see to walk on. The woods are very quiet, probably because we have put all wildlife on alert due to our presence. A few minutes later, we are frightened by the sound of a large animal running through the woods. We see two whitetail deer with white tail ends bobbing up and down as they scamper off swiftly and soon disappear. We've only been here for around ten minutes, but it's time to return, so we are not late.

We waste no time heading back. Decky and Junior are walking faster than I am. I want to stay up with them, but don't want to get my shoes dirty and dusty. They take a different course back. I sometimes lose sight of where they are, but eventually, I catch up with them. After a few minutes, we realize we need to pick up our speed. We break out in a rapid trot.

When we arrive, we are sweaty and hot. I quickly go to the farm water pump to rinse my face, arms, and hands. The musicians are playing their guitars and accordion. We don't have much time for hellos as the service is about to start. Quickly, we find a place to sit. Mom is proud that we arrived at church on time.

Grandpa begins the service by asking us to stand for the opening prayer. There's a good crowd; probably everybody at the morning service is here. It's almost considered a sin if you don't attend two services on Sunday and the Wednesday night service during the week. I've always been told that attending all three services shows that God is first in your life. Grandpa begins his prayer. Little by little, my secular thoughts move aside to make room for the spiritual. His prayers are seldom short but effective in preparing the hearts and minds of the congregation for the rest of the service. Pentecostal Sunday night services are usually a bit livelier than the morning ones, maybe because people are more awake. As Grandpa prays, the adults simultaneously pray in loud, audible voices. Hallelujahs and amens are generously sprinkled throughout Grandpa's prayer from the congregation. Grandpa builds up his tempo and volume. It sends forceful emotional waves through the congregation. The congregation is hungry and ready to come together in worship of God. Hands everywhere are lifted to the barn's ceiling, including the hands of Mom, Aunt Maruca, and Grandma. Mom and several other ladies have tears in their eyes, a sign of their thankfulness to God. I feel a shiver throughout my body, and my eyes drop a few tears, which I try to hold back. As usual, I don't want to show too much emotion in front of Junior and Decky. They would never ridicule me, but I still feel shy about it. I begin to forget about the woods, Lety, all my fun, and picking cherries tomorrow. I also block out thoughts of home, Bruno, and Jim. I forget about how sweaty I am from the hike to the woods. I remember the drawing I made of the church service in the barn last year. I still have the drawing. Mom liked it and wanted me to keep it. It's in the box of photos and memorabilia back home.

Grandpa asks us to sit down and motions the song leader to the podium. The song leader is lively and knows how to use the spiritual energy in the air. She asks us to turn to page 126 in the *Himnos de Gloria* red Spanish hymnal; the song is "Las Promesas de Jesus" (Standing on the Promises). We stand. The musicians play the introduction, and the song leader leads us as we sing. Dad and the other musicians are sounding so good. You can tell they enjoy playing their instruments. Good music adds so much to the quality of the service. It can also influence the tone of the rest of the service. Junior, Decky, and I join the many others clapping along with the music. The barn is filled with powerful, pleasing sounds of guitars, the accordion, voices singing, tambourines, hand clapping, and foot-stomping. The music is easily heard by all outside the barn. The next song we sing is "Yo Quiero Trabajar Por El Señor" (I Want to Be a Worker for God). The songs we are singing are some of my favorites. I'm tearing up again during this song. Junior and I have heard these songs all our lives—so many memories of hearing them at Grandpa's church in Wauseon. The song leader permits us to sit. We sing "Cuando Allá Se Pase Lista" (When the Roll Is Called Up Yonder). It feels good to sit down.

Church Service in the Barn

A church service is never complete without an offering. As the musicians play, two men go down the center aisle and pass the offering plates row by row.

The song leader opens the time for personal testimonies about what God has done for them. Several people share their testimonies. All three are excited to tell others what God has done in their lives. Their testimonies are inspiring. After each testimony, the musicians break out, singing and playing a chorus and verse of a song related to the testimony. As a congregation, we follow the musician's lead and begin singing.

Grandpa is ready to preach. The song leader sits down, and the musicians put down their instruments. Everyone stands for Grandpa's prayer for God's anointing as he gives the word of God. He prays that God will put us in a frame of mind to receive what God has for us so that our spirits will be nourished by the message. He prays for those who are present and don't know God that they might be saved tonight. After the prayer, we sit down. Grandpa directs us to turn our Bibles to John 3:16, "God so loved the world that he gave his only son that whoever believes in him will not perish but have eternal life." The scripture is a giveaway that his sermon will be on salvation. I follow along with Decky, reading the scripture in the Spanish Bible. I'm learning the essential salvation scriptures through Royal Rangers back at our church.

My mind wanders a few minutes into the sermon, and I think about Grandpa's salvation experience. It provides a fascinating glimpse into how we ended up being Pentecostal Christians. The year was 1927, and Grandpa was nineteen years old. It is said that Grandpa (Clemente Fuentes) killed a man. Some say he killed a couple of men. I never knew all the details, but Dad said that he went to prison. One day, a Pentecostal preacher visited the prison to minister to the inmates. The preacher preached a sermon on salvation. Grandpa was deeply moved by the salvation message and became a Pentecostal Christian. The preacher took an interest in Grandpa. Soon, a rapport between the preacher and Grandpa took shape. The preacher said he would try to get Grandpa out of prison. Shortly after that, Grandpa was released. Uncle Eli told me that we had an uncle in Mexico who was a well-connected lawyer, and that this is how Grandpa was released from prison.

Grandpa's family was elated that Grandpa was released from prison, but was shocked and angry to hear he had left the Catholic faith. They could not believe their ears. The Fuentes family was Catholic, just like almost everybody else in Mexico. How could any Catholic change their faith? His aunts and, especially his grandmother, were furious and could not believe he would do such a thing. Grandpa's older brother, Uncle Chon, was the only one who accepted his conversion. Uncle Chon figured he would support him if his brother wanted this.

After Grandpa's conversion, Grandpa started a new life in the USA. Grandpa left Mexico and found a place to live around Brownsville, Texas. Grandpa met and married Grandma Eucaria Herrera of Brownsville, Texas. Soon, they had children. After several years living in the Valley, Grandpa attended Bible School in San Antonio, Texas, for two years and graduated in 1937.

In 1937, shortly after graduating, Grandpa started the "Templo Calvario" Asamblea de Dios (Calvary Temple Assembly of God) Church at 1612 Jupiter Street, McAllen, Texas, the home of Maria Zambrano.

People are surprised to find out that I am Pentecostal and not Catholic. The Pentecostal faith is under the Protestant Christian umbrella. Pentecostals believe in miracles and the speaking of tongues. They are very emotional at church services. Some people make fun of my religion. I hear comments like "holy rollers" or "the Hallelujahs." Some people make fun of Pentecostals speaking in tongues. Pentecostals believe that the gift of speaking in tongues, as mentioned in the book of Acts in the New Testament, continues to this day. Speaking in tongues refers to a person speaking in an unknown language, inspired by the Holy Spirit. There will often be another person who interprets the speaking of tongues. This freaks out many people if they aren't accustomed to

Pentecostal services. I've invited friends to our church. Luis and Jim were startled and wondered what was happening when they heard people speak in tongues. They think it's weird and too much for them to belong to a church like this. I know I shouldn't feel this way, but I'm shy about inviting someone to church unless I know them well.

My mind snaps back to the service when I hear Grandpa say for us to turn to Romans 3:23, "For all have sinned and come short of the glory of God." Grandpa waits until everyone has found the passage in the Bible and then continues. Some children are beginning to squirm. Moms are telling their children to stop acting up, or they will get a spanking after church. I notice cousin Cheque drinking a baby bottle full of milk. He's a bit older, and I wonder when he'll stop drinking from a baby bottle. He doesn't seem to care what people think. The scent of Jergens hand cream is finding its way toward me. This always reminds me of Grandma Fuentes. She always has a bottle of it on her dressing table in her bedroom. I think it's coming from Aunt Maruca. Somehow, Junior found a Bic pen and starts to draw hot rod cars on a piece of paper. He shows Decky and me what he's drawing. I try not to pay too much attention. I want to stay focused on the sermon as much as possible.

Grandpa has us turn to Romans 6:23, "For the wages of sin is death, but the gift of God is eternal life through Jesus Christ, our lord." He shares some stories of people who lived without God and suffered the consequences of their actions.

I wander slightly as I think about Ted Esch's son, Larry. Larry was three years old when Grandpa and family started coming to the Esch Farm. Young Larry loved the aromas of Grandma's food: Spanish rice, refried beans, homemade tortillas, fideo (browned angel hair spaghetti), tacos, and more. He would tell Grandma that he wanted a taco. He especially loved Grandma's beans and rice wrapped up in a taco. Elsie Esch, Larry's mom, would get mad at him because he wouldn't have an appetite for the meal she prepared. Elsie also thought Larry was pestering Grandma. Grandpa told Elsie that he and Grandma didn't mind at all.

They asked Elsie not to get mad at Larry. Elsie agreed to let Larry eat what he wanted: Grandma's food. He did this every year when Grandma and Grandpa came to pick cherries.

When Larry was a little older, he would sneak up through the back entrance of the barn through the chicken coop to hear and see the Sunday church services. Nobody knew he was up there. He didn't know what they were singing about or what they were saying, but he loved it. He loved the music, the singing, the guitars, trumpets, accordions, and tambourines. It was a service quite different from his Lutheran Church upbringing. In our photo box is a black and white photo of young Larry, around three or four years old, with his older sister Janice, who looks like she's around six. They are on the side of the Esch house on the lawn.

Larry and his wife, Janice, are living on campus at Michigan State University this summer while Larry works on his bachelor's degree.

I'm snapped out of my wandering thoughts by Aunt Maruca, who snaps her fingers to get Ana and Marti's attention. They are whispering something to each other and giggling under their breath. Grandpa continues his sermon with Romans 10:13, "For whoever calls upon the Lord shall be saved." He then quickly takes us to Romans 10: 9-10, "If you declare with your mouth, Jesus is Lord, and believe in your heart that God raised him from the dead, you will be saved." Grandpa ties in another story of an unfortunate man with a drinking problem who lost his way through life and lost everything: his wife, his family, his job, and his money.

Grandpa's following scripture is Revelation 3:20, "Behold, I stand at the door and knock. If any man hears my voice, I will come into him and sup with him, and he with me." After explaining the meaning of the passage, Grandpa motions for the musicians to start playing and for us to bow our heads, close our eyes, and pray with him that the Holy Spirit will convict the hearts of sinners in the congregation. The musicians play "En la Cruz" (At the Cross). "Is there anyone who wants to accept Jesus? If so, raise your hand," Grandpa says. Nobody but Grandpa and the person with the raised hand would know. The Christian adults are earnestly praying. I always enjoy seeing someone get saved. I'm hoping that someone will. I can hear Mom crying and praying. Many others are also praying. The atmosphere is charged with emotional energy. No one comes forward to get saved.

Grandpa then asks those who want to be prayed for to come forward. Many people go forward. The elders are coming up to help Grandpa pray for those who have come forward. As usual, Grandpa puts the anointing oil on the person's forehead. A few minutes later, Grandpa opens the altar to whoever wants to come forward to pray. I go forward. The musicians and congregation sing "Todo a Cristo Yo Me Rindo" or "I Surrender All." I kneel and close my eyes at the wooden bench altar.

I thank God for allowing me to be around Grandpa, Grandma, and my other relatives here. Being at this service reminds me of the "camp meeting revival" services we have every summer at our church. The music is so alive, and it's great seeing Dad happy, playing, and singing. I hear someone speaking in tongues. I wonder what people outside think when they hear this strange language. The congregation is now singing, and the tambourines are playing. I have tears. It sounds so heavenly. I am at peace. I know God loves me. I am clean in his sight. I am a child of God. I have a sense of great possibilities for my life and a sense of closeness with my creator.

Once all of us praying at the altar are finished, we return to our seats. Grandpa has a big smile on his face. He is pleased with how the service went. We stand up for Grandpa's closing prayer. It's a prayer of thanksgiving and for God's hand upon all of us for the following week. I feel light and clean.

After church, we hang out at the Esch Farm for a bit; there's no rush to return to the Waterman Farm. I enjoy just watching people linger after the service. The musicians don't want to stop playing, and they make good background music.

On our walk back to Waterman's, I see a wild turkey feather on the side of the road and pick it up. This will make a nice pen. I've made a few. They are easy to make. You cut off the end of the feather tip and inject a ballpoint pen ink cartridge. I like writing with a feather pen. I think of George Washington and how people used feathered writing pens back then.

I walk to the quiet road and reflect on the day. Everybody else is already in the tent, getting ready for bed. So much happened today. It feels like two days' worth of experiences put into one day. I enjoyed the Sunday church services at the Esch Farm. It's so different having church inside a barn and having Sunday School under a large shady tree. It's so good to hear the church music in Spanish and hear Dad and the musicians play their instruments. I would love to erase from my mind the killing of the helpless porcupine that my cousins killed. I reflect on the bountiful and delicious Mexican food we had for lunch with relatives, including Grandpa and Grandma Fuentes. I think about the softball game and how nervous I was, and I'm glad I played. It allowed me to watch Lety as she watched us from the sidelines play. I'm grateful for the chance I had to meet Lety. I'm thankful she joined us in getting ice cream at NJ's Store in Lake Leelanau. How nice it has been to spend hours with Junior and Decky. I think about tomorrow and our first day of picking cherries. I know I'll make the best of it and enjoy it as much as possible. I'm not a stranger to work. Good night, world. I walk to the tent and prepare myself for sleep, trying to be as quiet as possible.

CHAPTER THREE

LA CHERRY DULCE

MONDAY, 28 JULY 1969

It's early Monday morning. It must be around four. It's beginning to sprinkle, and I hear thunder in the background. The wind starts picking up speed, and sprinkles turn into a light rain. With my sleepy eyes half open, I ensure that none of my items touch the tent or that no rain comes inside. Everything looks safe and dry. In ten minutes, rain is pouring down with lightning and thunder. As time passes, the storm becomes a free-for-all in the sky. Will our tent hold? The booms are beginning to scare me, although I must remember that it's lightning that I should be afraid of, not the boom sound. The tent starts to sway and dance in the strong gusts of wind. The tent seems to be able to withstand the storm's fury, but it's being challenged to its limits. Flashes of lightning illuminate the inside of the tent. I'm scared of being hit by lightning, but there's nothing I can do but ride out the storm.

Is anybody else in the tent scared? Will we be electrocuted? I can see the *Traverse City Record-Eagle* newspaper headline read "Migrant Farmworkers Die in Violent Storm." My body shudders after hearing the loud booms of the thunder. I can see everyone in the tent as clear as day. Dad has his eyes open, checking out the situation. This isn't my first time in a tent during a thunderstorm. The storm rambles through in 40 minutes. Moderate rain then continues to fall. The raindrops hitting the tent create a lullaby that puts me back to sleep.

It's our first day of picking cherries. Mom slips out of the tent. It must be around 7:30. She quickly walks through the rain to Aunt Maruca's to get information on when the picking will start. There is no picking when it's raining like this. On her return, Mom tells Dad the picking will begin no sooner than 9:30, depending on the weather. Lying in my warm sleeping bag, I'm delighted to hear the news. I can sleep a bit more! God, thanks for the rain. Mom goes back to bed.

Quietly, Mom dresses and exits the tent an hour later to start breakfast and make coffee for Dad. Within a few minutes, she returns with Dad's coffee and begins to wake us up. I'm feeling drowsy, as I usually do in the morning after waking up. I put on my work clothes and army boots that Uncle Dan gave me.

Everything outside is drenched. I don't look forward to getting wet. I'm so glad I brought my army boots. I can't imagine wearing flimsy canvas tennis shoes in this soggy mess. The air is fresh, courtesy of the front that moved through this early morning, but due to the heavy rain, there is a lot of moisture in the air and on the ground, which will likely create an uncomfortable, hot, and humid day later.

The farm is coming alive as other families are getting ready. I see Decky outside, and we greet each other. I'm going to the restroom, but then I see Lety leave her quarters. I don't want to see her until I'm much more awake. Thank God, she didn't see me. She's probably going to use the bathroom. She looks so pretty with her silky, long, dark brown hair in a ponytail and her new blue jeans that fit her young, feminine body perfectly.

I have my Kellogg's Corn Flakes breakfast on the picnic table outside our tent. Since everything is wet, I use a towel to wipe off the spot where I plan to sit. Mom urges us to eat quickly and finish anything else we need to do since we must be ready in twenty minutes.

I go to the bathroom and the water pump to brush my teeth. Now that I have some food in my stomach and my mouth is clean, I feel more awake and ready for the day.

We have a few minutes before we head to the orchard. Junior and I pretend we are World War II B-17 bomber pilots. It's a game that we occasionally play, especially after a heavy rainstorm. There's no problem finding the bombs we want for our game since the farm driveway is full of small gravel stones that make perfect bombs. Last night's heavy rain created several big mud puddles in the driveway, making perfect bombing sites. We pretend we are doing World War II bombing missions over Germany, just like in the TV series "12 O'clock High." With stones in hand and making sounds of B-17 Flying Fortress bombers as best we can, we slowly walk towards, or fly towards, the giant mud puddles, simulating we are bomber pilots and our targets are below: the mud puddles. "Bombs away!" we yell and release our load of bombs. Below, water splashes, and immediately, we see the explosion of fine, silty mud brought up by dropping our bombs. We modify our voices to create explosion sounds, providing audio of the destruction the bombs are causing below. We do around five bomb runs before meeting with family at the tent.

We're ready to start the work day. Dad put the Igloo, full of water, in the back of the pickup. We all walk to the main barn to get our pails and cherry harness/support straps. Some are cleaner and in better condition than others. Since we are the last family to arrive to pick, we can't be too picky with what is left. The one-gallon galvanized pails have small holes on each side where you put the two clips attached to the supporting straps. The supporting straps are made of sturdy, white-colored cotton mesh. The three-inch-wide straps crisscross your back. After assessing the available straps that are my size, I try one on. Every time I put on one of these supporting straps, I feel like I'm a soldier from the Revolutionary War or the War of 1812 because of the criss-crossed white wide straps. I like the feeling of the straps. I choose a pail with cherry stains, leaves, stems, and a little sand on the inside bottom. I clip the straps to the pail. I'm ready to pick! Mom tells Dad, "Honey, hurry up. We can't be the last ones to the orchard!"

At around 9:40 am, we head to the orchard. All the pails and support straps are loaded in the back of the pickup. All of us kids, except Timmy, sit on the tailgate while Timmy is in the cab with Mom and Dad. I spot the tractor in the orchard and hear its putt-putt sound. A few cars trail behind it as Dad follows Aunt Maruca's brown 1963 Oldsmobile 88 station wagon up the gently sloping two-track trail in the orchard.

We all love sitting on the tailgate with our legs hanging down as Dad drives slowly through the orchard. We feel every bump, and it makes us laugh. We pass other pickers on the sides, parking their vehicles and getting things ready to start picking. Each family chooses a row to pick. We pass by where Lety and her family will be picking. I only get a glance at her because we are moving farther up the orchard. We pass by an area with neatly stacked orchard ladders and a large mound of empty cherry lugs a few yards away. Dad takes the next available row and parks the pickup a few trees down the row.

All pickers are busy getting ready to start picking. I see some heading toward the ladders and cherry lugs. Other pickers snap on their pails and walk to their trees; a few are already picking.

We prepare ourselves for work. Since there are a lot of mosquitoes around us, the first thing we do is spray on mosquito repellent. Dad takes the first tree in the row, Mom takes the second, Junior takes the third tree, and I take the fourth one. Mom and Dad start walking to their trees to start picking while Junior and I, along with Sandy, Tito, and Timmy, go to the pile of empty cherry lugs to get a bunch of lugs we will need. We all choose the newest and cleanest lugs. With the new ones, you can smell the pine wood. I love that smell. Like the lugs we saw at the Esch Farm yesterday, they have names of various cherry growers and canning companies from around the Traverse City area imprinted on the sides. Junior and I carry four lugs at a time. The rest of the kids each carry one. Timmy is struggling with his. He takes a lot of breaks. I coax him on and tell him he's doing a great job.

As we walk back to our site, I hear cherries falling into the pails of those who have begun picking. I like the metallic sounds the cherries make as they land at the bottom of the pail. We find a spot by one of our trees and drop the lugs. We go back two more times and now have sufficient lugs to keep the family supplied for a while.

Junior and I go back to get our ladders. They aren't fun to move, so we drag them back to our area. We make several trips to get ladders for Mom, Dad, Junior, and me.

I hesitate to start because I don't look forward to getting more wet. There's so much rainwater on the trees and the tall grass surrounding them. My pants are already wet from carrying the lugs and ladders. It's also still a bit chilly. I'll feel even colder with my body wet. My walk to my cherry tree stirs up a bunch of mosquitoes. Now they know I'm around for their bloody delight. I approach the lush branches that droop under the weight of ripe, sweet black cherries. The rain enhances their shimmer, making them even more stunning.

I implement my plan on how I'm going to pick. I stand and focus on an area where I remain stationary and pick everything within my reach. I usually start with the branches that have the most cherries. After picking everything within my reach, I get on my knees and pick everything within reach. When all the cherries are picked, I move left or right of where I started picking and do the same routine. After picking all the cherries on the tree's exterior that are within my reach, it's time to find a place under the canopy to start picking. After I finish the interior, it's time to get a ladder to begin picking the cherries that are higher up and out of my reach.

Plink, plink, plink is the sound of cherries hitting the bottom of my pail. Before I get serious with picking, I satisfy my desire and have a short dessert time! A clump of cherries catches my eye. I rub them dry to get as much pesticide off as possible. In my mouth, they go. As usual, they are as tasty as they are plump.

I return to picking as I chew and savor the crushed cherries. The nippy air and rainwater make my fingers not want to cooperate as well as they should. The sky is still filled with grey clouds that drop spurts of light rain on us, only adding to my discomfort. I find a loaded branch, start at the top, and work my hands and fingers down as the cherries detach from the branches. It feels like I'm massaging the branch as the cherries fall into my pail. What a lovely sound they make as they enter my pail. My pail is half full from just this branch! This motivates me; it's just what I need to get my work rhythm going. This will help me warm up as well. The front of my pants and my long sleeves are all wet. The crisscross straps and bucket in front of me keep my torso relatively dry.

With all the moisture in the air, there appear to be more mosquitoes. My mosquito repellent does wonders and keeps them at bay. However, that doesn't mean I'm unbothered by the pests. Some fly close to my head. Though they don't land on me, it's annoying to hear their buzzing sound, which adds to the discomfort of my wet and uncomfortable body.

After picking another loaded branch, I fill my pail. Carefully, I unload my first pail of cherries into the lug I placed close to my tree. It almost fills half the lug. They look marvelous as they lie in the lug. A few more cherries go into my mouth as I walk back to start again.

As I walk back, I notice that my feet are dry. These black leather army boots are handy when I'm outside having fun, working, adventuring, camping, or doing anything else.

I fill my first lug! I'm so proud of myself. I'm still ahead of Junior in picking, but he isn't as motivated as I am. He's not motivated because he doesn't think Dad will pay us for picking. I think Dad will probably pay us. Even if I don't get paid, I still find this exciting. I would much rather be here than in Alma, where I would be doing the same things and also have to help Dad clean offices, churches, and car dealerships.

It must be around 10:45. It's starting to dry up, but I don't care because I'm resigned to being wet. I take notice of the mourning dove cooing, the crows cawing, and the robins and sparrows chirping. People are much more awake. I'm much more awake. I hear people talking, mainly in Spanish. I hear a mother scolding her child. Someone plays Tejano music from an eight-track tape player in their parked car. It reminds me of being at Luis Garcia's house. The Garcias have all the latest Ranchero, Tejano, and Norteño music on 45 rpm records. Dad is whistling some church hymns. It's a soothing sound. Junior and I talk back and forth in short dialogues and then return to the humdrum of picking. Sandy, Tito, and Timmy help Mom and Dad fill their pails as they choose. Sandy helps Mom the most. Tito and Timmy work in short spurts. I haven't seen Decky or Lety since we arrived at the orchard.

There's so much time to think about things, so I think about how Grandpa Fuentes came to Michigan. Even before Grandpa Fuentes came north to work the crops, there was a demand for seasonal farmworkers. Since the 1920s, Mexican Americans from southern Texas and Mexicans from Mexico have followed the agricultural circuit, preparing or harvesting sugar beets, cucumbers, strawberries, blueberries, raspberries, peaches, cherries, tomatoes, apples, grapes, cotton, and other crops.

Mr. Enrique (Henry) Vasquez Sr, of Ithaca, Michigan, introduced Grandpa Fuentes to Michigan. The year was 1946, one year after World War II. Enrique had a farm west of Ithaca, Michigan, and was looking for migrant farmworkers to hoe his sugar beet fields. Knowing he could get farmworkers from the Valley, Enrique drove to McAllen, Texas, to find workers. Since Enrique's roots are from the Valley and being a Pentecostal Christian, I'm assuming they met at Grandpa's church in McAllen. After hearing Enrique's need for farmworkers, Grandpa accepted the offer to work for Enrique. The Fuentes family packed their belongings and rode back with Enrique in his flatbed stake truck to Ithaca to hoe his fields.

Enrique and Grandpa established a good friendship. Enrique assisted Grandpa in every way possible with everything needed to keep Grandpa and his large family functioning. He helped Grandpa find migrant farmworker housing in the center of Shepherd, Michigan, on the side of the railroad tracks. Later, Grandpa and his family stayed at the long-closed sugar beet factory in Alma, where farmworkers were housed. Enrique transported the family wherever they needed to go.

One day, Enrique told Grandpa that farmers in northern Michigan needed pickers to harvest their cherries. Grandpa was interested, so Enrique offered to take Grandpa and his family to Traverse City, Michigan. He stopped at the farmworker employment station, which gave Enrique the name and address of a cherry farmer looking for migrant farmworkers: Theodore Herbert "Ted" Esch Jr., Esch Road, Lake Leelanau, Michigan.

Grandpa and Ted Esch hit it off so well that Ted changed his garage into an apartment for Grandpa, Grandma, and family to stay in when they came up to pick cherries. Ted also didn't mind Grandpa holding church services for the farmworkers. Ted never had any services held at his farm before. He was all for it. He liked the families that Grandpa brought to pick cherries. They were hard and faithful workers. They were family-oriented, respectful, and mindful of others. One of the following years, Ted Esch even received an award for Best Cherry Farmworker Camp. There was an article about this award in the local newspaper. It had photos of Grandpa leading the church service. The reporters even interviewed Grandpa. I've been told there was even a photo of Ted Esch and Grandpa Fuentes hanging on a wall at City Hall in Traverse City. I would surely like to see if it's true.

Grandpa and Ted's relationship was so strong that during the cherry harvest, Ted assisted Grandpa with buying a 1937 Chevrolet one-and-a-half-ton flatbed truck. Part of the deal was that Grandpa would return the following year and bring other farmworkers from Texas. As part of the deal, Grandpa would serve as the patron (foreman) for these families and act as a liaison between Ted Esch, and the workers that Grandpa recruited. Ted loved this because he didn't know much Spanish. Grandpa's duties as a patron would entail communicating with the workers about anything Ted wanted or needed to convey to them. Grandpa was also the communicator between the workers and Ted Esch. If there was anything the workers needed, Grandpa would let Ted know. It could be as simple as a farmworker needing another bed or reporting that a refrigerator in one of the worker quarters no longer worked and that another was needed. He also informed the workers when to show up regarding payday, which orchard to pick, and so on.

Grandpa kept his word; in 1947, he invited some families who attended the church he started in McAllen, Texas. The Acevedo, Chapa, Serna, and Arizola families were invited. Grandpa met the Tijerina family one summer at the Traverse City migrant farmworker staging area and invited them to pick cherries at the Ted Esch Farm. He always stopped here for a few hours before going to the Esch Farm to pick the annual cherry harvest. In 1957, the Rodriguez family from McAllen came with Grandpa. Some of these families still come to pick cherries for Ted Esch each year.

This became a yearly thing. As the years progressed, Grandpa and everyone he brought up from Texas worked the agricultural migrant farmworker circuit. They started in June, hoeing sugar beet fields in Ithaca, Michigan, then on to Lake Leelanau, Michigan, to harvest strawberries, followed by picking cherries. After three weeks of picking cherries, they went to Archbold, Ohio, to pick tomatoes for La Choy Food Products, where they would pick until around mid-September. Everybody stayed in the farmworker housing units across the street from La Choy and across the road from Yoder Frey Farm Auction Company. Uncle Eli said that the housing area used to be a World War II German prisoner-of-war camp. After tomato season, it was time to drive to Plainview, Texas, to pick cotton from October to December. By the end of December, Grandpa, family, and all the other migrant farmworkers who came with Grandpa were back at their homes in the Valley.

In 1948, Grandpa had two flatbed stake trucks. He brought his family and those who had traveled with him the previous year. They planted tomatoes around Archbold for La Choy Foods in May. They also performed road work for Fulton County, Ohio, and assisted farmers with baling hay. In June, they went to Ithaca, Michigan, to hoe sugar beet and cucumber fields for Enrique Vasquez, then to Lake Leelanau, Michigan, to pick strawberries, followed by cherries. Around mid-August, they were back in Archbold, Ohio, for the tomato harvest and later back to Plainwell, Texas, to pick cotton. This routine went on until 1952.

In 1953, Grandpa decided to settle in Archbold, Ohio. All the families he brought up from Texas also began settling around Archbold. This is the year Grandpa started the "Asamblea de Dios" (Assembly of God), a Pentecostal Spanish-speaking church outside Archbold. Years later, the church moved to Wauseon, Ohio.

Because we had a late start, Mom returned to the farm with Aunt Maruca at noon to prepare lunch. I now have five lugs to Junior's three and a half. I challenge him to see who can pick the most; he's not interested. He's consciously taking his time. I don't like working slowly. When I work slowly, I start feeling lazy and get bored. When I work fast, I get motivated. Time passes by quicker, or so it seems.

The blue sky is now filled with a lot of puffy cumulus clouds. I'm drawn to two contrails high in the sky, a jet is making. I wonder if the plane is coming from Montreal or Toronto and going to Minneapolis or Seattle. What do I know? I've never flown in an airplane before. I have a lot of time to daydream and to think about things.

I wonder how Luis is doing. Is he having fun? If so, what does he do? He told me that the farm where he'll pick cherries is halfway up Old Mission Peninsula. If you were to take a helicopter from where I am to where he is, it would be a short flight in a southeast direction. He's on the other side of the West Arm of Grand

Traverse Bay. It's a different story by car. It would take around 50 minutes to get there. You have to go through Traverse City. It might take longer due to the heavy traffic in the city.

My thoughts are interrupted by a pesky mosquito flying around my face. Whack! Whack! I miss my target. Patience is needed. A couple more slaps on my neck. Dead! Now I have blood and mosquito guts to add to the sticky cherry juice, dirt, and pesticide on my hands.

I now have another full pail and head to my half-full lug. I fill the lug and immediately take off my pail and support straps. It feels good to take them off. The wide straps trap my sweat and wet me, but the warm breeze will dry some of it.

I walk to the pickup truck and get water from the Igloo. Even though the water is not cold, it satisfies my thirst. I see Timmy playing in the sandy soil with his Tonka toys.

I have to pee. I've held it in long enough. I walk to an area where no other humans are present and attend to my business. Splash goes my release as it hits an ant hill target below. I'm just having fun. I didn't hurt them. In no time, they will rebuild their hill; this is how I rationalize my silly pleasure.

Back to the tree, I go. Crickets and grasshoppers hop around me as I walk through the orchard. I clip a flower from a Queen Anne's lace weed. Mom loves these, and so do I. I love the look and smell of them. I pass Tito and Sandy, who were helping Mom and Dad pick, but are now walking around and looking bored. I tell them to make a fort out of the cherry lugs. Smiles immediately appear on their faces as they embrace the idea. Off they go to the pile of empty lugs to bring back cherry lugs to make a fort. That will keep them busy, and I'm sure they'll have fun too. I wouldn't mind making one myself, but there's work to be done. I pass Timmy. He's busy playing in the sandy soil close to the trunk of a cherry tree with his toy trucks.

I'm back picking again, feeling refreshed and ready to finish the morning picking. I aim to pick six lugs by the time the farmer comes by to pick them up.

In the distance, I hear a hawny truck coming from the direction of the Esch Farm. I visualize Ted's 1958 Chevy two-ton truck fully loaded with cherries on its way to Frigid Foods Company just south of Suttons Bay on M-22. More than likely, the driver will join the queue of up to ten other trucks from other farms waiting to unload their fresh produce of cherries. It has to be the Esch farm truck. The driver goes through many gears as he drives up the steep easterly incline on Esch Road. Throughout the morning, I've heard other trucks and assume they, too, are going to Suttons Bay. There are several orchards farther west of the Esch Farm. Redpath Orchards is one of them. Their operation harvests more acres of cherries than Ted's, consequently hauling more loads throughout the workday. All the trucks sound like they're getting a good workout as they climb the hill.

I've picked everything I can by standing, kneeling, stooping, and stretching my body to pick as many cherries as possible off the tree. I need a ladder. I take off my pail and walk to where I left the ladder. It's so awkward to carry. I drag it. It feels as if I'm dragging a cross. I'm feeling low on energy; I'm so hungry and can't wait for lunch. I set the ladder up. It's in a perfect position now, but only after adjusting it several times due to branches that didn't want to cooperate with me and a spider web.

I'm motivated to pick faster as I hear the tractor in the distance. My speed picks up. My goal is to pick one more lug. I change my picking strategy and pick all the large clumps wherever they are. Wow! In no time, I will have a full pail. With purpose, I walk to where I have my five filled lugs and drop my cherries in an empty one. I jog back to start picking again. Meanwhile, the tractor's throttle increases as the operator moves to the next group of lugs full of delectable, black sweet cherries. The tractor now idles again as the farmer stops to pick up more lugs. The rhythm of the idling sound is pleasing to me.

Shortly after hearing the tractor for a few minutes, I see Aunt Maruca's car approaching. Mom arrives with our lunch and Dad's red plaid coffee thermos. We only have a few minutes before the tractor comes to our stack of cherries. Mom calls us to all work together on filling a lug before the tractor arrives. It works! We fill one.

Mr. Waterman is driving the John Deere orchard-type tractor we saw parked at the farm the day we arrived. He is about 75 years old, dressed in a khaki shirt and pants. His posture is slightly bowed, and he wears dark sunglasses while driving slowly. A ball cap conceals most of his grey-white hair.

As he parks the tractor in front of us, I notice a warm, gentle smile on his wrinkled face as he greets Dad. I love the tractor but wish it had a diesel engine, as I enjoy the scent of diesel exhaust more than the gasoline smell in the air. Mr. Waterman retrieves a pen and a small notepad from his shirt pocket, starts a new sheet, and writes down "Joe Fuentes." He counts our lugs and records the number in his notepad after confirming it with Dad. Mr. Waterman hands Dad two green tickets and two white tickets, which Dad promptly puts into his black leather wallet. Mr. Waterman goes back to the tractor while Dad, Junior, and I carefully place our 22 lugs alongside the filled ones already on the trailer. Several bees buzz around the lugs, drawn in by the cherry juice splattered on the wood floor of the trailer.

Off goes Mr. Waterman through the orchard, picking up more filled lugs from other pickers. The sound of his tractor lessens as he drives away, and the exhaust soon dissipates into the air.

The soiled and slightly cracked tickets are used as tokens representing the number of lugs a family or picker has given to the farmer. They are kept until

Saturday at noon, when it's payday. Then, they are turned over to the farmer for cash. Eighty cents is paid to the picker for each lug picked. The following is what each ticket is worth: white ticket = one lug; yellow = five lugs; green = ten lugs; red = twenty-five lugs.

Anticipating that we will be eating very soon, I run over to where Decky is picking and invite him to have lunch with Junior and me. I yell out his name as I walk through the orchard. It takes me a while to find him. He agrees to join us, and I return to our eating area.

I return just in time to hear Mom say, "It's time to eat. Wash your hands and only take two burritos." Mom gathers us for a group prayer before the meal. Junior and I grab some empty lugs for makeshift tables and chairs for lunch. Decky arrives with his food and sets up his table and chair nearby while Junior and I wash our hands. Once we're done, I fill my paper plate with two tightly packed flour tortillas filled with diced fried potatoes and ground beef wrapped in warm aluminum foil. I add a bit of salsa and a handful of Fritos corn chips before picking up a warm 16-ounce Coke.

I join Junior and Decky. It feels so good to relax and eat something. A few ants climb up my table. I flick them off. We've also attracted some flies who are circling our food. Although I could quickly devour my food, I choose instead to take my time chewing to stretch the pleasure. Warm pop is not something I prefer to drink back home, but here in the orchard, after a morning of hard work, I am delighted to drink it. The three of us chit-chat back and forth as we eat our food. The warm and delicious burritos are a delightful treat for my palate. Dad told us that Grandpa made tacos with fideo (angel hair spaghetti) and papas (potatoes). Grandpa was also known for his egg burritos and pieces of corn tortillas, which are the original corn chips. There are short, quiet periods as we are too tired to talk; besides, we feel so comfortable around each other that we don't need to.

Tractor in the Orchard

Mom and Dad are eating together by the pickup truck. They look happy. Dad is eating and sipping the hot coffee that Mom made. His plaid thermos is always close to him throughout the day.

After eating, I take a short break. I grab a blanket from the pickup truck, lay it under a cherry tree for shade, and take off my boots and socks. It feels heavenly to stretch my body and let my feet breathe. I close my eyes and rest for seven or so minutes. I know I'll have to get up soon, but lying here feels good.

My few minutes of peace dissipate as Tito catches my attention. He's all excited about something. From a distance, I see him give Sandy his Coca-Cola bottle. She takes a swig. Her eyes light up. Tito then asks Mom to taste his Coke. With an animated response, she tells Tito it's delicious. I ask Tito what's going on. Tito comes over to Junior and me and asks us to taste his Coke. I decline because I don't want his cooties on my lips or in my mouth. Junior tastes it. He's impressed. Tito says he added cherry juice to the Coke and calls it Very Cherry Cola.

Mom and Dad begin to get up from their eating area, giving a cue that lunchtime is over. Slowly, Junior and I get up to return to work. We throw away our paper plates and aluminum foil in the trash bag and place our empty pop bottles back in the pop crate. Decky says goodbye and heads back to start picking. How quickly the half hour for lunch went by. I head to the water Igloo to get a glass of lukewarm water. On go my support straps and pail. I'm ready to start picking again.

The sun is beating down on us, so I choose a shady part of the tree to start picking. A large clump of cherries catches my eye. They make an excellent dessert after lunch, so I grab a few, clean them up with my napkin, and they go straight into my mouth. I never get tired of eating cherries. I quickly get back into my routine and think about things to pass the time away.

I'm in a food coma. The best way to get out of this is to pick up the pace and sing. I start humming the melody of Sugar Sugar by the Archies and interject as many lyrics as I can remember: "Sugar, ah honey honey, you are my candy girl, and you got me wanting you." On and on, the melody and lyrics come out of my mouth as I sing the song the best I can while making sure nobody can hear me.

A lot of activity is around me. Several mosquitoes fly around my head and arms. They are persistent in sucking out some of my blood. A yellow jacket flies too close to me. Several dragonflies zoom by. I hear muffled, unintelligible conversations in Spanish from other pickers. I hear a child cry and a mother scolding the child. I hear a car starting. It must belong to a picker moving his car farther up his row. Tejano music is coming out of someone's car speakers. A handful of daddy longlegs spiders are within reach, crawling around on the tree trunk and branches. These harmless fellows get a bad rap. A lot of people are scared of them and end up killing them. I like to pick them up and let them crawl around my arms. I hear Timmy and Tito arguing. Timmy goes into his classic "siren" sounding cry a minute later. This gets Mom's attention. She tells them to stop, or they will get in trouble with Dad. Above are several turkey vultures flying high and effortlessly as they catch and take advantage of the higher winds. They make wide 360-degree turns while looking for their next tasty meal of putrid and rotted carnage. Even higher up is a jet leaving behind a thick white contrail. I notice the dime-a-dozen sparrows, occasional robins, and a cardinal flying by. At times, I see a white or yellow moth. I see flies and ants on the trees. I hear the rustling of the wind through the orchard. I hear the occasional traffic on Esch Road.

Since there are a lot of other sounds around me, I feel it's safe to hum and sing a song. I start humming and singing the song "Sweet Caroline" by Neil Diamond. I don't want anybody to hear me as I make mistakes singing. I love this song. It came out a few months ago. I'm finding out that I can sing this fantastic song. I can't sing most pop music because the songs are too high for my voice. My baritone voice is suited just right for this song. Over and over, I sing the lyrics. *"Where it began, I can't begin to know it, but then I know it's growing strong..."*

Picking is tedious work. You have to become creative to get through the boredom. One method I use is to reflect on a specific topic or thought, such as the box of family photos and memorabilia we have back home. Out of the box of photos, I can vividly see pictures taken in the late 1940s and early 1950s of Mom and Dad, relatives and friends picking cherries here at the Waterman Orchard, at Ted Esch's orchard, and at other places where they did farm work. I also see photos of us kids in places around Traverse City. Almost all of them are in black and white. There are several photos of Dad outside, standing up and playing his accordion at the tomato migrant farmworker camp in Archbold, Ohio. He must be around 16 or 17 years old. In the background are some tomato bushel baskets and a washboard leaning against a migrant living quarters. Dad's all dressed up. I wonder if the photo was taken after a church service. There are many photos of Dad with his prized 1948 Chevrolet hawny truck that he used for hauling cherries and other crops. Several photos have the back of the truck covered with olive green thick canvas. There are a couple of pictures of Sandy and Tito, ages three and two, sitting in the grass at Clinch Park in Traverse City in front of the zoo and another one of Sandy, around 20 months old, sitting on the lawn at the Waterman Farm with one of the migrant farmworker housing units in the background. I have no previous memories of staying at the Waterman Farm.

I like the photo of Dad on the side of the Esch house with his dog Brownie taken before I was born. Brownie was the first dog we had when we were growing up. Dad is squatting down on the side of Brownie. I just found out that Brownie used to be Grandpa Fuentes' dog. He was such a faithful dog.

One of my favorite photos is of Uncle Eli, Aunt Rebeca, and Aunt Ester. Their ages are approximately ten, seven, and five years old. Uncle Eli and Aunt Rebeca have shoulder harnesses and buckets. Uncle Eli's bucket is full of cherries. He looks like he has a stone and is ready to throw it. Aunt Rebeca is blowing a bubble with her gum. Aunt Ester isn't wearing a harness or carrying a bucket. She's drinking a soda, looking like she has no care in the world. In the background is the cherry orchard. Kids will be kids. Another picture shows two men loading a trailer in the orchard with filled cherry lugs.

Decky surprises me as I'm picking and standing on my ladder. He's going to get more cherry lugs and yells to me, "See you later, alligator." This is one of the silly sayings he likes to say.

I'm getting antsy and want to know what time it is. I fill my lug and place it where all the other family lugs are. I see Mom and ask her what the time is. A smile overcomes me, and I realize we only have an hour and a half to pick. One good thing about starting two hours late is that we are still quitting at the regular 5 pm time.

I put my mind into "machine mode" and just pick for the rest of the work day. This helps me to quit thinking about the time.

I am tired, hot, sweaty, hungry, and probably somewhat dehydrated from not drinking enough water. I look forward to removing these straps, pail, and dirty, sweaty clothes.

Quitting time has come. It's time to get in the pickup, return to the farm, and prepare for the beach. All of us are dirty but enjoying the bumpy ride down the two-track that leads us to the farm and our tent. Crickets and grasshoppers are flying everywhere and in all directions. I love the sound of the tall grass on the two-track path hitting the bottom of the pickup. Sandy giggles every time we hit a small bump. A smile is on my face. I love it here.

Soon, we'll be at the beach. Township Park is the actual name, but we call it "the beach." Dad did say we would be going to the beach during our vacation. Although we could take a cold shower at the farm, it's much more fun to go to the beach after a hard day picking cherries.

The beach is on the northeast side of North Lake Leelanau, in the middle of the scenic Leelanau Peninsula. The lake is 21 miles long. At its widest point, it is one and a half miles wide. It's an impressive size for a Michigan inner lake. North Leelanau and South Leelanau Lakes make up the entire Leelanau Lake. A narrow passage through the village of Lake Leelanau joins them. North Lake is smaller than South Lake, which is around three times bigger.

The farm is alive with all kinds of activities, mostly related to washing up and eating. Children of all ages are running around and having a great time.

I see Lety on my way to the water pump and bathroom. With a big grin, I say hello to her. She smiles back and says hello. My heart is racing again. I get so excited whenever I see her. My problem is that I'm so shy with girls, and I can't stand it. I know that I'm missing out on many opportunities by being this way. I sense she has feelings for me, but I hesitate on what to say or do. God, please show me what I should do. I feel so awkward. I don't want to regret not knowing her because of my shyness.

I catch her giving me a furtive glance. It encourages me. I give her one in return. We both smile at each other again. She is so pretty, even when she is sweaty and dirty like me, although she doesn't look sweaty or dirty like me. I get a boost of energy from my encounter with Lety. She makes me feel good.

Soon after, I'm at the water pump to wash my face, arms, and hair. There is already a short line. After priming the pump and bending down, and with my head under the spigot, I let the cold water gush out over my head. The chilly well water shocks me into a vibrant state of mind. I feel so alive! This is how the lake water will feel. A few minutes later, I'm back at the tent and grab a towel, toiletries, and clean clothes to take to the beach.

Finally, we're all in the pickup and off to the beach. Everybody is excited. It's the usual seating arrangement. The beach is less than seven minutes from the farm. Dad makes a right turn onto Esch Road. We pass several hawny trucks loaded with cherries heading to Suttons Bay. We pass the Esch Farm and, shortly afterwards, Redpath Orchards. We pass by some bare fruit trees, which have been recently harvested, but most of the trees still have cherries. Redpath is at the bottom of the hill and on the other side of the curve in the road. Their operation has amazed me for as long as I can remember. It appears they have more orchards than Waterman or Esch combined. I've always liked the layout of their farm, including its barns, farm tractors, trucks, and other machinery I've seen in past years. I love their Case Orchard tractor. I can see some of the farmworkers busily about at Redpath. Farmworkers are unloading lugs full of cherries off a trailer and loading them onto a hawny truck. I would love to explore their farm and orchards.

At the end of Esch Road, Dad turns onto North Lake Leelanau Drive, County Road 641. The road follows the east coastline of Lake Leelanau. The drive is very scenic. The road curves often as it parallels the shoreline. The blacktop road is narrow and well-maintained. The median white stripes always seem to be freshly painted. Tall trees shade many parts of the road. On certain parts of the road, you feel like you're going through a tunnel. At times, you get a free strobe light show caused by the sudden bursts of sunrays popping out between the openings of the tall trees. It annoys my eyes. We hear the obnoxious and high-pitched sound of a cicada bug. We pass many well-maintained cottages and houses that dot the coastline. They are all unique, with beautiful flowers and landscaped yards. Many of the cottages have boat ramps in their backyards. I can only see the lake in glimpses due to the many cottages and thickly planted tall trees. We pass a large wooded area on the east side of the road and a few large cherry orchards. Junior spoils the pleasant drive to the beach by letting off a stinky SBD fart. He is pretending he didn't do it, but I can tell by his sly little smile that he did. Sandy, Tito, and I are gasping for fresh air. Then he breaks out in a laugh and proudly takes the credit for our misery. A minute later, he points out a dilapidated wooden house that's on the side of the road. He yells out that it's Sandy's house. Sandy gets mad and almost starts crying.

She quickly regains composure as Dad pulls into the park's white stone gravel parking lot. He parks on the north side by the woods, as he usually does.

Shortly after arriving at the beach, Timmy vomits near the shore. Dad saw him and reminded Timmy of his previous warnings about eating too many cherries. Dad had caught Timmy several times eating a bunch of cherries from the full lugs we picked and finally told him he should slow down or he might get sick.

I'm excited to be here! Soon, we'll be swimming in the lake, but first, Junior and I need to set up the picnic area. The path by the pickup leads us to a picnic spot with several tables nestled in a small, dense cedar wood sprinkled with birch trees, giving it an enchanted feel. We often choose this part of the park for its privacy and the shade it provides. The ground is cushioned with dead ferns, small sticks, and twigs. A fallen log blocks the path, and a long birch branch rests nearby. Stripped white birch bark lies on the ground, and I can't help but wonder if this is where Mom found the birch tree bark she used to write a love letter to Dad in the late 1940s. She keeps that love note in our family photos and memorabilia box.

A different path at the picnic area leads to the shoreline. I explore the coast, where the roots of cedar trees are partially exposed due to erosion, resembling the mythical head of Medusa. Small sticks and twigs are washed ashore by the lake's waves. The sea foam on the beach reminds me of shaving cream. A dead fish covered in flies lies on the shore.

I return to the pickup to fetch the cooler and other items for our picnic spot. Meanwhile, Mom sets up the table and prepares the food and utensils for dinner. Dad focuses on starting the grill because we're having hot dogs tonight! Afterward, we'll finally have the chance to go swimming.

Walking back to the pickup to prepare for swimming, I pass by a cedar tree and cut off a small fern. I cut small pieces with my thumbnail and index finger and rub them back and forth. Out comes the pleasing aroma of cedar resin. Doing this always reminds me of this place and Mom. Smelling cedar resin brings feelings of harmony, serenity, happiness, joy, peace, and well-being, as well as a belief that all is well with me and that God has my back. I started doing this when I was around ten years old. It started here at this park. I still do it wherever I go.

At the pickup, I crawl into the back camper and prepare to go swimming. It feels good to take off my dirty work clothes and put on my swim trunks. Looking across the road as I get ready, I see the strawberry field where we picked one year ago. There are no strawberries since the season has passed. Picking strawberries is hard work. Your back hurts as you stoop over to pick, or if you choose to kneel, your knees will ache. Add this to the sun beating down on you with no chance of any shade. The only thing I liked about picking strawberries was choosing and eating the giant strawberries of my choice. Ummm, they tasted so delicious! By far, I prefer picking cherries over strawberries.

With a towel in hand, I'm ready to walk to the beach. I wish I had sandals or shower shoes because these stones in the parking lot are killing my tender feet. This is so painful. Why are my feet so tender? I've always been amazed at how most people can walk barefoot without being bothered, but not me. The balmy breeze from the lake takes my mind off the pain in my feet.

Junior stands on the white-painted pier, ready to jump into the lake. Splash! In he goes. He fully immerses himself and comes up excitedly, yelling how cold but refreshing it is. In no time, he's swimming underwater and moving everywhere like a big fish.

Timmy stays at the little beach and plays with the sand and small stones.

Tito, Sandy, and I step into the chilly water and slowly walk towards the deeper water. Junior is swimming toward us, threatening to splash us. The three of us quickly plead with him not to, but I feel he will do it anyway. He loves to play King of the Hill with his siblings. He likes to be the big ape. Since he is the oldest and strongest, he usually gets his way. Diplomacy is the only way I can get anything out of Junior.

The water is crystal clear, and the sand at the bottom of the lake is pleasant to walk on. My only annoyance is the large rocks scattered randomly on the lake floor. Some areas are worse than others. There aren't as many once you go out 20 feet or so. I hold on to the side of the pier as I walk further out into the lake. This is how I always enter a lake: slowly and cautiously. It feels so chilly. Why do I torture myself by going in so slowly? I want to jump off the dock and get it over with.

Dad and Junior are the only ones who know how to swim. I can swim underwater for a short distance, but nothing else. I don't feel confident, but I want to learn. I don't like having a fear of water.

The water is now up to my waist. It's time to immerse fully. Here I go. I pinch my nostrils tight with my fingers, and down I go. The shock of the cold water rushes through my body. In a few seconds, I come up for air. I am elated. I am energized. I feel awesome! It only takes half a minute to acclimate to the chilly water, but I must continue moving my body. Tito is now totally in the water, and Sandy is still taking her time as she slowly walks into deeper water.

Now that I am all wet, Junior swims towards me and splashes me vigorously. I do my best to do the same to him. I'm blinded by the water furiously hitting my exposed eyes. He comes closer and closer to me, continuing his splashes of water. I can hardly see because my eyes are closed most of the time. Junior is having a blast. There is nothing more I can do. He only backs off after I tell him I surrender. The water fight with Junior revitalizes me. I now feel hyper-alive. I am full of energy. All the weariness I felt after picking cherries all day is gone. I'm ready to have fun.

I notice that Sandy still isn't all the way in the water. An obnoxious idea comes to my mind, which I accept to do. I know that she told me not to get her wet, but I can't resist getting her wet like Junior did to me. She can tell by how I approach her that I have something unpleasant in mind. Warnings blurt out of her mouth for me to stay away from her. I must have little devil horns on because I'm enjoying playing the prankster; I'm only helping her so she can start having fun. I swim to her as fast as I can and splash her. Screams come out of her mouth, but I can tell she's starting to enjoy it.

Now, it's time to start jumping off the pier. Since the water is very clear, it's easy to gauge the depth. I find a perfect spot where the water is around four feet deep and has a sandy bottom. Pinching my nostrils tight, I jump into the water. It's so fun. I do this four times. Afterward, I practice some underwater dog paddling—just the basic stuff.

I need to learn a great deal about swimming. I swim with my eyes closed, while Junior swims with his open. I want to be able to see underwater, which would open a new world to me.

I walk to where Junior is in the lake. We have a couple more splash fights, then he swims to water over his head. The water level is at my lower neck. This is as far as I go. It feels good to walk around and swim in the lake. I pass through several microcurrents of cooler water. After 20 minutes of playing in the lake, it's time to get out and prepare for dinner.

Walking to the picnic table, I think about how this place is so different from Alma. I'm under a magical spell when I come to this place. The God-given beauty is abundant everywhere. I take in the panorama of Lake Leelanau and its shoreline. The other side of the lake is around half a mile away. Here in Michigan, we are blessed to have the Great Lakes around us. Lake Michigan is a stone's throw away from us. I'm having a blast. I love Michigan in the summertime. It's my favorite season. Michigan has a cold season that is too long, and I always look forward to summertime. I hope we can go to the Lake Michigan beach at Leland sometime this week. I want to stay longer than one week; this area has many fun things to do.

Mom has prepared the meal. We're having delicious grilled hot dogs, potato chips, Fritos corn chips, and canned baked beans. For refreshments, it's cherry-flavored Kool-Aid. Mom leads us in a prayer once we all sit at the picnic table. I am so hungry. These hot dogs are so delicious. Dad grilled enough hot dogs so that we all get two. I go for my second one, choosing the most burnt hot dog. Carefully, I spread ketchup on one side of the bun and squirt mustard on the other. I add a bit of relish, spread it across the bun, then carefully place the hot dog. We don't have grilled hot dogs often, which makes them all the more delicious. While eating, I think of my brothers, sister, and Mom and Dad. It feels good to be with them.

I'm starting to feel like I'm on an actual vacation, that is, if I block out the drudgery of picking cherries for eight and a half hours a day and forget how hot, sweaty, and dirty I get. I'll play Dad's game and say we are on vacation. However, from a broader perspective, I am grateful for my unique "vacation" experience. I can't wait to tell all my friends back home about my great time.

I won't tell everybody, though. Some people would scoff at me if I told them I did migrant farm work and that I consider that a vacation. Some people would find it silly for me to think that although I am going to the beach, having picnics and sightseeing, and staying in a tent, I'm not really on a vacation because I'm working. Other people, I wouldn't tell because they are prejudiced against Mexicans and Mexican Americans. They have no interest in knowing about the migrant farmworker's life. They know nothing about these hardworking people or their lives. They would never think of doing such menial hard work; it would be below their dignity and too hard for them to do. They would find living in a barn or some other quarters on a farm unacceptable.

We are poor and don't have money for regular vacations, but Mom and Dad are resourceful and always find inexpensive ways to do things. I guess this is one of those times.

I compare my "vacation" to those of other students at school who have gone on vacations with their parents to amazing places like Rocky Mountain National Park, Yellowstone National Park, Niagara Falls, Daytona Beach, Florida, Washington DC, Mackinaw Island, Chicago, New York City, Disneyland in California and other cool places. I think of the many other students who go camping with their families, staying at the many state parks and other camping sites scattered throughout Michigan. I think of the students who vacation at their family cottages around Michigan. Some students have vacations around Traverse City, staying in nice motels. I know the "vacation" I'm on doesn't compare to these, but I still love the time I'm having. Plus, I'm making money while on "vacation," or at least that's what Dad says.

I'm feeling so good. My spirit is calm and peaceful. My body is clean from the pristine lake water. The weather is steadily cooling down, but it is still warm outside. It feels terrific. The chirping of the birds in the background adds to the peaceful feeling I'm experiencing. Suddenly my state of bliss is interrupted by Dad slapping Mom in the butt as she walks by him. "Chotas en daddys," he says. He always says this when he slaps Mom's butt. It's a saying he made up. He's been saying it for years. Mom is annoyed. "Honey, stop it!" Dad laughs and does it again to annoy her. I figure it's time for me to leave the table. I'm done eating anyway. After cleaning up and thanking Mom for the meal, it's time to feed the seagulls.

Junior and I take the lead on preparing to feed the seagulls. We rip up small white Wonder Bread end-pieces and half-eaten hot dog buns. We share the fragments with Timmy, Tito, and Sandy. They are much more excited than Junior and I because we've done it a few more times than they have. There must be 15 seagulls flying above us, following our every move. They are eager to take the gifts we bring them. We start throwing the pieces in the parking lot. Immediately, they begin swooping down to land, each taking their chosen morsel. At different times, a fight erupts over the same morsel of bread. Timmy is laughing with glee and wants to get closer to them, but they fly away for a few seconds when he does. Junior repeatedly tells him not to get too close. The fun ends after a few minutes when we run out of bread.

Before we leave the beach, Junior and I hike along the path that parallels the lake. We do this every year we come here. The well-worn path stretches for around three to four hundred feet. At the end is a private house. The path is slightly curvy and uneven. There is snake grass on both sides. We are familiar with snake grass because it's also found on the shore of the Pine River at Conservation Park in Alma. Tito, Sandy, and Timmy are following us. They want us to slow down so they can join us. We ignore them because they will only slow us down. We know we have little time left before returning to the farm. To our right is the lake; how beautiful it appears. The sun gleams off the surface and blinds us if we look too long in its direction. The leaves of the many white birch trees around us sound similar to waves hitting a beach as they flutter in the wind. I reflect on how this place may have looked before European settlers arrived.

I wonder about the local Native Americans, the Grand Traverse Band of Ottawa, and the Chippewa Indians. I visualize Native Americans walking on this path and how beautiful this place must have looked before the houses, cabins, asphalt roads, telephone poles, wires, and motorized vehicles appeared.

The combination of Spanish and indigenous Mexican blood resulted in the Mestizos, who make up the majority of Mexico's population today. This is my identity: a mix of Mexican Native American, and Spanish ancestry.

I am proud to be an American, but I don't want to forget about my Mexican heritage. I can have both and take pride in both. I'm eager to learn more about my Mexican heritage, as it helps me better understand my identity. I don't want to give up my Mexican culture; I want to live a blend of both Mexican and American cultures.

All my life, I've been around White people by way of school, church, community, and neighborhood. Generally speaking, we have been accepted by the majority culture. I know of some people back home who are racist, but for the most part, White people are accepting of us.

In contrast to my Michigan upbringing, the culture of Mexican Americans from Texas, where Dad was raised and where Mom lived as a young child, is so different from my upbringing. Generally speaking, White people and Mexican Americans from Texas don't mix. Many of my Mexican American peers back home have White girlfriends, just like I had last year. You won't find this in Texas.

I also find that many of my Mexican American peers from the Valley aren't as open to trying new things that take them out of their comfort zone as I am. Many times, when I do something different, I'll be told by some Mexican Americans that I'm only trying to show off and that I should tone it down. Some say, "Are you trying to be a gringo? or "That's for White people, that's for gringos." I won't accept that or believe it. I don't like people holding me back from what I want to do.

I'm snapped out of my thoughts by Dad's loud whistle. It's our cue that it's time to head back to the truck and the farm.

As we get on the road, I think of the fun we will have at the chicken coop clubhouse tonight. Junior and I are excited to spend the evening with Decky and the other guys.

Back at the farm, I quickly write a note to give to Lety. I hope she doesn't mind me writing to her. I'm nervous, but I'm going to take a chance. I see Ana and ask her to give it to Lety for me. I prefer giving it to Lety, but sometimes it's hard to catch her outside. Ana says she'll give it to Lety, but it will cost me a stick of gum.

No problem. I pull a pack of Doublemint chewing gum from my right front pant pocket and give her a stick.

Dear Lety, how are you? I'm doing fine. I'm having a lot of fun here. I'm glad we met. I think you are cool. I hope you don't mind if I write notes to you. I think it's cool that you're from McAllen, Texas. My dad grew up there. We have many relatives who live in the Valley. I've never been there, but I would like to go one day.

Bob Fuentes

PS: Please write back

Walking to the chicken coop clubhouse, I have butterflies in my stomach. I wonder if I'll fit in. I've already met Jaime and Moises, but I wonder who else will be there. Will they make fun of me or look down on me for not knowing how to speak Spanish? Will some think I'm trying to be a White person? Can I be honest with them and explain why I don't speak Spanish? Can I tell them I'm proud of my Mexican heritage and love being around my people? Can I tell them that I have many White friends and Mexican American friends back home? It doesn't matter to me what color your skin is. Jim is White. He's my best friend. Luis is Mexican American; he's my other best friend. Can I be myself?

We enter the coop and find only Decky. He tells us other guys will be coming. I'm glad only Decky is at the coop before us. This way, I have time to adjust to my surroundings. I pick a cherry lug to sit on and ask Decky how the beach was. He went to the Lake Michigan beach at Leland. The beach is much larger than the Lake Leelanau beach we went to. Decky tells us he had a blast and that there were a lot of pretty girls in bikinis. Junior and I listen intently as Decky tells us how pretty they looked.

Shortly afterward, Moises, Jaime, Cousin Abel, and a few other guys walk in. Everybody grabs a cherry lug for their seat. Several conversations are going on at the same time. We need someone to get everyone's attention, welcome everyone, and do introductions. I mention the idea of doing so. Decky and Junior laugh at me for thinking we need to do this. I sense people are nervous but don't want to show it. They don't see the value of having an introduction so that everybody gets to know each other. It's not a clubhouse if you don't know your fellow members. It's not good for trying to build relationships.

I feel foolish when I ask everybody to please introduce themselves. I tell them that I will start. "Hi, I'm Bob Fuentes; I'm 14 years old. I live in Alma, Michigan, about three hours south. I don't speak Spanish. I wish I did, but Mom and Dad didn't teach us. I love hearing it, and I want to learn Spanish. I love being a Mexican." I sound so corny, but I don't care. I figure that letting them know about me might help stop their negative perceptions of me, given that I don't know how to speak Spanish. I also don't want them to perceive that I'm trying to be a White person. Two boys don't understand what I am saying. Decky interprets for them. By their smiles, I sense they accept me. I'm feeling in the groove.

Everybody takes turns introducing themselves. There are many chuckles and nervous laughs as, one by one, everybody tells us who they are. The place is beginning to come alive. I feel much more at ease because I know a little about everyone present, and they know a little bit about me. I now know who can and cannot speak English at a conversational level. This will help me when I want to talk with them.

Decky suggests that we play a game where we get in a circle. The goal of the game is to be able to fart every time it's your turn to do so. If you cannot fart, then everybody gets to pinch or hit you in the arm. You decide beforehand whether you want to be pinched or hit. All of us laugh and think it's a great idea. Decky starts. He has no problem providing us with a fart. The next person is

Jaime. He has no problem. Then it's Abel's turn. He has no problem. Everybody can fart for the first round. Why do guys think farts are so funny that they would even play a game about it? I'm not sure, but everybody is laughing and busting a gut. The chicken coop is not well-ventilated, so the place is beginning to smell very gassy and rank, but nobody cares; the smellier, the funnier.

The second round starts. We all succeed, although some of us had to try really hard to produce one. Junior had no problem. By the sound of his two farts so far, it appears he has a lot of reserves. I'm doing alright, but I wonder if I can produce more for the upcoming rounds. I don't want to be pinched or hit.

Round three starts. Half of us could not fart, including me. Seeing some of the guys get slugged makes me choose to be pinched. Here comes the pain. Seven guys pinch me! I tense my arm every time I'm about to be pinched. Anticipation is part of the pain. Peer pressure has certainly kicked in. If the other guys are hanging in, so will I.

I'm trying hard to collect enough gas for the fourth round. Out comes a small toot. I made it! Four guys weren't able to fart. Now it's time for me to have some fun pinching and slugging.

My hits might not be as forceful as the other guys, but my pinch is something to contend with. It always gets a person's attention. I learned how to do it from Dad pinching us. I don't use my nails. I use the technique of rubbing the skin in opposite directions. You place the skin between the upper index finger and the thumb on the other side of the skin. You move your index finger and thumb in opposite directions. If done right, it can deliver a good amount of pain.

By now, everybody has been pinched or slugged. We all feel the pain, but decide to do one more round. I can't fart. Here comes another round of pain! I choose to be punched. I take the punches on both arms to balance out the pain. I laugh during the hits to take my mind off the blows.

After the game, we open the door to release the horrendous gas smell. We talk about the different types of farts we heard (or smelled); the squeaky, the SBD, the trumpet sound, the loud fart, the soft and wispy fart, the long-lasting fart, the juicy one, and others with no names. This definitely is a guy thing.

I feel a lot closer to the other guys. The fart game served as a perfect icebreaker. I feel closer to Moises and Jaime and find it easy to talk with them. However, I still feel somewhat uneasy around Jaime because I like his younger sister. Mexican males can be very protective of their sisters, so it keeps me on a slight edge. I don't want him to tell me to stay away from Lety.

I find out that Jaime will attend one of the high schools in McAllen, Texas, this fall.

I find out a little bit more about Moises. He goes by the nickname "Moi." This fall, he will be a freshman at Archbold High School in Archbold, Ohio. Moi attends the Rodriguez church, Archbold's Spanish-speaking Asamblea de Dios (Assembly of God) church. His older brother, Miseal, is the pastor.

This fun cannot stop. I want more. I don't care that it's hot in the coop, or that I am in pain, and that my abdominal muscles are hurting from laughing so hard. I get Junior's attention and take him aside. "Let's show the guys how to make a hand-held-controlled fly toy," I tell Junior. He laughs and thinks it's a great idea.

We get everything ready to show the guys our fly demonstration. Quickly, I run to find Mom to see if she has a piece of thread for us to use while Junior captures a giant fly. He won't have any trouble because there are two flying around in the coop. I'm back with a piece of thread around 20 inches long in no time. Everybody is wondering what we're up to. We go to a corner of the coop, away from the guys, and begin to tie a noose around the slim neck of the fly. Now it's time to test it. Junior holds the opposite side of the thread. The fly is flying but is under the control of Junior, who is holding the thread. We are ready!

It's time to show the guys! "Gentlemen, may I have your attention, please? I introduce to you the magnificent new toy that every kid will want. Now you too can have your own fly toy!" Junior walks out, holding the thread as the giant fly flies under Junior's control. Everybody is amazed and bursting with laughter. Junior and I got the idea from the electric wire control aircraft toys that are advertised for Christmas. Junior does a few 360-degree turns as he walks around the coop, passing in front of every guy. Jaime, Moi, and Decky take turns flying the fly inside the coop.

The rest of the time at the clubhouse is spent talking about girls, muscle cars, Big Time Wrestling, and professional baseball. Before I know it, it's time to leave. It's turning dark outside. I love these long summer days. Everybody slowly clears out and heads back to their abodes to prepare for bed. Until tomorrow, goodbye, clubhouse!

It's around 10 pm. I just finished cleaning up before heading to the tent to sleep. I walk to the road to be alone. No cars are driving by. In the background, the ever-present sound of crickets and katydids is constant. The farm is tranquil. Only a couple of lights around the farm are on. I look at the clear sky with all its stars. I reflect on the long, purposeful, weary, fun, and happy day. Day one of picking cherries is over. I now have an idea of what to expect from here on out. My body is achy, not only from the fart game but from picking. I think of Lety and hope she doesn't mind me writing notes to her. I think of the refreshing time at the beach and all the fun guys at the clubhouse. I think about all the beauty around me in the forms of cherry orchards with their delicious fruit, the freshwater lakes, the hilly terrain, my family, and how nice it is to be doing things together. I am happy about the risks I took today, like writing a note to Lety. I'm stretching myself. It doesn't feel comfortable, but I'm praying she will like it. I'm happy that I started the introductions at the clubhouse. I was nervous, but it paid off.

Closing my eyes as I lay in my sleeping bag, all I can see are thousands of cherries. I see my hands picking them. I see huge clumps of cherries on branches. I see cherries in my bucket and the full lugs. Cherry images are burned in my mind. I see orchards full of cherries. I open my eyes for a second to get rid of the continuously changing images of cherries coming into my mind's eye. Thoughts of the lake, thoughts of Lety, and the clubhouse whiz by. What wonderful thoughts. I could think about things for a long time, but I need sleep for tomorrow's work and fun. My body is achy, but it feels good. I can't wait to tell Luis and Jim about everything I'm doing. I think about whether Dad will pay Junior and me for picking cherries. I think about what I might buy. I don't want to leave this place.

TUESDAY, 29 JULY 1969

It's time to get up and get the day started. Off I go to the bathroom, hoping nobody will see me. I pass by Lety's uncle's truck, which looks pretty cool. It's a 1968 red Ford 450 stake truck with a wood plank floor and a ladder made of wood to get into the back, with wood sides and thick green canvas enclosing the back. It's a single axle with four tires in the rear. The truck looks brand new. Decky told me that Lety's uncle is a patron and has a few families he brought up with him from McAllen, Texas, to pick cherries.

It's time to start day two of picking. We will work from 8 am to 5 pm, with a 30-minute lunch break. That's an eight-and-a-half-hour workday. Like yesterday, Tito, Sandy, Junior, and I ride in the back of the pickup, sitting on the tailgate and heading out to the orchard where we left off yesterday.

I struggle to get motivated to start the work day. I don't want to get drenched from all the dew on the weeds and cherry branches. After a few minutes, I'm in the groove and doing my best to forget the discomfort of being wet and chilly.

Junior is picking close to me. He makes a perfect target. I give in to my childish ways and pranks and throw a cherry at him. It hits him in the back. I pretend not to know what he is talking about as he accuses me. We get back to picking. A couple of minutes later, I throw another cherry at Junior. "OK, I know it's you. You're going to be sorry." The cherry fight is on! We aren't too concerned that our clothes will probably be stained. I'm hit, he's hit. I'm hit more than he is. Junior is not one to be overcome by a younger sibling. I'm taken by surprise as he charges at me and throws volleys of cherries at me. Behind me is the cherry tree I'm picking that blocks any escape route. I'm in his direct line of fire. I'm riddled with cherry bullets at close range. My shirt shows the evidence of where cherry bullets hit me. With a grin, I surrender and promise not to do it again. The cherry fight was a short diversion from the tedious work of picking. The fight has helped me to stay motivated as I pick.

While I pick, I can't stop thinking about Mom's side of the family. Grandpa Jose Maria Ramon was born and raised in Ciudad Mier, Tamaulipas, Mexico, a border town near Roma, Texas. Grandma Antonia Canales Ramon is from Cuero, Texas, between Houston and Corpus Christi.

At the end of 1935 or early 1936, Grandpa and Grandma Ramon, along with their two children—Uncle Ernie, who was six years old, and Mom, who was three— moved from Cuero, Texas, to Mt. Pleasant, Michigan, with Grandpa's brother-in-law Tio Arnulfo Martinez and his wife, Tia (Aunt) Estefanita "Fane" Martinez. I've also heard her name was Sanjuanita. Grandpa Ramon and Tia Fane are siblings. Tio Arnulfo had already been to Michigan to scout for a good place to work, where there wasn't a lot of racism. All the families related to Grandpa and Grandma Ramon had strong ties and always sought ways to help each other.

Other relatives who came to Michigan with Tio Arnulfo in his 1937 Chevrolet stake truck included the newlyweds Tio Sisto (Grandpa's brother) and Tia Chula, Tio Cecilio Martinez (Tio Arnulfo's brother), his wife Tia Leocadia (Grandpa Ramon's sister), and their two children, Tio Mateo Castillo and his wife (I don't remember her name), along with their child. I wish I could remember all their names.

Soon after, the Ramon family moved to Shepherd, Michigan, and stayed in migrant farmworker housing. Initially, Grandpa did farm work, hoeing sugar beets, beans, and other fields, helping with the hay harvest, and other farm labor. Later, Grandpa bought a stake truck and did different jobs, including hauling sugar beets, tomatoes, and logs, as well as taking migrant farmworkers to and from their fields to hoe sugar beets and other crops.

In 1943, Grandpa Ramon and his family received a "Certificate of Farm War Service." It's a certificate from the United States Department of Agriculture signed by the Secretary of Agriculture, Claude R Wickard. The certificate is in our box of photos back home. It says, "This certifies that this family is enlisted in all-out farm war production, 1943." It was a program from 1940 to 1945 to assist in farm production during World War II. Many young men were sent off to war, and there was a critical need for farmworkers. It's funny the things I remember.

Grandpa later moved to Maple Rapids after purchasing a parcel of land he paid fifty dollars for to build a house. On the land was the concrete foundation of a former shoe repair shop, and Grandpa built his house on top of it.

Grandpa and Grandma planted a garden in the backyard, where they mainly grew potatoes. Uncle Ruben told me they ate potatoes at least once and sometimes two times a day, and that he was sick of eating them.

A few years later, Great-grandma Mercedes Vera, Grandma's mother, moved in with Grandma and Grandpa. A few things I know about Great-grandma Mercedes are that she had a spice garden on the side of the house. Great-grandma didn't speak English, and she never went anywhere. Uncle Ruben told me that a man came to the house one day for some reason. He could smell the tortillas that Great-grandma was making. Great-grandma could tell by his non-verbal expressions and tone of voice that he liked what he smelled. Even though Great-grandma couldn't communicate in English, she handed him a plate with a hot flour tortilla. He loved the gesture and the tortilla. Soon, he left the house and immediately returned with a Mason jar of canned tart cherries, which he gave Great-grandma as a gift for her kind hospitality.

I think about how Grandpa and his family had their world turned upside down when Grandma Ramon passed away in 1947 due to birth complications, a few months after giving birth to Uncle Peter. Grandpa couldn't work and care for all his children, so relatives and friends stepped in to help. This continued for a couple of years.

There was serious talk of splitting the family up. Some of Mom's siblings would be leaving the household and living and growing up with relatives in Saginaw, Michigan. Mom wanted nothing to do with this. Fourteen-year-old Mom agreed to quit school and take over the role of being a mom. She put her life on hold to focus on keeping the family together. She was now responsible for Aunt Martha (age thirteen) and uncles Bernie (age ten), Daniel (age nine), Filemon (age seven), Joe (age six), Ruben (age 4), and Peter (age one). Uncle Peter told me Mom never yelled at them and was nurturing and kind to her siblings. She always had a positive attitude and could change bad moods into happy ones. I can hardly imagine the responsibility and work at such a young age.

Many residents of Maple Rapids were aware that Grandma Ramon had passed away and that Mom was taking care of the children. Through her natural ability to form friendships, Mom made friends with some neighbor ladies who taught her how to can vegetables and fruits, bake, and cook various dishes. Some neighbor ladies also helped Mom improve her sewing and clothing-making skills.

In the mid-1950s, the Ramon uncles traveled to Free Soil, Michigan, to pick cherries. Cousin Gary Martinez, one of the Martinez cousins, also joined them. This was how the uncles could buy school clothes and other things they wanted. Grandpa worked full-time for General Motors at the Fisher Body Plant in Lansing and could not leave his job to pick cherries.

Uncle Bernie told me Grandpa Ramon would drive to Free Soil and drop them off (Uncles Bernie, Daniel, Filemon, Joe, Ruben, Pete, and Cousin Gary). Uncle Bernie, who was the oldest, was in charge. Grandpa would leave a big cardboard box of food for the young men that needed to last them for the entire week. It consisted of basic food items like bread, eggs, peanut butter, jelly, and cans of beans and vegetables. One summer, Grandpa gave them a box of bread, peanut butter, jelly, and a case of kidney bean cans. Uncle Pete never wanted to eat another kidney bean for a long time. A couple of migrant farmworker families at the camp beside my uncles knew what they were eating and occasionally offered them a warm Mexican meal. Since they had no vehicle to get around in, they would walk into town to enjoy their time off. They would go to Johnny's Skating Rink to roller-skate. This is where they met some local girls and dated them. They would also go to the park downtown, where free movies were shown outside on a large screen.

My mind takes me to how Mom's family and Dad's family met. It was late spring of 1946 when the Ramon and Fuentes families met each other. They met at Enrique's Spanish Pentecostal Church in the country outside of Ithaca, Michigan. The church was built on property belonging to Enrique Vasquez. I can only imagine the excitement at the church when Grandpa and Grandma Fuentes visited it with their nine children for the first time. Spanish Pentecostal churches are usually small and rare in Michigan. It's always an exciting event when a new family comes. Later, this church was moved to La Curva, only 50 yards from our old house. As a young child, I saw it every day until we moved to Alma. The Fuentes family fit in with ease. Since Grandpa was a preacher, in no time, Grandpa was invited to preach occasionally. Also, Dad was invited to play his accordion and guitar. Grandma, Aunt Maruca, and Aunt Chacha also brought and played their tambourines.

I can easily visualize the young Mexican girls in church checking out Uncle Cone, 16 years old, and Dad, 14. I can visualize Uncle Cone and Dad checking out the girls. Dad must have received added attention when he played the guitar or his accordion. Mom was one of these girls.

In no time, Mom and Dad were discreetly gazing at each other. Chemistry was beginning to brew. Soon, warm smiles appeared as they looked at each other. They had to be careful not to draw too much attention from the adults because the Pentecostal ways are very strict, and there is no room for young puppy-love adventures.

In the box of photos and memorabilia back home, we have an 11-inch by 17-inch black and white photo taken in 1946 of the church where Mom and Dad's families met. The church still looks the same today. In front of the church are around 130 people. The Ramon and Fuentes families and the Castillo and Martinez families are in the photo. These are relatives on Mom's side of the family. It's hard for me to imagine that all these people were able to fit inside the tiny white-painted wood church. On each side of the church, there are three windows. On top of the church is a small cupola with a bell inside that rings when church services are about to begin. As you enter the church, you enter a small vestibule before the sanctuary. The only aisle runs down the middle. Males and females sit on opposite sides of the aisle. In the back of the church is a platform about six inches tall, with the pulpit, piano, and a few seats for the pastor and other speakers.

We have another large black-and-white photo that shows a group of teenagers in front of the little church, all dressed in church clothes. The girls are wearing white blouses and black skirts that fall below the knee. The boys wear various colored shirts. In front of them is a banner that says "Embajadores de Cristo," 2 Cor. 5:20, Iglesia Belem, Organizada el 14 de Julio 1945, ITACHA, Michigan." The translation is "Christ Ambassadors, 2 Corinthians, chapter five, verse 20, Bethlehem Church, organized July 14, 1945, ITACHA Michigan." Ithaca is not spelled correctly. In the group of around 30 teens are aunts Martha, Maruca,

Chacha, and Uncle Ernie (Mom's older brother). Some of the people in this photo are here picking cherries this year.

Mom and Dad wasted no time getting to know each other. Romances back then were conducted covertly. Mom and Dad used all the acceptable and available times to get to know each other better. These times included Sunday School for teens, the periods before and after the two Sunday church services, and the Wednesday night service. Seeing each other in the sugar beet fields, hoeing, or other farm labor was also possible, but it didn't give Dad and Mom any time to hang out. People had to work, and it wasn't the time to be sociable and make goo-goo eyes at each other.

Mom and Dad began writing notes to each other. Mom kept all of these notes, which are in the box of photos. The first time I read the notes, I couldn't believe Dad could write such a beautiful love note. It seemed to me that a different person wrote them.

In the late 1940s and early 1950s, the Ramon family went several times to Lake Leelanau to pick cherries with the Fuentes family. Dad and Mom were delighted; they would have almost three weeks to spend as much time together as possible after work.

Their romance continued to sprout and blossom, and as luck would have it, they had their first kisses at the Esch Farm. They were unique kisses. Dad would come to the Ramon living quarters to visit Mom. They were only able to talk through the screen door. Great-grandma Mercedes kept her eyes on Mom and Dad. In the short times when she wasn't watching, they placed their lips on the door's screen and kissed. You can't stop love.

Dad didn't stay with us very long this morning. To my surprise, starting today, Dad will split his work time by picking cherries and then leaving the orchard to prepare and load them onto the flatbed semi-trailer parked at the farm. I don't know all the details yet. Dad loves to operate machinery and drive vehicles. Back home, one of Dad's previous jobs was being a school bus driver for the Alma School District. In the late 1940s, he drove for the Esch Farm, taking cherries to the processing plant in Traverse City. Sometimes, he would drive the tractor in the orchard to collect the cherries.

My body is sore from yesterday's picking, partly because of all the positions I put my body in when picking cherries. I'm also sore from the hits and pinches I received yesterday from the fart game we played at the clubhouse.

A few monarch butterflies flutter by. One lands on a branch nearby. I'm thrilled. It repositions itself as it approaches me. I think it's lucky to have one land on you. Slowly, I stretch out my arm, hoping it will settle on me. It lands on me! The butterfly stays on my arm briefly. In the meantime, I remain as still as possible. Smiling, I gently move my arm so the butterfly can fly away; I need to return to picking. Perhaps I'll have luck with Lety.

It's around 10 am, and the tractor is approaching to pick up the first load of freshly picked cherries. I always feel excited when I hear it coming. It motivates me to pick faster to fill another lug before it stops for our cherries. As it gets closer, I see Anne Waterman driving the tractor. This is the first time I've seen her. She is fair-skinned, blonde, and slender. Her short bob haircut emphasizes her five-foot-five-inch frame. She has a simple and natural beauty. She looks fashionable in her work clothes. With a big smile, she approaches us to collect our lugs. Dad chats with Anne while Junior and I load our lugs onto the trailer. I always take pride in the number of lugs we've picked. The number we picked is recorded in the notepad Mr. Waterman used yesterday. Anne gives Dad the tickets for the count of lugs we've picked. Timmy, Tito, Sandy, and I wave goodbye as she leaves to pick up the stack of filled cherry lugs from the next family down the row from us.

I go back to picking and soon remember when Sandy almost got run over by a tractor. Around six years ago, we came up to pick cherries for a few days. We'd just arrived in the orchard and were getting things ready to start picking. All of a sudden, a young male farmworker driving a tractor is yelling out over and over at the top of his lungs, "Haste un lado" ("get to one side"). He was in a panic and driving erratically, steering left and right. He didn't know how to operate the tractor. He even went in a big circle around several cherry trees several times, yelling and with a terrified grimace on his face. Nearby, children around five or six years old, including Sandy, were playing in the orchard when this dangerous and unpredictable situation occurred. The guy almost ran over Sandy! I was standing only feet away and saw it happen. Dad screamed out to the guy what to do to take control of the tractor and stop it. Thank God all ended well. Sandy didn't appear too concerned or afraid. I don't think she knew what was happening. Dad and some other men scolded the tractor driver, who had no business operating it. Mom was in shreds and crying because she also saw it happen. It turned out that the driver jumped on the tractor to move it out of his way so that he could move his car closer to his picking spot. He forgot where the clutch and brakes were on the tractor.

The sound of Aunt Maruca's car brings joy to my ears. Mom gets out of the vehicle with the lunch and yells, "It's time to eat." Like yesterday, she rode back with Aunt Maruca to prepare lunch. We are all looking forward to eating and taking a short break. Mom made ground beef and potato burritos tightly wrapped in aluminum foil. We have strawberry Kool-Aid and Lay's potato chips to add to our meal. Mom says a short prayer, and in minutes, my siblings gobble down their food. Not me. I want to extend the pleasure I get from these savory burritos.

I join Decky and Junior in the shade of a cherry tree with their food. I arrange some empty cherry lugs for my table and chair. Our faces are sweaty. We don't talk much because we're tired and hungry. Several flies are flying around our food. They ignore our attempted whacks. We're too slow for them.

With the food settling in my stomach, I have around ten minutes to lie on the blanket before returning to work. How good it feels to rest in the shade. The warm, gentle breeze is a godsend. There are blue and green dragonflies flying around. They look pretty, but I'm afraid to touch them. Although they don't sting, they can bite out of self-defense. I leave them alone. Several flies are buzzing around me, disturbing my rest.

Junior and I say goodbye to Decky as we throw cherries at each other and tell him we're looking forward to the beach with him and chicken coop clubhouse time. We all agree to bring our baseball cards. Decky says he'll also bring his Mad magazines. Back to work, we go.

The afternoon picking is uneventful and tedious. I start thinking about the paper I wrote for a class about the origin of cherries and how cherry farming came to Michigan. I found out that the ancient Chinese grew them. Some scholars say that cherries originated in Turkey and the Caspian Sea area. Cherry growing in Michigan started in 1852, when Peter Dougherty, a Presbyterian missionary, planted cherry trees on Old Mission Peninsula. Much to the surprise of the local Native Americans and White settlers, the trees flourished. Soon, other farmers in the area started planting cherry trees. In 1893, the first tart cherry orchards were planted at Ridgewood Farm, close to Peter Dougherty's orchard. By the early 1900s, the tart cherry industry was established around the Traverse City area and along the Lake Michigan coastline in Michigan. The demand for transporting cherries around the country was met by ships anchoring at Traverse City, where cherries were loaded and sent to ports all over the Great Lakes. The Traverse City area is excellent for cherry growing, with its sandy soil for good drainage and rolling hills for airflow. This creates a favorable microclimate for growing cherries. Lake Michigan plays its part by tempering the cold arctic air and winter winds and cooling the cherry trees In the summer.

I think about the history of the Esch Farm. I discovered that in 1907, John Esch bought one hundred and sixty acres from the Stephens family. Three years later, his brother, Theodore Herbert Esch Sr., bought it from him. Theodore started to grow potatoes. In the 1920s, he cleared some of the woods to grow cherries. Theodore Herbert Esch Sr. is Ted's father.

Today, the Esch Farm has around 80 acres of sweet and tart cherries. I counted around eleven cherry orchards on his land, consisting of different types of sweet cherries and tart cherries.

It's around two hours before quitting time. It's time for me to get on the ladder and pick the top branches. The sky is mostly clear with minimal haze. I'm in a sleepy state of mind as I climb up the ladder. To my surprise, I see a long reddish-brown colored iron ore ship sailing west on Lake Michigan! I immediately tell Junior. He gets on his ladder to check it out. Almost as soon as the ore ship is out of view, we see another ore carrier going in the opposite direction. This sure is helping the work go quicker for me. Ships have always interested me. I'm proud that we live in a state surrounded by the freshwater of the Great Lakes. Nowhere else in the world will you find such an expanse of freshwater. Seeing the ship snaps me out of my grogginess, brought on by the tedious work. I wonder where the ship is going. Chicago? Maybe Gary, Indiana, to one of the steel mills I learned about in geography class.

Behind the ship, I can see the North and South Manitou Islands. The islands are not clear, but they are visible. There is a ferry out of Leland that takes passengers to both islands. The islands are part of Sleeping Bear Dunes National Lakeshore. These are the islands known in the Native American Ojibwe legend about two bear cubs that drowned trying to swim across Lake Michigan from Wisconsin with their mother. Mother bear made it safely to mainland Michigan, but the cubs did not. The Great Spirit covered the cubs and the mother bear with sand. The two islands and Sleeping Bear Dunes symbolize a mother bear waiting forever for her little cubs to swim safely across the lake. I can see the dunes on the southern end of North Manitou. They must be huge if I can see them from here. The view from the top of the tree offers a splendid panoramic view of where we are. In the foreground are cherry orchards, then the Mitchell orchards, then the Esch orchards, and on to Lake Leelanau, followed by Lake Michigan with the Manitou Islands in the background. What a view! It's free, and I'm on vacation!

It's time for a break. I need water. I'm so thirsty. Why do I wait so long? Dragging my tired legs to the pickup where the water jug is, I see Mom standing on a ladder, picking with a smile as she sees me walking her way and asks me, "How are you, mi hijito?" She always calls me that. It's a term of endearment for "my beloved son." She is wearing a head scarf that covers half of her head, a short-sleeved blouse with tails out, and a pair of light brown pants. The pant bottoms are slightly rolled up. She seems out of place with her stylish look, but most ladies and girls do the same, including Lety. She never seems to be too dirty when she's picking cherries. I think of the photo of Mom and Dad standing in front of a cherry tree taken at the Esch Farm. It's cherry harvest time in 1950.

Mom has her hair in a ponytail. She's 17 years old. She looks voguish in her denim jacket, with sleeves slightly rolled up, accented by a paisley-style scarf tied in a front knot, the two ends of which are slightly above her waist. Dad has a blue and white plaid shirt, with tails out, and jeans with a narrow roll on his pants legs. Mom looks so pretty, and Dad so handsome. Mom snaps me out of this memory by asking me again how I'm doing. "I'm doing fine. How are you? I'm here to get some water and stretch my legs," I reply. Dad has already left for his other job of preparing the cherries for shipment to the cherry plant. I sit on the tailgate while I drink my water. Mom is never short of having something to say, so she tells me one of her memories of picking cherries here a generation ago.

I sit on a cherry lug and drink my water. Sandy, Tito, and Timmy play hide-and-seek nearby. I notice that we have nine lugs, which we picked since Anne went through and picked up the others we had. Several minutes later, I head back to work.

Mom Picking Cherries

On my way back to my tree to start picking again, I think of some of the photos in our photo box back home. I see the photo taken at an onion field around Imlay City, Michigan. The Ramon and Fuentes families picked side by side here when Mom and Dad were teenagers. It is here in the onion fields of Imlay City where Mom and Dad had their first real kiss (no screen between their lips). I think of the picture of Dad playing a Gibson electric guitar outside the tomato migrant farmworker camp near Archbold, Ohio. In the background is a washing machine with drying rollers on top. I can hear Dad playing his guitar now.

There's a photo of Mom's cousin, Ester Martinez, picking cherries. She now lives in the Saginaw area with many other relatives on Mom's side. Her big smile is welcoming and contagious; that's how it is even today. She's dressed for work and looks fabulous. Her hair is covered with a tied bandana and a bow in front. Her sleeves are rolled up above her elbows. Cousin Ester's shirt is under a pair of baggy bib overalls. She's wearing her harness with a pail attached that is almost filled with cherries. I wonder if I'm picking in the same orchard where this picture was taken. There's another photo taken in the late 1940s of Dad and a couple of his siblings, Aunt Chacha and Uncle Abran, in their work clothes, sitting on a fallen tree trunk on the side of a cherry orchard. One photo that stands out is of Dad with his curly hair at age 17, Aunt Chacha at age 15, wearing stylish sunglasses, and Uncle Abran wearing a wide-brimmed hat at age 13.

There's a photo taken in August 1956 of Aunt Rebeca with her frizzed-out hair under a straw hat with Aunt Chacha and another girl standing in front of cherry trees with filled cherry lugs. I see the photo taken in 1967 of Mom picking cherries. She's on a ladder with a big smile as she picks and looks straight into the camera. She wears a bandana covering part of her head, a short-sleeved light-colored blouse, and khaki pants. The tree is loaded with gorgeous-looking, sweet black cherries. Behind her is our parked 1964 tan-colored GMC pickup truck with the tailgate down. Inside is a toolbox and a cooler. To the truck's left are around six or seven filled cherry lugs neatly stacked, with one partially filled.

My thoughts continue, and I think about Mom's side of the family and how they changed from Catholicism to Pentecostalism. Mom told me they switched after Tia Fane's miracle. When Tia Fane was pregnant, she developed intense cravings to eat dirt. Her family was shocked at seeing her, for the first time, eating dirt. They tried every way they could think of to stop her. Nothing worked. Her cravings increased. Her intake of dirt increased. Uncle Bernie told me that she was eating weeds and not dirt. In either case, she usually found a sneaky and creative way to satisfy her craving. Some relatives thought she had a mental illness. The family was at odds as to what to do.

Meanwhile, Tia's physical condition was deteriorating as well. One of the relatives suggested asking the preacher to come over from the big-top tent where "Pentecostal camp-meeting services" were being held. The tent was located in the country, near their home in Cuero, Texas. This relative had attended some of these services and saw the miracles that were taking place. It was so different from the Catholic way of spiritual life. The family agreed to invite the preacher. The traveling preacher came to Tia Fane's house. As soon as he entered the house, he made it clear that before he prayed for Tia Fane, they would agree to hear him explain how to become a Christian and receive salvation. They agreed, and the preacher told them that the only way to eternal life was by accepting Jesus Christ as their savior. Tia Fane was moved by what the preacher said and immediately said she wanted to become a Christian. The preacher then prayed for her healing. After this, she had no more cravings to eat dirt (or weeds) and was back to being healthy in a short time. This miracle moved the family so much that, one by one, they all turned to becoming Pentecostal Christians.

I'm tired of standing and want to change my picking position. I find a place under the shady tree and begin picking on my knees. It feels good to take a break from standing as I pick.

I continue to think about Grandpa and Grandma Ramon and their commitment to their faith. The story of Grandpa Ramon's car accident is an excellent example of their faith and has always amazed me. It was around 1942 when Grandpa and Grandma Ramon were on their way to the little Spanish Pentecostal Church outside of Ithaca. This is the same church that was moved to La Curva. Their seven children were also in the car. The car couldn't have been packed any more, but no one complained much; everybody was used to it.

Suddenly and so unexpectedly, a farmer driving his tractor hit Grandpa's car broadside. The sudden and forceful impact sent the car flipping onto its opposite side. Heads, arms, and legs are all jumbled up. Back then, there were no seat belts, so everybody was scrambled about inside the vehicle. Everybody in the car was in a daze. There are a few cries from the younger children due to the hits their bodies sustained and the shock of what just took place. Grandpa and Grandma assess the situation as they look around as best they can to ensure everybody is alive and to see if there are any injuries.

Meanwhile, outside the car, the farmer almost has a heart attack after seeing what he has caused. He wonders if his grave error killed or injured anybody in the car. His heartbeat increases as his fears climb, thinking about a possible lawsuit for his negligent driving. The farmer quickly began to assist the passengers out of the vehicle. It was a miracle that no one was seriously injured. There were only a few scrapes, bruises, and sore bodies.

The shaken farmer profusely apologized to Grandpa and Grandma. He was willing to do anything they wanted him to do. He offered to pay and wanted everybody to go to the hospital to be checked out and make sure everybody was medically okay. The farmer was astonished when Grandma told him he could help by helping to get the car right side up and running so they could continue their way to church. After a few minutes, the car was right side up and running, and off the Ramon family went on their way to church. When I think of this incident, I know why we rarely miss a church service.

Uncle Bernie has a slightly different version of the accident from what Mom has always told us. He says that a farmer driving a car hit Grandpa Ramon's vehicle. In either case, the Ramon family car was broadsided.

Uncle Bernie likes to joke around a lot. He says the accident made the front page of the *Gratiot County Herald* with the headline "Flying Saucers Go Rolling Down Road After Car Hit by Tractor." According to the article, people close to the accident scene thought they saw flying saucers coming out of the car. Uncle Bernie says that what they thought they saw was really the stack of tortillas that Grandma Ramon made for the after-church meal as they scattered down the road.

At last, it's quitting time! The afternoon picking seemed to go on forever. Junior and I are happy that the workday is over. I picked 22 lugs today. That's around a lug per 24 minutes of picking; it's not too shabby. Now it's time to have fun! Since Dad is loading the semi-truck, Junior will drive the pickup truck back to the farm. He's so excited to drive. Mom and Timmy are in the front with Junior. Junior slowly and gently maneuvers the pickup through the orchard as he returns to the farm. Goodbye, cherries, until tomorrow!

I'm getting butterflies, wondering if Lety will like my note. Will she have one for me? I hope I see her before we go to the beach.

My wish has come true! I see her before we go to the beach. She gives me a big smile and says she will be right back and not to go anywhere. A quick minute later, she hands me a note. I tuck the note inside my pants pocket and walk to the water pump. I can't wait to read it.

Ana and Marti see me from a distance and call for me to join them. "Hey, try this," Ana says. She holds one of Mattel's Magic 8-Ball fortune-telling toys, which predicts your future. We have one back home. To use it, you ask a question, then shake the ball. One of the twenty responses appears. Marti and Ana are eager to ask me questions. The first one is, "Are you in love with Lety?" She shakes the ball and turns it over to see the answer. "Signs point to yes," it responds. I like this. Ana then asks, "Is Lety in love with Bob?" The answer is, "Outlook good." I'm feeling positive vibes. The last question they pose is, "Is our cousin Bob crazy?" I smile at them as they shake the black ball. The response is, "Cannot predict now." Marti and Ana tell me they are sure I am.

As usual, I dash to the water pump to clean my face, hands, and arms. After a hard day picking cherries, this always feels refreshing.

I see Dad placing a cherry tank onto the flatbed semi-trailer. Curious about his work, I watch for a few minutes. From what I can gather, the process goes like this: the full cherry lugs, recently brought from the orchard by tractor and trailer, are taken to the "cooling pad" on the farm. The cooling pad features a concrete surface with three cooling stations, where Dad works. Each station has a white cooling tank, with "Waterman Orchards" stenciled in red paint on the sides. Each tank holds 1,000 pounds of cherries—equivalent to 40 lugs! Each station has two large plastic water hoses pouring cold, clean well water into the tanks. The cherries are manually dumped into the cooling tanks filled with water, while empty lugs are tossed aside to be reused in the orchard. The cool water washes the cherries and keeps them as fresh as possible before they head to the processing plant. After each tank is filled with the dumped cherries from the lugs, Dad drives in with a tractor fitted with forklift tines at the rear. The tines are hydraulically operated, allowing Dad to lift the cherry tanks onto the flatbed trailer. Several tanks are already on the trailer. Once all the cherry tanks are loaded, Dad secures them tightly to the trailer with white mesh straps. They're ready to be transported to the cherry processing plant in Suttons Bay. Since Dad will be busy, he won't join us at the beach today.

I put my hand in one of the cooling tanks and feel the cold, refreshing, clean water, and swish around some cherries. It's incredible to see so many. When I'm ready for sleep tonight, I will have these images in my mind's eye. I take a small handful of cherries from the tank and rinse them under one of the water hoses that gushes out fresh, clean, well water. The cherries go into my mouth. How delicious they are!

Decky barks, "Whoever is riding with me, start getting in the pickup because I'm leaving in a few minutes." He's ready to head to the beach. Junior and I are excited to spend time with Decky at the beach, though I'm a bit anxious about riding with him. I don't feel safe when he drives, but peer pressure makes me ignore my sense of fear. Down the hill he goes, driving the pickup west down Esch Road. Sandy, Tito, Marti, and Ana are with us, riding in the back of the pickup truck with the cap on it. Decky speeds down the road, as I expected. The sudden accelerations and decelerations, along with the hilly and curvy roads to the beach, make Tito feel nauseous. All this, combined with the engine exhaust filling the back of the pickup, is too much for Tito.

Decky is a great swimmer, so he and Junior spend time in water that is over my head. But most of the time, the three of us hang out in water that reaches my neck. Tito, Timmy, and Sandy don't come out this far. As usual, the water feels incredible. What a relief from all the cherries I picked today. I feel rejuvenated, refreshed, and fully alive as soon as I enter the lake.

I want to swim with my eyes open underwater. I tell Junior about my plans and ask for his advice. Will it hurt my eyes? He assures me it won't hurt and that I'll have much more fun underwater with my eyes open. I'm scared but determined to try it. Under the water I go, and I quickly open my eyes. My instinct tells me to shut them, yet I resist. It doesn't hurt at all! I practice this over and over while dog paddling underwater. This is amazing! It opens up a new dimension of enjoyment in swimming for me.

Decky, Junior, and I are having a blast at the lake. We engage in a few water fights, and during these, it's tough for me to keep my eyes open. They love to swim underwater to target my legs and knock me off balance. When I don't see them around, I get anxious and scan the water to see if they're approaching me. We also spend some time jumping off the pier. Decky and Junior dash down the pier and leap into the water. I go to the edge and jump in. I still have a lot to learn about swimming.

While in the lake, I see Aunt Maruca driving her car and entering the parking lot. She and Mom get out and find a spot for us to picnic. Fifteen minutes after seeing them arrive, I leave the lake and head to Decky's pickup truck to get changed. I can't wait to read the note that Lety wrote me.

For supper, we're having bologna and cheese sandwiches on Wonder Bread. I spread mustard and mayonnaise on my sandwich and enjoy it with Lay's Potato Chips, canned baked beans, and fresh carrots. Everyone brought their appetites with them. I eat much faster than usual because I want to read Lety's note as soon as possible, and with nobody around. After eating, I walk to the cedar woods for privacy and open her note.

Dear Bob, I'm doing fine. Thank you for your note! No, I don't mind if you write to me. I would like that a lot. Hey, I hope you don't mind if I call you Robert. Is that OK? I mean, you don't look like a Bob. I love the name Robert. Did you work hard today? Are you having fun? Ana and Marti tell me you are crazy. You have pretty eyelashes. I want them! Please write soon.

Lety,

PS: What do you like to do for fun?
PSS: I don't mind if you don't speak Spanish. I like your accent.

After reading Lety's note, I feel like I'm in heaven. The swim and the food in my belly rejuvenate me. My heart melts as I read Lety's note several times. I smile.

Adrenaline rushes through me. I sense that she likes me. Wow, wow, wow! This vacation is turning out to be quite an enjoyable experience.

Junior and I walk over to Decky's place to see if he's ready to head to the clubhouse. We see him carrying a bag of chicharrones (salty, crunchy pork rinds) and a brown paper bag filled with his baseball cards. Junior and I have our baseball cards, too. In addition, Junior has a stack of hot rod and racing car magazines he wants to show the guys.

I suddenly remember the stack of newspapers I saw in the barn on Saturday when Decky gave us the farm tour. I tell Junior and Decky I'll meet them at the clubhouse. I walk to the barn and grab a stack of newspapers to take to the clubhouse.

A lot of conversations are going on as I enter the clubhouse. I begin to review the newspapers. The top right corner of each edition of the *Traverse City Record-Eagle* newspaper says, "It is a privilege to live in Michigan." In the Monday, July 14, 1969, edition, there's an article about astronauts Neil Armstrong and Edwin Aldrin and their tasks when they land on the moon. In the sports section, there's a piece about Joe Namath of the New York Jets, who is butting heads with pro football Commissioner Pete Rozelle. Supporters of the grape strike are facing charges, with nine adults arrested for backing the California grape workers' strike. The incident occurred at a Kroger grocery store in Detroit, where they demanded that the store manager remove all California grapes from the shelves. They threatened to walk out with unpaid items if their demand was not met, and they did.

The Wednesday, July 16, 1969 headline says, "Apollo Hurtling Toward Landing on the Moon." Under Classifieds, there's a 1955 Ford two-ton flatbed truck for sale. It catches my eye because I was born the same year. There's a U-Pick ad featuring Queen Anne, black Schmidt, and Tartarian cherries, along with another ad for cherry pickers needed. There's an article about the grape strike supporters facing charges, but all charges have been dismissed. Fisherman's Cove has an ad; the restaurant is in Leland, Michigan, not far from where we are. They offer fresh lake white fish from Lake Michigan. Leland is known as Fishtown and is famous for its fish. Decky loves coming here. There's also an ad from Thriftway: "Fresh tortillas, 18-pack for 25 cents." They're not as fresh as the ones I get.

Thursday, July 17's headline reads, "Apollo Unerringly Races Toward the Moon." Another article states that the rocket is halfway to the moon. There's also an article about the cease-fire between Honduras and El Salvador. I remember the guy we saw on the freeway riding his motorcycle, with long, dark brown hair and a license plate from Nicaragua. One day, I would love to visit the countries of Central America. Tempo Department Store is having a sale on bell-bottom jeans, and I want a pair. Decky always wears bell-bottom jeans. Dad says they are from the devil; he associates bell-bottom jeans with hippies. Doesn't Dad know that all US sailors wear bell-bottom pants? It's one of their uniforms. Because of this, Junior and I don't have any. Another article mentions that President Nixon is scheduled to meet the astronauts when they return on the aircraft carrier Hornet.

The Saturday, July 19 paper features an ad for a new 1969 Mercury Cougar two-door hardtop with a 351 V8 engine, 250 horsepower, automatic transmission, bucket seats, sequential rear turn signals, and front concealed headlamps, all priced at $3095. Cougars are among my favorite cars. I love their sleek design, the hideaway front lights, and the rear turn signals. I enjoy going with Dad to clean Lyon's Mercury car dealership in Alma. I sit in all the cars of my choice in the garage and showroom. I've sat in several luxurious and sporty Cougars at Lyon's showroom. Among all Cougars, my favorite is a 1969 burgundy XR7 Cougar with a four-speed manual stick shift, burgundy leather seats, an eight-track tape player, and a 351 cubic inch engine. I've spotted a few of these on the road. Maybe one day I'll own one.

Chicken Coop Clubhouse

It's time to talk about baseball. We set up a makeshift table with cherry lugs to showcase the baseball cards. Decky shares his bag of chicharrones, and everyone helps themselves.

Although Jaime and Moi don't have any baseball cards, they're excited to look at ours. Everyone except Jaime likes the Detroit Tigers. Jaime's team is the Houston Astros, and I can see why since he's from Texas. I can't wait to see Decky's Tigers cards. Since the Tigers won the World Series last year, there's a lot of hope among us fans that they'll do it again this year. Decky has been telling Junior and me about his Mickey Mantle New York Yankees baseball card, and we're eager to see it.

I'm discovering that Moi, Jaime, and Decky know the most about Major League Baseball, especially Moi and Decky. Baseball runs in Moi's family; his brother, Abel, often listens to a Detroit Tigers game on the car radio here at the farm. I've seen him with his girlfriend, Regina Perez, sitting in lawn chairs by his car near the barn as they listen to a Tigers game.

Decky is the first to show his baseball cards. He carefully removes the rubber band that holds the cards together. With over 800 cards, he has several piles stacked up. He's primarily a New York Yankees fan but also likes the Tigers. Decky proudly shares his favorite Yankees cards and is excited about his Mickey Mantle card. Mickey Mantle is an excellent player who plays center field, right field, and first base, wearing number 7 for the Yankees. Decky is an ace regarding the statistics of his favorite players in the entire Major League. I'm always amazed by how he can rattle off the stats of hundreds of baseball players. Decky mentions that he likes Yankees player Yogi Berra, catcher, number 3, as well as Yankees pitcher Whitey Ford, number 16, and outfielder Roger Maris, number 9 of the St. Louis Cardinals. He tells us that Mickey Mantle retired after eighteen years with the Yankees this past March. We all share our thoughts about Mickey Mantle. I'm sad to hear this. Decky says we can look at all of his cards after Junior and I talk about the ones we have.

Decky then shows us his Detroit Tigers cards. He starts with Al Kaline, number 6, an excellent right fielder and hitter, and goes on to Willie Horton, number 23, who plays outfield. He has all the best Tigers cards that include pitcher Denny McLain, Mickey Lolich, Don McMahon, Dick McAuliffe, Bill Frehan, Mickey Stanley, and Jim Northrup. Junior and I like Jim Northrup a lot and find it exciting that he grew up in the small village of Breckinridge, Michigan, around ten miles from our house.

We discuss other players. Reggie Jackson from the Oakland Athletics, Pete Rose of the Cincinnati Reds, and Willie Mays of the San Francisco Giants become part of our conversations. Decky brings up the player Tito Fuentes, number 29, who also plays for the San Francisco Giants. Occasionally, someone I meet or know asks me if I'm related to Tito. My usual response is that I'm not related to the famous baseball player, but I have a brother with the same name. It would be cool if we were related. We also talk about players like Don Drysdale, the Los Angeles Dodgers pitcher, and Hank Aaron of the Atlanta Braves. Although Jaime is a Houston Astros fan, he joins in and talks about some of his favorite non-Astros players. He likes Harmon Killebrew, the Minnesota Twins' first and third base player, and Mike Cuellar, pitcher for the Baltimore Orioles.

I feel left out of the lively conversations that are taking place about all these players, mainly because of all the stats on the players that the guys are talking about. I don't fully understand the statistics of each player on the back of each baseball card. I don't have a deep interest in knowing all this stuff, but it's fun hanging out with the guys and listening to the ones who know their stuff. During this baseball talk, my thoughts drift to Lety and her note. My mind is in two places: baseball and Lety.

Junior starts talking about his favorite cards. He has around 250 cards, which I think is a lot. However, compared to Decky's 800 cards, it doesn't even compare. He has several doubles. Decky has many cards that Junior is showing us, so it didn't take too long for him to talk.

Next, it's my turn to show my cards. Since I don't know much about my players, Decky and Moi point out key statistics for some of my cards. Decky notices a couple of cards I have that he wants to trade for. He wants one of my doubles, so I'm pleased to make the trade. It didn't take long to show the 100 cards I have.

Now it's trading time. I have a Cincinnati Reds pitcher, Jerry Arrigo, card that Decky wants. Since I don't care for any Ohio teams, I'm pleased to make the trade for a Tigers Dick McAuliffe. Decky, Junior, and I go back and forth, trying to get the best deals as we trade. Decky is a shrewd businessman, so I must pay my fullest attention. Junior has no cards I'm interested in because we made our trades back home. Meanwhile, Moi and Jaime look over the hundreds of cards Decky brought.

After all the card dealing, baseball conversations continue. I'm getting a bit bored with all these baseball statistics, so I stretch and walk around the inside of the chicken coop. Looking outside the window, I see Lety with Ana and Marti. At this moment, I wish I were with them. I admire how beautiful she looks. I wish she could see me looking through the window at her to exchange smiles and gaze at each other. I head back and join the guys.

Junior and I have another private meeting in the corner of the chicken coop. I want to change the vibe and do something silly and fun. I suggest we do our rendition of "Tip Toe Through the Tulips" by Tiny Tim. Junior agrees to it. We can't stop laughing and imagining doing this in front of the guys. We've never done this together or in front of anyone before. Junior tells me he doesn't know all the lyrics, and I admit I don't either. "We'll make up our lyrics. Let's go and have fun," I say. Tiny Tim released "Tip Toe Through the Tulips" last year, and since then, it has received a lot of airplay on pop music radio stations. Tiny Tim is a recording artist with a voice that sounds like an old lady's—frail, squeaky, and high-pitched. He accompanies the song on his ukulele. Tiny Tim is quite the sight with his six-foot frame and long, thick, messy hair. Junior and I are confident that all the guys know the hilarious song. In preparation, I grab two sticks from the ground near the chicken coop. They will make excellent props for our ukuleles.

It's show time! Junior and I walk out from the corner of the coop, singing the song in our best falsetto voices and playing our ukuleles on our tiptoes. It's ridiculous, but everybody laughs as we prance around the room, singing and playing. We quickly discover that we hardly remember any of the lyrics. It doesn't matter. We make up our own and add silly things about Decky into the lyrics. Everybody begins to laugh even harder. Junior and I struggle to stay in character as we try to hide our laughter. My heart is racing. I've never done anything like this before.

It's getting dark outside, so we all leave the chicken coop. We say goodnight to Moi as he walks back to his place in the barn. The rest of us head in the opposite direction, baseball cards in hand. Junior and I exchange goodnight wishes with Decky and Jaime before making our way to our tent.

Quietly, I grab my toiletries, go under the starlit sky to the bathroom, wash my face, and brush my teeth. I'll pee one more time before I go to bed. I hate having to get up in the middle of the night to pee, and it's even worse to hold it in. I can't win either way.

Walking back to the tent through the dew-covered grass, I take in my surroundings. I gaze at the sky, marveling at the stars and planets. The wind rustles the leaves, their sound blending with the chorus of crickets and katydids that create a whole symphony, only occasionally interrupted by the few cars passing by. This place feels so peaceful right now, including the Mitchell Farm and Esch Farm down the road. Most people are in bed, hoping for a good night's sleep to prepare them for tomorrow's hard work day.

I stroll down to the road. In the far distance on Lake Michigan, I'm thrilled to see the red lights of a ship! I wonder where it's headed, where it came from, and what it's carrying.

I stand on the quiet road and reflect on the day as I gaze at the heavens. I think about how much fun it is to be with Moi and Jaime, and just the other day, I worried they might not have accepted me. They contribute to making my "vacation" even more enjoyable. I reflect on how I can now open my eyes underwater and how I've improved my doggie paddle swim stroke. I think about Lety and the note she wrote me, expressing that she wants me to keep writing notes to her. I'm discovering that she's upbeat and enjoys laughing and giggling. How pretty she is! I reflect on the long day that was filled with exciting experiences.

I close my eyes and prepare for sleep; I see thousands of images of cherries on the trees. I visualize the thousands of cherries in the white cooling tanks. They won't leave my mind's eye. I try to change it, but I only see other images of sweet, black, plump cherries running through my head. I work hard to stop the thoughts and fall asleep after ten minutes.

WEDNESDAY, 30 JULY 1969

It's around 6:30, and Mom is already moving about. I still have half an hour to stay in my warm, somewhat cozy sleeping bag. A melancholy thought runs through my mind that we'll head home in a few days. I don't want to go. There's a strong scent of pesticide in our tent; it comes from all the work clothes we have inside. My body feels achy, and I don't want to get out of my sleeping bag.

I feel more awake as I enjoy my Kellogg's Corn Flakes at the picnic table by the tent. Thoughts of Lety and hanging out with the guys at the chicken coop after work motivate me and help me start the day right.

At the orchard, as usual, everything is covered in dew. I apply the mosquito repellent, then put on my harness and pail. I don't look forward to getting wet, but I have no choice, so I might as well deal with it. Now that I'm soaked, nothing matters except moving my body to stay warm. After ten minutes, I'm in a good mood to work.

I love it when I finish picking all the cherries off a tree. I feel a sense of accomplishment when I have picked just about every cherry, and then I am motivated to start on another tree loaded with cherries.

The hardest part of picking cherries for me is usually the very top. It's always the last place I pick. Picking the top is typically more strenuous because I stretch my body as far as I consider safe while standing on a ladder. Dad says I don't need to be as thorough as I am, so for safety reasons, I leave a few clumps here and there that are out of reach and hard to get.

After picking four lugs, I walk to the pickup for a water break and pass by Tito, chatting with his imaginary friend, Suitcase. Tito and Suitcase have been friends for a couple of years. From the looks of it, Tito and Suitcase are having a great time on this vacation. Occasionally, I hear Tito engaging in dialogues with Suitcase. Tito always includes him in his playtime.

When I return to the pickup for a water break, I see Timmy and Sandy. Timmy plays with his Tonka toys in the sandy soil beneath a cherry tree. He makes all the sounds of a tractor and semi-truck and talks like the drivers of those vehicles. Sandy is helping Mom pick cherries. I also notice the new fort that the kids built from cherry lugs. They did a great job.

I walk down the row to find the next cherry tree I want to pick from. I'm a bit picky; I don't want one that is too tall because it's harder to reach the top, and I'm looking for one with the most cherries. I find one that suits me. I start picking under the tree, taking advantage of the shade. I choose a branch loaded with hundreds of black cherries, ready for someone to pick. I grab an empty cherry lug to use as a stool while I pick. With my pail placed under the weight-burdened branch, I begin picking. It's so enjoyable collecting these cherries with ease. My fingers move nimbly, only slightly nudging the cherries to release themselves from the mama tree. Clumps of cherries, sometimes as many as 35, quickly tumble into my bucket, making that musical sound as they hit the bottom of my galvanized pail. Usually, it takes me about 24 minutes to fill a lug, but today, I'm racing against myself and want to fill one in less time. I want to see how fast I can fill a lug, and I manage to do it in around twelve minutes!

As I pick, cherry trivia and other pieces of information come to mind to pass the tedious time. I begin to think about as many things as I know about cherries and other things related to this area. Bits and pieces I've gathered through the years come to my mind. Mr. Esch was a big help in providing me with a wealth of information I had never known about cherries.

Not only are cherries as tasty as candy, but they are also good for you. They are high in antioxidants and have a good amount of fiber, potassium, and vitamin C.

Traverse City is known as the Cherry Capital of the World. The area's orchards produce more tart cherries than elsewhere. These cherries are used to make cherry pies, various desserts, juice, juice concentrate, jams, preserves, and more.

The cherry harvest in Michigan occurs between mid-July and the end of the third week in August. Depending on the weather, it may start early or late during this span of time.

Approximately forty percent of the U.S. cherry crop comes from Michigan.

There are four quarts in a pail. A pail of cherries weighs around ten pounds. It takes two and a half pails to fill a cherry lug. A full lug weighs around 25 pounds.

The dimensions of a cherry lug are 20.5 inches by 11 inches by 6 inches. The front, back, and bottom are made of 3/8-inch pine wood. The sides are 3/4-inch wood, with indentations on both ends for easier lifting.

There are approximately 85 cherry trees per acre, with trees spaced 25 feet apart. Young trees do not produce fruit until their third year. Cherry density varies based on the age of the tree and its pollination. Yields improve as the tree matures.

The Waterman Orchard consists of about 75 percent sweet cherries and 25 percent tart cherries, almost the opposite of the Esch Orchard. Waterman Orchards grows the Montmorency tart cherry. I love eating them, especially after they've been chilled in the refrigerator. I enjoy popping a few in my mouth to savor the delicious tart juice.

Waterman Orchards grows sweet varieties, such as Schmidt, Napoleon, and Ulster, similar to Esch Orchards. They also produce Black Tartarian and Windsor cherries. The Black Tartarian is a sweet cherry with purplish-black fruit, perfect for making preserves and eating fresh. The Windsor is a soft and juicy dark red cherry, featuring a heart-shaped appearance. One downside of the Windsor is its vulnerability to fruit splitting from excessive rain.

Growers are paid per pound, varying from seven to fifteen cents. The Esch Orchards produce approximately 200,000 pounds of sweet cherries, while the tart harvest varies between 150,000 and 400,000 pounds.

In the 1960s, cherry pickers earned between 50 and 80 cents per lug. This year, we're getting 80 cents a lug.

A really good picker can pick around 25 to 30 lugs per day. Uncle Ruben and Cousin Polaco are the fastest pickers of all my Fuentes relatives. They also work more hours per day. It's common for them to start around 6 am and work until 6 pm, compared to our regular 8-5:00 pm workday. Sometimes, they turn on their car headlamps to illuminate their work area in the morning. Individually, they pick 35 or more lugs per day!

If I maintain my average of 22 lugs during an eight-and-a-half-hour workday, plus add the 18 lugs I picked Monday (the short work day), I will have picked 106 lugs. On Saturday morning, I will pick seven more lugs, bringing my total to around 113 lugs of cherries picked.

Soon, it will be time for lunch. I've picked eleven lugs so far, and I'm glad I chose this tree because I'm getting a lot of cherries from it.

A few tiny black and white streaked "jumping spiders" are near where I'm picking. They freak me out, but not enough to stop me from doing my job. They're common spiders, and I'm scared of them. They move fast, and I don't like how they dart around; I never know which direction they'll go next.

To combat the monotony of picking, I recall memories of previous years when we stayed in Ted Esch's barns when we came to pick cherries. Although we stayed in several locations within the barns, they generally shared a similar description. The living quarters resembled where Aunt Chacha and her family are staying this year. I picture it vividly. You walk into the barn, where several living quarters are on the main floor. You can often hear the other tenants inside. The quarters are separated by thick, dark green canvas, likely US Army surplus. My siblings and I always use the Spanish word "lona" to refer to canvas. While I enjoy the smell of lona, too much of it can make me nauseous. There are no doors to the entrances of these living quarters. To enter, you separate the two overlapping lonas. Mom always placed a small rug at the entrance to keep out the sand and dirt we would track in from the farm.

Inside the living quarters, a broom, dustpan, mop, pail, trash can, and washboard were positioned along the canvas wall. Nearby would be a table with a two-burner kerosene stove and its clear glass kerosene basin not far from the canvas

135

wall. Food preparation took place on the table beside the stove, which had two basins for washing dishes and a dish-drying mat. At the back of the table were two wooden shelves where Mom stored all the cooking items. On the shelf was a box of long wooden matches for lighting the kerosene stove, and a can of Maxwell House coffee. Below the table, Mom kept laundry detergent, dish soap, steel wool, and other cleaning supplies on a shelf. A refrigerator was constantly present. I swear all the fridges I saw at the camp were from the early 1950s or perhaps the late 1940s, featuring brands like Frigidaire, Philco, and Maytag. They might have looked their age, but they were consistently reliable. On the floor, a couple of plastic laundry baskets held either clean or dirty clothes.

In the middle of the room, a naked light bulb with an on/off switch dangled from the ceiling above the wooden dining table, surrounded by four wooden chairs. Mom always used her plastic, red-and-white checkered cloth, which was easy to wipe down and clean, to cover the table. On top of the table sat the salt and pepper shakers, Tabasco hot sauce, toothpicks in a holder, and the Pan de Vida (Bread of Life) Bible verses. Several empty cherry lugs served as extra chairs when we all ate together.

The rear wall was part of the barn structure. We used the hooks on the wall to hang clothes, towels, bathing suits, work clothes, and other items. Inside the living quarters were two smaller rooms with canvas walls that served as bedrooms—one for Mom, Dad, and Sandy, and the other for us boys. Both rooms had bunk beds. Junior preferred to sleep on the bottom bunk, while I mostly enjoyed the top bunk. However, I didn't like being so close to the ceiling, fearing a spider might crawl up one of my nostrils, into my mouth, or bite me while I slept. I always checked my sleeping area for any spiders.

Dad would always set up a flycatcher with its yellow sticky ribbon dangling down, ready to lure flies to their impending doom. Even now, I enjoy examining flycatchers up close to see if any new flies are stuck on the ribbon; usually, I spot one desperately trying to free itself from the lethal trap.

A typical morning at the barn living quarters began with the sound of Mom getting up to make freshly brewed coffee for Dad. After brewing the coffee, she would prepare a hot breakfast for Dad, usually huevos rancheros (scrambled eggs with fresh salsa), refried beans, and some homemade flour tortillas. Although I'm not a coffee drinker, the aroma of the freshly made coffee delighted my sense of smell. Then I would hear Dad getting up. The scent of Mom's cooking would motivate me to get out of bed when the time arrived. While Dad had his breakfast, Mom called us kids to get ready for breakfast and the day ahead. We usually had cereal for breakfast.

If we didn't go to the beach after work to wash up in the lake and have a picnic, Mom would make dinner in the barn. Dinners usually consisted of refried beans, Spanish rice with chicken, fideo (browned angel hair spaghetti), salsa, fried potatoes, handmade flour or corn tortillas, and migas (fried cut-up corn tortillas) mixed with scrambled eggs, along with homemade ice-cold sweetened lemon tea or Kool-Aid. If Mom didn't feel like cooking or didn't have the time, we had bologna, hot dogs, cheese sandwiches, or peanut butter and jelly on Wonder Bread, potato chips, and canned pork and beans. Of course, Mom always had some vegetables for us, just like she does now.

My reminiscing about where we've stayed suddenly stops when I hear Mom calling us for lunch; it's so nice to hear her voice. The morning went by quickly, probably because I thought about many family memories and relatives picking cherries here and at Ted Esch's orchards. I get off my ladder, unbuckle my half-filled pail, and take off my cherry harness. The slight breeze evaporates the sweat beneath the weight of my pail and cherry harness. My shoulders feel better now that the burden of the straps, pail, and cherries is no longer on me. I head to the water jug to wash my sticky and dirty hands. I'm feeling drained of energy and a bit slow. This all changes when I feel something small and forceful hit my mid-back. It's a cherry! Another one, and then quickly, a third cherry hits me. They're coming from Decky. I throw a few at him, and we continue our cherry fight for a few minutes on our way to lunch.

After Mom prays for the food, we join the line for food and drinks. Mom made refried beans and scrambled egg burritos, tightly wrapped in aluminum foil, for lunch. We're also having Lay's Ruffled Potato Chips and grape Kool-Aid. The burritos are piping hot and look so delicious. Tito and Timmy are jumping up and down, eagerly waiting to eat.

Junior and I join Decky, who is already eating his food under a cherry tree. I find a shady spot near Decky beneath the cherry tree and set up my cherry lug chair and table. For the first five minutes, no one speaks. Everyone is hungry, hot, sweaty, and exhausted. As I expected, these burritos are absolutely delicious.

Right after lunch, I unfold the old bed sheet I use daily and spread it over the softest, smoothest spot under the shade. I settle onto the sheet and attempt to take a ten-minute nap. It feels nice to rest. The gentle breeze helps evaporate some of the sweat on my face. A few flies buzzing around are trying their best to annoy me, while a couple of ants crawl across the bed sheet and onto my arms. I flick them off while waving my hands in front of my face to shoo away the flies. I suppose I won't get that quick nap, but it still feels good to lie down.

It's time to start the afternoon picking. The sun beats down on us with full force, so I begin picking on the inside of my tree to stay in the shade. The inner part usually doesn't have as many cherries as the outside, but I don't mind; they need to be picked, and I want to be in the shade. Mariachi music plays from a car's eight-track tape player. I hear several people faintly talking to each other in Spanish. In the background, I hear a hawny truck.

Lunchtime in the Orchard

The sound of the hawny truck brings to mind the time when Dad almost had a severe, potentially fatal accident while hauling cherries to Traverse City. It was the summer of 1950, and Dad was eighteen years old. He drove his 1948 Chevrolet stake truck, army green in color, for Ted Esch to transport the cherries to the processing plant in Traverse City. Dad was on Highway 204, the road from Lake Leelanau to Suttons Bay, when he put the truck into a lower gear to slowly descend a steep section of the road. Suddenly, the car behind him began to pass. Danger lurked ahead, as there was an oncoming car directly in the path of the vehicle passing Dad. The driver quickly realized her grave situation and swerved back into the right lane in front of Dad's truck, which was too close for comfort. Dad frantically tried to slow down, but the low gear and brakes weren't functioning correctly. Even the handbrake wasn't working as he needed it to. At the bottom of the long descent was a stop sign marking where Highway 204 tees into busy M-22. Just yards from the intersection with M-22 lies Grand Traverse Bay. Charged with adrenaline, Dad descended the hill, barely managing his brakes. He says he doesn't know how he safely made the right turn onto southbound M-22 towards Traverse City. Once he regained control of the truck, he parked it and assessed the damage. To his amazement, only three or four lugs were lost, and he had a blown tire. The best part was that no one was injured, and Dad's truck came out without a scratch. Still shaken from the frightening experience, Dad said a simple but heartfelt prayer for the miracle that had just taken place. I'm sure he felt much closer to God that day.

Another memory comes to mind. I remember a Leelanau County tri-fold tourist brochure from around 1950 with Aunt Martha, Mom's sister, on the cover. It's stored in the box of photos and memorabilia at the house. The brochure has a color photo of Aunt Martha picking cherries from a ladder in an orchard. Behind her, numerous cherry trees display their abundant, delicious-looking fruit. Aunt Martha looks lovely, fresh, and pure with her inviting smile and bright eyes. She draws attention to the brochure and must have been around 16 years old. Because of this brochure, we believed she was the Cherry Queen for the annual

Cherry Festival in Traverse City. Occasionally, we would hear one of the uncles teasing Aunt Martha in a friendly way, calling her the cherry queen. This all stemmed from the brochure for which she posed. I wonder how she was selected for the brochure; she looks like a professional model.

There's another photo of Aunt Martha at age 18 with a warm smile, posing for the front page of the Leelanau Enterprise and Tribune, July 23, 1953, newspaper. She's sitting on a ladder with her pail, picking tart cherries. The headline reads, "And the Cherry Harvest Rolls Right Along." The article says that "Miss Martha Ramon" is one of 5000 itinerant workers in Leelanau County that include Whites, Mexicans, and Negroes that are here to harvest the cherries.

Beneath Aunt Martha's photo is a photo of Grandpa Fuentes leading a Sunday School class on Theodore Esch's lawn, along with the students and musicians. The article mentions that Grandpa serves as the "picker boss" while preaching on Sundays. He is also the work foreman and works with his congregation on other days during the cherry harvest. The musicians in the photo are two teenage boys with electric guitars and Dad with his accordion.

My thoughts drift to other photos we have back home. One of my favorites is a picture of Dad taken around 1951 at the Esch Farm in front of the Esch house. His hair is neatly styled, and he's wearing a white shirt with rolled-up sleeves and khaki pants.

There's also a picture taken around 1951 of Mom and Dad sitting together in a white wicker loveseat on the Esch lawn. Mom is dressed in a long plaid dress with a V-shaped lace design around the front, while Dad sports a shirt with broad horizontal stripes. They look so young and full of life. In the background are a hawny truck and Grandpa's car.

There's a 1949 photo of three lovely teenage migrant farmworker girls standing in front of the west Esch barn. Their hair is neatly styled, and they wear white skirts, indicating the photo was likely taken on a Sunday before or after church.

I think of the picture of Dad and his siblings hoeing sugar beet fields near Ithaca, Michigan.

There's a photo of young Olivia Chapa taken around 1949 in front of the back of a hawny truck, which I assume was taken at the Esch Farm. (The Chapa family is one of the families Grandpa brought up from Texas.) She is wearing a white dress and seems ready for church.

There's another photo of Uncle Abran and Uncle Bernie when they were around 15. Uncle Abran is wearing a cherry harness. The picture looks like it was taken after the end of a workday.

A photo from the late 1940s or early 1950s shows about a dozen people standing and singing while Dad and other musicians play their instruments during an outdoor church service. Dad is playing his accordion, and a man is playing guitar. Dad rests his foot on an upside-down tomato bushel basket as he plays. Grandpa held church services outdoors in the open field where La Choy Foods in Archbold is today.

I think of the photo taken around 1961 of Junior, Sandy, Tito, and me at a Lake Michigan beach. I'm five years old. In the background is Lake Michigan, with the Manitou Islands visible. We're all waving. Junior is wearing jeans and no shirt. I'm dressed in checkered shorts and a horizontally striped shirt. They don't match. I have a shy look on my face. Sandy is dressed in a white dress, sporting a warm smile. Tito is wearing white cotton underwear and no shirt, with his arms raised high in the sky. His big smile shows he's having a great time with no cares in the world.

I snap out of my thoughts about family photos and wonder what to write in my note to Lety. I need to respond to the questions she asked me in her note. I'm anxious about exactly what I will say. Guys and girls are so different. Will she find my interests boring or exciting? Will there be a continuation of the spark we both feel for each other? I hope so.

I walk to my fourteenth lug and fill it with the cherries in my pail. Since I usually pick about 22 lugs before quitting, we have three hours left to work. I then head over to Junior's tree to check on him and notice he's taking his sweet time picking. I give him a brief motivational speech and remind him we're halfway through our cherry-picking for the week. He seems a bit unimpressed but manages to give me a faint smile.

The daylilies at the edge of the orchard catch my eye. Since childhood, I've always found these flowers beautiful. I see them everywhere in Michigan—along the roadsides, fence lines, and gardens. The sight of these flowers takes me back to when I was seven or eight years old, returning home from Sunday morning church service. The sun shines brightly, and I'm in a cheerful mood. I'm sitting in the back seat while Dad drives the car. I asked Mom if we could stop to pick some of the orange flowers that dotted the roadside. Dad blurts out, annoyed and gruff, "Flowers are for girls. They're not for boys." He didn't appreciate my interest in flowers. I was angry at him and embarrassed for having asked. I felt a deep hurt. We never talked back to Dad; there was no arguing with him. I don't like the machismo attitude some Mexican men have. Nevertheless, that didn't stop me from loving flowers.

The monotony and good work rhythm end when I feel the impact of a cherry hitting my back. I look around and see Decky tossing cherries at me. I have to defend myself. I get hit again in the chest, but I manage to hit Decky, too. This is a much-needed break from the monotony of picking cherries for hours.

On my way to take a potty break, I see Decky and catch up to him. He's headed to get more empty lugs. We pass by Ana and Marti, picking cherries from the same tree. I tell them to get to work. With a frown, they stick their tongues out at me, but the frown quickly turns into a smile and a laugh. Afterward, we walk by a car with Mexican music playing on the eight-track tape player. Decky tells me the artist is Paco Jimenez. This guy can really play the accordion.

The car music has been playing for two hours, setting a good cherry-picking mindset and making time go by faster. The tractor will be here soon to pick up our last lugs for the day. I've already picked 23 lugs, one more than my usual amount. Junior and I are excited to wrap up the workday and start the fun!

Sitting on the pickup tailgate on our way back to the farm, I'm still unsure what to write to Lety. When we get back to the farm, I ask Mom for a piece of her stationery, grab my pen, and start writing my note to Lety.

> *Dear Lety,*
> *I hope you are fine. I just read your note. You can call me Robert. I don't mind. Nobody has ever called me by my formal name before. I kind of like it if you do. I like your accent, too. What do I do for fun? I like adventure. I like to bike ride, hike, swim, camp, read history books, make car models, watch Hogan's Heroes, look at cool and fast cars, and watch car racing. I like ice cream too! I'm so glad we were able to go together to get some the other day. What do you like to do? Robert*

I look around the farm where I usually find Lety. I see her coming out of her living quarters. Her face glistens with sweat, almost as if it were intentionally applied as part of her makeup routine. She looks stunning, even when she's sweaty and dirty. Her hair is slightly tousled from a day spent picking cherries. Lety appears mildly exhausted from the hard work, yet a gleam sparkles in her eyes. I feel the same sparkle, too. We both understand that we don't have much private time together, so we quickly share how our workday went. Lety expresses her excitement that the work day is over and looks forward to hanging out and having fun; I feel the same way. I hope there will be something we can do together tonight. I hand Lety the note and return to our tent area for my shower items.

Since we won't be going to the beach today, I'll have to take a cold shower. I rush to the bathroom to keep my body heat up and take advantage of the sun's warmth while it's high in the sky. Everyone has the same idea of showering after work, so if I wait too long, I'll get stuck in line to use the shower. I see Dad, who is busy preparing the cherries to take to the processing plant in Suttons Bay.

There's no line! Off come my clothes, and into the shower I go. Someone left a bottle of Prell hair shampoo behind. A tiny bar of Zest soap is also lying on the floor of the shower stall. I begin my classic dance before turning on the cold well water. I quicken my dance steps to generate some body heat to counter the shock of the cold water. Out it comes. I dance even faster as the cold water sprays over my chilled body. Goosebumps appear on my legs and arms. I only want to wet my head. I start again, only getting my head wet to shampoo my hair. I shut the water off, give my hair a brisk but thorough shampoo, and then turn the water back on for a good rinse. I'm getting used to the cold water now, and I leave the tap on as I wash and rinse the rest of my body. Keep dancing! I hear someone enter the bathroom and think he will probably want to shower. Another person is taking a shower in the other stall. To be courteous, I move as quickly as possible to get out of the shower, dry myself as best I can, and head out. The guy I noticed gives me a quick greeting in Spanish. As soon as I'm out, he steps in.

Walking back to the tent area to drop off my towel and dirty clothes, I feel refreshed and renewed—like a new person! These work clothes need a good wash, so I'm grateful we brought two sets. I'm looking forward to wearing my clean work clothes tomorrow.

Tonight, we're having Mexican food at Decky's place. Since there are so many mouths to feed, we take turns eating. Decky, Junior, and I eat together; the food is so tasty. We're enjoying freshly made flour tortillas, refried beans, and rice with chicken. Even though the chicken leg isn't my favorite part, I'm savoring it tonight. These tortillas are delicious; I could eat four or five, but I stick to two since others want some. The aromas make me want to linger here as long as possible. For drinks, we have strawberry-flavored Kool-Aid with ice! It feels good to have something this cold. Living in the tent for a week has made me more grateful for our comforts at home, like having ice whenever we want. We eat quickly to get to the chicken coop for clubhouse time.

I'm so happy it's clubhouse time. It's time to enjoy being a teenager. Everyone is in good spirits and eager to talk and have fun. We stay on a topic for a few minutes and somehow find ourselves on a different subject.

We start by discussing the Three Stooges. Every guy I know is familiar with the Three Stooges. Moe, Curly, and Larry are the stooges who always mess something up, even when things seem to go their way initially; they can never get it right. Some episodes feature Shemp or Joe, who step in for Curly. Junior, Decky, and I have watched all the half-hour slapstick comedies they've made. We've seen each of them at least three times, and there are about 90 in total! They frequently find themselves in trouble and often hit each other, either accidentally or intentionally. They never come out on top because they are stooges. Decky and Junior always want to play the role of Moe. Moe is the bossy one. I prefer to play Larry, who is more easygoing.

The conversation shifts to Big Time Wrestling. Wrestlers' names are mentioned, such as Bobo Brazil, Dick the Bruiser, The Crusher tag team, and Tony Marino, to name a few. Tony is Decky's favorite because he is from Toledo, Ohio, less than 50 miles from where Decky lives. I'm starting to think that all this Big Time Wrestling is staged, unlike how I felt a few years back.

Next, we talk about Hogan's Heroes. This weekly television show is a half-hour comedy set in a World War II prisoner of war (POW) camp in Germany. U.S. Army Colonel Hogan leads a group of American, British, and French prisoners who secretly carry out sabotage raids and espionage missions against the Germans while also assisting escaped POWs in finding their way back to England to rejoin the war effort. They lend support to the French Resistance whenever possible. All this occurs under the watchful eye of the clumsy, incompetent, and arrogant Colonel Klink, the German officer overseeing the POW camp.

I tell the guys that my favorite episode of Hogan's Heroes is when Colonel Hogan and French POW Corporal LeBeau go on a mission to rescue a top French Underground prisoner named "Tiger," who the German Gestapo has in custody in Paris, France. The episode is titled "A Tiger Hunt in Paris." Colonel Hogan finds a way to get Tiger released; he's a master at accomplishing the impossible. We all love the head German Sergeant Schultz, who is often somehow tricked into aiding Colonel Hogan and his men in many of their covert activities. After discussing Hogan's Heroes for a while, I'm convinced that Decky, Junior, and I have seen all the episodes.

The dialogue then changes to comic book action heroes like the Hulk, Decky's favorite, Superman, Spider-Man, Batman, Captain America, and Thor. My favorite is Thor.

We start talking about cars. I listen half-heartedly to what Junior is saying as I pull out the newspapers I retrieved from the barn and glance at them. He's going on about the superiority of Mopar muscle cars, and everything he mentions, I've heard countless times before.

Since I'm familiar with his conversation, I focus on the *Traverse City Record-Eagle* Wednesday, July 9, 1969 edition. Today's paper is quite thick, and I quickly realize it's because the annual National Cherry Festival in Traverse City took place from July 9 to July 13. The complete Cherry Festival program is included. A large photo of Cherry Queen Barbara Ann Beckett is on the front page. We've never attended the Cherry Festival, but some kids from school have gone with their families.

Based on the schedule of events, I'm sure I would have a fantastic time. There are parades, barbecues, beach activities, live music, and so much more. There's a "cherry hunt" for kids; while I'm too old to participate, I'm curious about what it involves. An ad for the House of Flavors ice cream shop in Traverse City showcases a black cherry sundae with toppings for just 39 cents—I'd love to have one right now. Another ad from Tom's Food Market & Family Center notes that the Cherry Festival began in 1926. Over the years, we've frequently stopped at this grocery store on our way to Lake Leelanau. I look at the ads for the Tempo Department Store in Traverse City. We have a Tempo in Alma, too. They offer a 20-inch Hiawatha Innovator boy's bike featuring a banana seat, a tall safety bar, and a red reflector in the back. Many kids ride banana bikes, but I prefer my 24-inch male-frame bike. There's an ad for cherry jelly, cherry preserves, and hot cherry pies; yum! I love everything cherry. Dad enjoys cherry pie with his coffee. Mom occasionally treats him by making a cherry pie from the Esch and Waterman Orchards cherries that she canned. Murdick's Fudge has an ad for their black cherry fudge. I want some!

In the Thursday, July 10, Record-Eagle, another advertisement for the House of Flavors showcasing their special black cherry sundae topped with black cherry syrup. There's a photo of the plaque left by the astronauts on the moon, which reads, "HERE MEN FROM THE PLANET EARTH FIRST SET FOOT UPON THE MOON JULY 1969 WE CAME IN PEACE FOR ALL MANKIND." Johnson's TV in Traverse City promotes the smallest, most powerful AM/FM pocket radio for $19.95. The Bake Shop at Milliken's in Traverse City offers cherry breakfast rolls, cherry-filled coffee cakes, cherry jelly rolls, and cherry turnovers. I wonder if Dad knows about this place.

I look over the newspaper from Monday, July 21. The headline reads, "Eagle Blasts Off Moon." A subheading states, "Americans, World Watch Walk on Moon." Jim and I heard the news of the moon landing while we were riding our bikes in downtown Alma. We were in front of the library and got off our bikes to listen to the news on Jim's portable transistor radio about the astronauts landing on the moon. It was Wednesday, July 20, and we were so excited to hear the fantastic news. There's an article about the Vietnam War, mentioning that American B-52 bombers targeted locations just below the Demilitarized Zone between North and South Vietnam. I think of the two B-52 airbases we have in Michigan. I've never seen them, but I would love to. In the cinema section, The Cherry Bowl Drive-In Theatre is showing "The Trouble With Girls," starring Elvis Presley, while the Michigan Theatre is featuring Disney's "The Love Bug."

The Tuesday, July 22 newspaper features some intriguing articles. The headline reads, "Apollo Heading for Thursday Splashdown." An ad promotes sweet black cherries available by the quart, lug, or case. There's also an ad for orchard ladders and another that says, "Attention Cherry Farmers," advertising a 1963 430 Case tractor for sale, complete with a forklift and plow. In sports, a subheading notes, "McLain Faces Carleton on the Mound." Detroit Tigers pitcher Denny McLain and center Bill Freehan are in the starting lineup for tonight's All-Star Baseball game between the National and American leagues. McLain will be pitching against the National League's "Tex" Carleton. The Tigers are currently in third place in the American League. An ad sells used three-legged cherry ladders, available in eight, nine, and ten feet. An advertisement for a 1963 430 Case tractor for sale catches my attention, noting it's perfect for moving cherry tanks. There's also an ad for U-Pick cherries on Bugai Road, offering black sweet cherries by the quart, lug, and case, and Montmorency pie cherries at the Incochee Farm on Ramsdell Road. Under sports and baseball, there's an article titled "Babe Ruth Named Greatest Player of All Time," along with a sub-article about Joe DiMaggio being the greatest living player. We have a lot of respect for these players—names we've heard all our lives. The Little Red Barn Fruit Stand features an ad stating, "sweet cherries by quart and lug, Mrs. Ray Seaberg, Bluff Road, Traverse City." Another ad reads: "The Big Cherry Is Open. Big Black Sweets, Schmidts, Tartarians, and Queen Annes at Benjamin Twiggs Cherry Products, 3 ½ miles Center Road, Peninsula." Playing at the Traverse Drive-In

Theatre in Acme, Michigan, is a double feature of horror films, The Green Slime and Ghosts Italian Style, starring Sophia Loren.

Once Junior finishes talking about cars, I set my newspaper aside and ask him if he'd like to put on another performance for the guys to shake things up and keep the fun going. He agrees to join me for what we call the Arm Pit Fart song, which is performed to the tune of Johann Strauss's "Blue Danube" Waltz. We aren't classical music enthusiasts, but we know the song mainly from a Three Stooges episode. We've heard it in other shows; it's a familiar melody. The guys will recognize the tune when they hear it. Junior's role is to create the armpit farts while I hum the melody and pretend to be the conductor with my baton. I'll use a stick I found outside the chicken coop as my baton.

Out we go, in front of all the guys, and start our performance. Right away, the guys begin laughing when Junior does his armpit farts. I realize this is just a guy thing. I've never met a girl who finds farts that funny. I invite the guys to join in. Everyone decides to participate. I have a quartet of the finest armpit farters you'll ever find. It's such a blast that we choose to do it to the tune of "Jingle Bells." It's a bit more challenging since the guys make their armpit farts on every note of the melody line.

Decky tells us that Mr. Waterman has given him the job of loading and taking the weekly farm trash accumulated throughout the week to the Lake Leelanau dump. He does this every Friday afternoon and loves driving the International Harvester 4x4 pickup truck. Even though he's only 15 years old, we all think it would be cool to have this job.

Decky continues, "After I dump the trash, I always grab an ice cream at NJ's. There's a pretty girl who works there. She has long blonde hair and a great smile. We always smile at each other." We all laugh and tease him about being in love. "It's cool that Mr. Waterman trusts you to drive his truck," I say to Decky. He tells us he needs to be careful, or he might lose Mr. Waterman's trust. He mentions this because Mr. Waterman recently caught him driving through the wheat field between his house and the farm, going in circles and peeling out, with dirt flying everywhere. Mr. Waterman witnessed it all from the window of his living room and couldn't believe what he was seeing. Immediately, he came down to the farm to see who was driving and to scold Decky. Decky says he'll never do that again.

After leaving the chicken coop, Decky, Junior, and I decide to catch fireflies, also called lightning bugs. They're fun to catch. They are a type of beetle and not a bug. I love the fluorescent green light they produce. Junior and I have always found them fascinating. I can't imagine a summer without lightning bugs. To me, they are part of the summer magic in Michigan.

We have no trouble finding jars with lids. We walk to the trash drop-off area on the farm, and each of us selects a glass jar. I'm using a cleaned-out pickle jar. We make slits in the metal lids with Decky's jackknife so the captured lightning bugs can breathe.

Scores of lightning bugs are hovering near us tonight. I continue to marvel at how they create the yellow and green fluorescent light within their bodies.

Above the lightning bugs, I observe several bats flying erratically. They swiftly alter their paths to catch the insects buzzing around.

The key to catching lightning bugs is to concentrate on one and follow it as it flies around or to note where it lands. I track a lightning bug, and with the jar open in my left hand, I bring the jar close to it and quickly slap it into the jar with my cupped right hand. As soon as I can, I screw on the cap and search for other lightning bugs to catch.

Catching Lightning Bugs

I notice Lety with Ana and Marti as we continue catching lightning bugs. Lety is wearing a pink T-shirt, jeans, and a wide white bow made of shiny ribbon as an accessory at the back of her head. She looks so girly; she's my type. They seem interested in what we're doing, and I'm glad they are. "Do you want to catch one?" I ask Lety. This could be an excellent way to spend some time together. Excited but shy, she accepts my offer with a big smile!

As she walks over to me. I'm mesmerized by her sparkling eyes. I'm nervous, but I'm also delighted that she's accepted. Lety tells me she's scared of them, thinking they can bite or sting her. While I listen to Lety, I notice Junior and Decky have each caught two lightning bugs. I assure Lety that lightning bugs are harmless. She begins to relax and feel safe. If she's afraid of lightning bugs, I shouldn't tell her that the two things above us that are diving, ascending, and swooping are not birds but bats. Of course, they are harmless and help humans by gobbling up hundreds of insects, including mosquitoes that are flying around us. She might be so scared that she decides to go inside her dwelling. I tell Lety that catching lightning bugs is magical; she loves hearing this. Being around Lety is magical; the lightning bugs are doing their magic. I place my hand in the jar and gently grab a lightning bug to show her how harmless they are. She nervously laughs as I ask her to touch it. Lety doesn't want to, but she enjoys watching me hold the one in my hand. I feel so joyful and alive.

The stars start appearing as I catch more lightning bugs, and an idea crosses my mind. Stargazing is enjoyable and exciting. Would Lety be interested in exploring the wonders of the sky with me? This would be a great way to spend more time with her. She seems open to trying new things. I know the only way she would be able to join me is if Ana and Marti want to do it, too. I'll probably have to convince my cousins by offering them pieces of gum.

Lety is thrilled that I invited her to stargaze. Ana and Marti are excited, too, and I didn't even have to bribe them with gum! The girls head to their dwellings to ask their parents if they can stay out later. As they leave, I chat with Decky and Junior about stargazing, and they're interested.

It's stargazing time! It's a beautiful summer evening, and a gentle, warm breeze flows through the air. All thoughts of my tedious work picking cherries feel distant now. I'm thrilled that Lety and my lovely cousins can join us. With minimal light pollution, the sky glows with thousands of stars and a three-quarter moon. Our attention quickly shifts to the heavens. For a moment, no one speaks as we take in the splendid view before us. Nights like this spark questions in my mind: Are there other living beings similar to humans on other planets within our galaxy or in other galaxies? Where do humans fit into the bigger picture? How vast is the universe? Is there an end to it? Are there other intelligent forms of life on distant planets? Stargazing often reminds me of my smallness in comparison to the vastness of the cosmos. I'm in awe of what God has created, and I feel proud and grateful to be part of this greatness.

I ask Lety some of the questions I think about when gazing at the night sky. Ana tells me not to be so strange for asking so many questions. I'm a bit annoyed by Ana's remark, but I realize that not everyone cares about having a curious mind or a sense of wonder. I can see from Lety's warm, bright smile that she wants me to ask her more questions. Her expression shows she's enjoying every moment of stargazing and being with me—my confidence grows. I strongly sense that Lety likes me, and I'm also showing her I like her.

Stargazing

Lety tells me she knows little about the night sky or the universe besides the moon and planets. I explain the constellations and point out the Big Dipper, describing how it points to the North Star and how people on land and sea have navigated by using it for thousands of years. I show Lety the constellation Cassiopeia, calling it "The Lazy W." I notice how sparkly Lety's eyes resemble the starry diamonds above. In her eyes, I see the joy she's getting from this experience. Her facial expressions show that she is captivated by what she sees. Lety takes in the awe-inspiring natural beauty before her. While I don't know much about the night sky, I continue sharing what I know. Most of my knowledge comes from the Royal Rangers, where Commander Jerry Crawford taught us about land navigation, including how to find our way using the North Star. Lety mentions that she has heard of the Big Dipper but never learned how to identify it.

To our delight, there's a meteor shower happening! "Did you see that?" Ana yells in excitement. She spots another one before I see my first. All eyes are glued to the sky, and everyone is trying to find the next falling star. Lety's excitement increases a notch, and mine does too. Now, everyone has seen one. "Why do stars fall like that?" Lety asks. I explain that they aren't stars but meteors entering the Earth's atmosphere, which usually disintegrate due to the immense heat generated upon entry. I continue by saying that occasionally, one hits Earth with an explosive, destructive force. Ana tells me to be quiet because I'm scaring her.

I notice that we can see the Milky Way! I rarely see it back home because of all the lights in my neighborhood. I point it out to Lety and everyone else. Ana tells me to stop showing off. Lety looks at me and silently indicates that I'm doing well and that she wants to learn more about the night sky. I tell her there are billions of stars in just one galaxy, Earth is within the Milky Way galaxy, and there are billions of galaxies. It makes me think about how microscopic my life is compared to the big picture. A few jets fly high in the sky, and as I often do, I wonder where they are coming from and where they are headed.

I see a satellite! Excited, I point it out to the group. Satellites are visible because they reflect the sun's light. At first, identifying one is tricky since they can blend in with the stars. You might mistake it for an aircraft, but it's far too high for a jet, and all aircraft have green and red lights. The satellite moves steadily across the night sky, high above Earth. Shortly after, we spot another satellite.

I don't want the day to end, but the night is getting late, and time is running out. It's time to get ready for bed. We see a few more shooting stars and then exchange our goodnight greetings. I thank Lety for coming and shake her hand slowly. I pause the shake, hold her hand, and gently squeeze it as I look into her eyes with a smile. My fingers feel her silky, soft hands. She gently squeezes my hand in return. Oh my God, I can't believe how warm and soft her hands are! They are so lovely. I would love to stroll around the farm holding her hand. As she leaves, I immediately think of the hit song "Sugar Sugar" by the Archies.

As usual, I walk down the dark road before the farm, reflecting on the day. Everyone else is already in the tent. So much has happened since we left Alma. The day's highlights included spending time with Lety, catching lightning bugs, stargazing, and holding her soft hand. They are even softer than I imagined. I love feminine, smooth hands. I don't want this week to end; I want time to slow down. I want more time with Lety. I want more time with Decky and my new friends.

As I close my eyes to sleep, images of cherries and Lety fill my mind, just like every other night. I remember the black cherry sundae advertisement I saw in the paper. I think about the astronauts landing on the moon. Reflecting on all the exciting things that happened today, I would love to linger, but I need a good night's sleep to prepare for tomorrow's work and adventures. Off goes the thought switch in my head, and slowly, I fall asleep.

THURSDAY, 31 JULY 1969

It's the usual morning routine. Even though I slept well, it takes me about 15 minutes to shake off my grogginess. Splashing cold well water on my face always helps. I spot Lety in the distance, and we wave at each other. There's no time to talk in the mornings because we are both too busy getting ready for work.

I'm ready to start the workday. I'm sure that my excellent night's sleep has put me in a good mood for work. Seeing Lety this morning also gave me a boost of energy. These fresh, clean work clothes feel great, too.

I head to the tree where I left off yesterday and start picking. After a while, I begin softly whistling some church songs: "Amazing Grace," "There is Power in the Blood," and "I've Got a Mansion." I lower my volume so that no one else can hear me; that way, I can make all the mistakes without anyone laughing at me. It's a great way to pass the time while I pick.

Uncle Joe, Decky's dad, is the best whistler I know. I love listening to him and try to imitate his melodic style. The last time I heard him was yesterday afternoon in the orchard, which helped me take my mind off the tedious work. I felt like I was at a concert.

It's around nine-thirty in the morning. I've already picked four lugs of cherries. This is one of my favorite times to pick cherries. I like it because I'm fully awake. I love it because I'm outside, surrounded by cherries in beautiful Leelanau County. I enjoy the sounds of the mourning dove and other nearby birds' cheeps, tweets, and twitters. I appreciate the beauty of the orchard and the dark purple cherries glistening in their morning dew coats. I like the solitude that this time of the workday offers me. I've always been a reflector and am grateful for this time alone.

As I pick, I reflect on how I've been foraging since I was seven or eight. I love searching for wild blackberries, raspberries, blackcaps, strawberries, cherries, pears, apples, and grapes. The woods between Jim's house and ours are filled with blackcaps, some wild strawberries, and cherries. Mom always agrees to make a shortcake and fresh whipped cream whenever I offer to go foraging for blackcaps or wild strawberries. Off I go with a mixing bowl and start picking. I enjoy the solitude, the time to reflect while I forage, and the connection I feel with nature. It doesn't sit well with me to see free, delicious fruit go to waste. Foraging has helped me develop patience and set goals. I always aim to fill the mixing bowl three-quarters full with fruit before heading home. Sometimes, it takes me two and a half hours to reach my goal, but the reward is worth it.

It's time to pick the top of the tree. I readjust the ladder and hear the tractor coming. Picking the top of the tree is the most challenging part because I have to stretch my body a lot to gather as many cherries as possible before moving the ladder again. It's also the most dangerous part of cherry-picking. For safety reasons, I need to concentrate on what I'm doing. The spectacular view makes me forget about the difficulty of picking up here. I see more ships in the distance with the islands behind them; it all looks like a postcard. The view makes my picking feel less menial. I can see the occasional car or truck passing by on Esch Road. I scratch my arm on a branch as I reach for a large cluster of cherries. Several cherries drop to the ground. With one hand holding the ladder, I go for another hard-to-reach clump. Once again, a few cherries slip from my hand and fall. This often happens when picking fruit from the top of a tree. The breeze feels nice above the trees. I try to be as safe as possible with every move on the ladder. As a backup plan, I look for a branch to hold onto if I slip. Close to me are a couple of thick branches I stand on to reach a hard-to-get area with many cherries. I finish picking the top of the tree and gather a pail and a half of cherries. Now, it's time to move on to another tree.

After two hours of picking, it's time to have some fun. Junior and I engage in another cherry fight. This time, he doesn't mind participating. We're both enjoying ourselves. As usual, he hits me more often than I hit him. We don't mind the minor distraction from work.

I think about the life of a migrant farmworker and how challenging it is. This work is tedious and wears down the body. Migrant farmworkers constantly move across the nation to follow the crops that need harvesting. They are continuously uprooted from their homes. Children of migrant farmworkers often struggle with their education because they frequently change schools. I can only imagine how hard it must be to adjust to a new school and curriculum. Since they also work in the fields, this leaves less time for school and homework. How difficult it must be to make friends. It must be hard to say goodbye to friends you just made and then start again making friends at the next new school. They have minimal time for leisure activities because they are working. Many migrant farmworkers do not speak much English, making communication with mainstream Americans challenging. This leaves them vulnerable to being taken advantage of. They bear the burden of constantly relocating for work and moving all their belongings to live in temporary homes. Migrants often live in basic, sometimes substandard housing conditions. They also face prejudice. Although I enjoy picking fruit, I wouldn't want to do this kind of work day in and day out, week after week, and month after month, like many farmworkers here picking cherries around the Traverse City area.

I think about how Mom and Dad left the migrant farmworker lifestyle and ventured into other jobs that offered better pay and a permanent home. I'm glad they made that choice. To make it personal, I can't imagine having to help pick crops while attending different schools in various states each year. I would always have to say goodbye to friends I had made. Making new friends isn't easy for me. I wouldn't have a bedroom to store my things. I wouldn't be able to enjoy my summers while school is out. I wouldn't have the freedom to take bike rides whenever I wanted. I think about how Junior and I help Dad with his commercial cleaning business. Sometimes, I complain about having to help out, but I would rather do this than spend months picking crops or hoeing fields far away from home.

It's almost time for lunch, and I start thinking of a story that Uncle Bernie (Mom's brother) told me about Aunt Rebeca and Aunt Ester. In the late 1940s, Aunt Rebeca, at age eight, and Aunt Ester, at age six, would use their little wagon to take the hot lunch Grandma Fuentes prepared to the orchard where all the other Fuentes family members were picking. Their precious load included freshly made burritos, a coffee thermos, plates, forks, spoons, knives, napkins, and everything else for lunch. I picture my young aunts struggling as they maneuvered the wagon over tall weeds and rough terrain, slowly making their way through the orchard to deliver the food.

I'm so happy that it's lunchtime. As usual, Decky joins Junior and me. Mom made burritos filled with ground beef and diced potatoes, and I savor every bite. My tummy is also filled with grape Kool-Aid, potato chips, and pork and beans. While we're eating, Decky has a big smile, which means he has something cool to share with us. He tells us the exciting news that Moi's older brother will be drag racing against another racer and that the race will take place on Esch Road after dinner. Junior and I are thrilled to hear this since we've never seen a drag race. This news is another exciting thing to look forward to after work.

Decky, Junior, and I break into a cherry fight at the end of our lunch break. We don't care if the cherries stain our work clothes. One of Decky's cherries hits my neck and stings because he throws it fast. It's all good; I'll get him back later. It's time to get back to work.

We've been back at work for 40 minutes, and the heat, the picking, and the lunch I had are making me feel drowsy. I need to do something to jolt me out of this lethargy, so I hum and sing "Cherry Cherry" by Neil Diamond, "Baby loves me, yes, yes she does...."

The topic of racism comes to mind. Mom tells me that life is different in the South compared to Michigan. Mom was three years old when they moved to

Michigan. She says that in the South, there's a lot of racism, and that's why she doesn't want us growing up there.

Mom had told us several times about when she and Dad were returning to Michigan from McAllen, Texas. Junior was a baby. She needed to use the bathroom, and Junior needed food. Dad pulled into the parking lot of a store. Mom saw the sign that read "Whites Only" at the entrance to the bathroom. Dad tried to convince her not to go in, but she didn't care. With baby Junior in her arms, she bravely walked into the bathroom. She had no trouble at all. No one said anything.

Uncle Abran shared stories about gas stations and stores that refused service to Grandpa and other migrant farmworkers traveling from Texas to Michigan and Ohio for field and orchard work.

Uncle Ruben mentioned that racism was present while growing up in Maple Rapids. He said, "You're okay as long as you know where your place is." He also told me that whenever he faced racism, he would remind himself, "Who's he to make me feel bad? It's his problem, not mine." Generally, his peers didn't give him much trouble. He wasn't a small kid; Uncle Ruben had muscles, which he believed helped deter many kids from bothering him. His strength kept the bullies at bay.

Uncle Pete said he had no racial experiences in Maple Rapids, but he did when Grandpa Ramon and his family moved to Lansing. Uncle Pete was dating a girl in Lansing whose father didn't want her to date any Mexicans. As a result, he couldn't go to her house to pick her up for a date. However, Uncle Pete found a clever way to date her. His White friend would pick up Uncle Pete's date at her house, while her father believed Uncle Pete's friend was her date. Uncle Pete would wait down the street in his car. Afterward, his friend would drop her off at Uncle Pete's car, and she would then get in Uncle Pete's car to start their date. This arrangement continued for a long time.

Some of my personal experiences with racism come to the forefront of my thoughts. Several times, I've been called a "spic." I didn't know what it meant the first time I heard someone say it. Others have labeled me "greaser" or "wetback." I'm so sensitive that these racial remarks often put me in a depressing mood. I want to become emotionally stronger. I know who I am; I'm not a second-class citizen. People should treat each other with respect and strive to get along.

I think of my occasional friend who lives in the neighborhood. His father doesn't like Mexicans, but his mother is nice to us. Junior and I sometimes went to his house to play in his bedroom. He had the best and coolest toys. After an hour of playing, his mother usually brought us cookies and milk.

There are several girls in junior high school who I heard don't like Mexicans. They never say anything bad to me, but they also never say hello or start conversations. My former girlfriend's father didn't want her to have anything to do with Mexicans, let alone have a boyfriend who is Mexican. Decky's next-door neighbors are racist and dislike Mexicans. The Confederate flag is displayed in one of their windows. I always feel uneasy when I walk past their house.

I remember what Luis told me about the time his family faced discrimination. The Garcia family had been working for a farmer outside St. Louis, Michigan. At the end of the week, the farmer came to the field where they were finishing up. Luis's dad was shocked when the farmer ordered him to leave the land and said he would not pay them. The farmer believed the Garcia family was in the US illegally and thought he could treat them however he wanted. Unsure of what to do, Mr. Garcia drove to the IGA Grocery Store parking lot in St. Louis to reflect on what had just happened. A man named Benjamin Santana noticed the confused look on Mr. Garcia's face and asked if he needed help. Mr. Garcia explained to Mr. Santana what had just occurred. Mr. Santana assured Mr. Garcia that he could help them get paid. The Garcias were in luck; Mr. Santana worked on a farm owned by the county agriculture extension director. He spoke with the extension director about the situation. Shortly after, the director contacted the farmer, who paid the Garcia family their hard-earned wages.

I have never felt any racism or discrimination from the Esch and Waterman families. Some of my Fuentes relatives have worked for these farmers for 23 years. There's a strong relationship built on respect, loyalty, commitment, and mutual support.

Because I know that racism and prejudice exist, my senses become sharper whenever I'm in a new environment with strangers around me. The question of whether they are prejudiced against Mexicans constantly looms in my mind. If people are quiet and don't interact with me, I wonder if they are prejudiced or shy. Are they conceited and believe they are better than I am? Are they going through a tough time and not in the mood to meet new people? I'm realizing that some individuals I thought were prejudiced are, in fact, just shy. And some who I believed were prejudiced are not, but are simply self-centered. Then some don't have good social skills and don't know how to start a conversation or make others feel welcome around them. I grow tired of wondering if someone likes or dislikes me because I'm Mexican.

I thank God that I haven't had too many experiences with racism. I know some people don't openly express their racism but are still racist. I thank God that the majority of people I encounter, no matter where I go, are kind and treat me well.

Mom is great at building relationships with people and bringing out the best in them. She doesn't worry about what others might think of her. She's confident in herself and treats everyone with kindness. She doesn't fret about whether someone might not accept her for being Mexican. Her warm and friendly personality wins people over easily. I aspire to be like her.

After returning to the farm, Lety and I see each other, talk briefly, and exchange notes. We go our separate ways; there's much to do after work. I wish I could talk with her longer, but neither of us can wait to get cleaned up and prepare for the evening activities.

My note to Lety reads:

Lety, I hope you had a great day at work. I had so much fun with you yesterday, catching lightning bugs and gazing at the stars. Your hands are so soft; I love them. I thought about you all day at work. I hope we can do something else soon. Could you send me a note with your perfume on it?

Thanks, Robert

Walking to the tent, I admire how Lety folds her notes. Nobody is in the tent. I sit at the picnic table and read Lety's note.

Dear Robert, I like getting notes from you. So, you want to know what I do for fun. I like to hang out with my girlfriends. I like to ride bikes too. I've never camped, but I'd like to try it here in Michigan. You told me you would like to go to Texas. You better visit me if you do. Thank you for showing me how to catch lightning bugs. I had fun last night. Now I'm not scared of them. I loved looking at the stars with you, too! I like talking with you. No, I don't think you are crazy. You make me think about things I never have thought about before.

Lety

After reading the note, I see Sandy walking toward the tent. She shares the hilarious news about Dad falling off his ladder after dozing off. She was nearby when it happened and was startled to see him fall to the ground. Once Sandy realized he was okay, she wanted to laugh but held it back, unsure how Dad would react. She mentioned that after Dad fell, he seemed too embarrassed to say anything, so he just got back up and climbed the ladder again, acting as if nothing had happened. We had a good laugh after she told me the whole story. Dad is putting in extra hours at his new job, and it must be catching up with him.

I've heard other stories about people falling off ladders. Abel Rodriguez told me he fell off a ladder while picking cherries after dozing off. Uncle Eli recounted a migrant farmworker who fell from her ladder. After crashing through several branches and limbs and hitting the ground, she noticed farmworkers staring at her. With grace and total composure, she said to those around her, "I'm okay; this is my usual way of getting off my ladder." I should pay more attention because it could happen when I'm in one of my tired states of mind, standing on a ladder, and picking.

Mom and Dad are discussing the possibility of staying longer. I hope we do! I'm thrilled that they are even considering it. I told Mom that I want to stay longer. With conviction and passion, I made my case to her about why we should extend our stay. If Mom and Dad leave this Sunday, I asked her if I could stay behind and return with Decky and his family to finish the cherry harvest. They could drop me off at the house since it's on their way back to Ohio.

Ana and Marti are blowing bubbles and invite me to join them. I often see them chewing bubble gum and blowing bubbles, which reminds me of the chewing gum wrappers I've saved for Ana and keep in a small brown paper bag. I run to the tent to get them and return to where the girls are.

I give the bag to Ana, and she asks if I'd like some chewing gum. I put the pink, sweet, hard bubble gum in my mouth and start chewing. "Make the biggest bubble you can," says Ana. It always seems like someone else can blow a bigger bubble than I can. I've never blown one as big as the ones I'm making now. I've never had this type of bubble gum before; it's a different brand. I wonder if I can make one as big as the ones they are blowing. You can tell they've had a lot of practice. I usually don't chew bubble gum because the flavor doesn't last long.

My first bubble isn't anything impressive. They ask me to blow another one. I manage another one; they cheer me on to make more bubbles. I blow one slightly bigger than my face; I'm impressed. To my surprise, Ana bursts my bubble with her quick hand, leaving gum in my hair above my forehead and on my nose. Ana and Marti can't stop laughing. I figured they were up to something. Next time, I'll have to be more cautious around them. Ana and Marti tell me not to leave until they come back. A minute later, they appear with the gum wrapper necklaces they made from the wrappers I gave them the other day. Ana puts it around my neck and tells me they gave one to Lety, too.

After supper, Decky comes over to tell Junior and me that the drag race will happen in a few moments. We spot two cars parked near the farm entrance, just a short distance from our tent. We walk toward the cars and see two guys and Moi standing nearby. The two guys argue back and forth, their emotions running high as they passionately debate which of their vehicles is the fastest. I learn that one of the guys is Moi's older brother, Yrineo Rodriguez.

After a few minutes of listening to their friendly yet firm argument, they both climb into their cars and rev their engines. The challenge is on! Yrineo will race his 1965 maroon Ford Mustang 2+2 Fastback, which features a 289 cubic-inch high-performance engine with 225 horsepower. The other car is a 1966 red Ford Fairlane automatic with a 390 cubic-inch motor producing 315 horsepower.

Both cars are in pristine condition, resembling new vehicles. You can see the pride the drivers have in their cars. One advantage of helping Dad with the car dealerships is that Junior and I get to sit in many muscle cars in the showrooms and maintenance shops. It will be thrilling to watch some muscle cars demonstrate their power. We all believe that the Fairlane will win due to its larger engine with more horsepower; there's no doubt about that. The drivers repeatedly rev their engines to showcase their power. This reminds me of gorillas beating their chests to assert their dominance.

Accelerating rapidly and peeling out, they race down the hill to the Esch Farm, where the event is set to begin. A strong smell of engine exhaust fills the air, accompanied by the roar of muscle car engines. Inside, my body shakes with excitement. The race will conclude at the top of the hill at the Waterman Farm, where we are currently located. It's approximately half a mile from the Esch Farm to the Waterman Farm. We will have front-row seats for this spectacular event, and I can't wait to share it with Jim.

Immediately after the cars take off, we all stroll to the road. I step onto the freshly laid black tread marks left behind by the racers. From our vantage point, we can see the cars below lining up side by side, occupying both lanes of the smooth blacktop road.

We hear the roar of revving engines as racers prepare to compete. Someone at the Esch Farm shouts, "On your mark, get set, go!" Still standing by the road, we watch the cars speed off. Both cars swerve as the drivers adjust to the instantaneous torque provided by their engines. The tires screech on the asphalt. Birds are startled and take flight from both sides of the road, desperately trying to escape the loud, menacing sound of the accelerating engines unleashing their furious power.

Before the cars pass the Mitchell Farm, we exit the highway for safety reasons. The cars speed up to around 90 miles per hour as they cross the finish line. To our surprise, the Mustang wins by a significant margin. We're amazed that the smaller engine with less horsepower comes out on top.

The drivers quickly get in position to race back to the Esch Farm. They have decided to hold three races. I plug my ears for the upcoming crescendo of engine noise we are about to hear. Moi signals them: "On your mark, get set, go!" Off they go, like fierce hunting dogs focused on their prey. Back on the road, we walk over the freshly laid tire marks. Around halfway through the race, we can see that the Mustang is already ahead of the Fairlane. The Mustang wins again.

The third and final race begins at the Esch Farm and finishes at our location. This time, the drivers do a rolling start. The race concludes in just a few minutes, with the Mustang claiming victory again.

We discuss the race, and Junior mentions that he now understands that while engine horsepower is important, weight is also a crucial factor. In this situation, the Mustang, being about 1000 pounds lighter than the Fairlane despite its extra horsepower, won.

After the race, I realize I'm running low on gum. I thought I had brought enough Doublemint gum for the whole week. I'm running low because I give Ana and Marti sticks of gum almost every day. I ask Mom if she has any chewing gum. She chews Juicy Fruit and usually has some to share. Mom is out of gum, too! I won't even ask her to drive me to NJ's in Lake Leelanau just for gum. It's too far away to go for gum. She has more important things to do. Decky tells me a farmworker runs a store at one of the Esch barns, and they probably sell chewing gum. Junior and Decky offer to go with me to the store. I head to the tent to grab some money and quickly meet up with Decky and Junior.

Off we go with a quick pace to the Esch Farm. Passing the Mitchell Farm, I see several teenage boys kicking a ball and a group of pretty girls walking together, laughing and chatting in the open area of the farm. Tejano music plays from a parked car where a young farmworker sits in the driver's seat with the door ajar. Decky says the guy is playing a Little Joe and the Latinaires song that he likes. I like it too. I like the Mexican yell in the song. A few other farmworkers are around, attending to their tasks or enjoying some leisure time. Many of the parked trucks and cars have Texas license plates.

At the Esch Farm, we immediately go to the big barn where the store is. There isn't much time to waste; the store will close soon, and we want to return for clubhouse time. This is the barn where Aunt Chacha lives, and it's also where the tire swing is located. We spot a pretty lady with medium-dark brown hair, about

35 years old, sitting in a chair in front of two shelving units filled with various items for sale. I find it interesting that a migrant farmworker runs a store as a side business. Grandpa Fuentes had a store at the Esch Farm in the late 1940s and early 1950s. We arrive at the store just minutes before the 8 pm closing time. I'm relieved to see a couple of people in line, giving me a moment to catch my breath and look at what she has for sale. I get in line and start scanning the shelves. I don't see any Doublemint, but I do spot Juicy Fruit. I'm fine with Juicy Fruit; however, the flavor doesn't last as long as Doublemint. I notice various items on the shelves that people at the work camp would need or want.

There are toiletries like toothbrushes, toothpaste, Zest, Dial, Ivory bar soap, shampoo, shaving cream, razor blades, and feminine products. Several boxes of Tide laundry detergent, bleach, borax, and Pine-Sol are neatly arranged on one of the shelves. I see salt, pepper, Crisco shortening, flour, sugar, Clabber Girl baking powder, Arm and Hammer baking soda, tomatoes, jalapeños, and garlic. The lady has several packs of Marlboro, Lucky Strike, Camel nonfilter, and Salem cigarettes, with even single cigarettes available. There are also Mars and Snickers candy bars, jawbreakers, penny candies, bubble gum, and Juicy Fruit gum.

Decky assists me by asking the lady if she has any Doublemint. She doesn't. I buy two packs of Juicy Fruit. Usually, a pack costs five cents, but the lady charges double that amount. I'm okay with it; tomorrow, I'll be able to get some when Dad and Mom go to Lake Leelanau.

Now that I have my gum, we quickly head back to the farm to spend time at the chicken coop. On the way, we see Jaime and Moi and tell them that clubhouse time is about to start. Because of the races and the trip to the store, the sky is a bit darker than usual when we arrive at our clubhouse. Someone suggests we tell scary stories. Everyone is excited to hear and share a frightening tale. When it's my turn, I share the story of the teenage girl from Maple Rapids, Michigan, where Mom grew up. Mom sometimes tells us this story whenever she wants us to listen and feels we aren't paying attention. I've heard it since third grade. I know the story so well that I can clearly see it happening. I add some flair to the story while staying true to the original story. I begin telling my scary story to the guys.

There was a teenage girl, the only child of a widowed mother. She would not listen to anything her mom wanted her to do. She was very stubborn, cocky, mean, nasty, and full of pride and acted like a brat, not just to her mom but to everybody she encountered. Because of this, no one liked her in the small village of Maple Rapids. Her mother tried everything possible to get her rebellious daughter to mind her. Days and nights, her mother would pray for her dear daughter to change her wicked ways.

One day, the girl was walking home from school when she heard a loud, bizarre sound about 500 feet away. To her, it sounded like something enormous and brittle was breaking. She had never heard anything like it before. The noise grew gradually louder. Then, she could see what seemed to be the ground cracking and opening up, forming a deep chasm. She tried hard to understand what she was witnessing, thinking it could only be an illusion. The ground continued to crack and split slowly. She soon realized her eyes weren't deceiving her. Her heart started to race like never before, and she now saw the crack moving in her direction.

The mean girl is just a block from her house. Panic sets in. She tries to stay calm but is overwhelmed by fear. She's never faced a situation where she had no control. She begins to run as fast as she can to get out of the way. As she runs, she realizes that she might not be able to outrun the crack. She changes her direction only to find that the crack changes its course to match hers. She changes direction several times with no success. She's running so fast that she trips and falls twice. She doesn't care about her bloody and scraped knees and arms, nor the pain. Survival is all she can think about.

The ear-splitting sound of the bedrock cracking nearly overwhelms her as she makes her way to the front yard sidewalk that leads to the porch and door of the house. She climbs the stairs and trips again, injuring her right arm. She gets up, and only feet away from the door, the ground opens beneath her. Down she falls into the deep crevice, screaming in horror at what is happening to her. In an instant, the Earth stitched itself up. The sidewalk and front porch returned to their previous state, leaving no evidence that anything had occurred. The only witness left behind from this tragic event is the mother. I finish the story. The guys like it and ask questions. I then ask who else has a scary story to share. No one offers a story, so I tell them about the flying pig.

As far back as I can remember, I've always known about the flying pig; all my siblings know about it, too. This is another story that Mom would share with us kids over the years. I've had my share of scary nights thinking about the flying pig. The older I get, the less frightened I am of the dark. However, I occasionally get what I call the heebie-jeebies when I'm alone in the dark, and I wonder if I'll see the flying pig!

At nine, Dad's oldest living brother, Uncle Clemente "Cone," was a little rascal. Julio, the oldest, had passed away at eight months. He never listened to Grandpa or Grandma Fuentes, was hard-headed and mean, and always insisted on having things his way. Grandpa wasn't shy about spanking one of his kids if they didn't do what they were supposed to do, but even this didn't stop little Uncle Cone from being a selfish and mean brat. Grandpa and Grandma were at their wits' end, wondering how to deal with their stubborn and unruly child.

One night, everything changed. It was a dark, hot, and humid night. Everyone was fast asleep at Grandpa and Grandma Fuentes' house in Harlingen, Texas. Grandpa and Grandma were in their bedroom, in their bed. All the children were in the other bedroom, sleeping in their bunk beds. Little Uncle Cone was sleeping in his bunk bed by the bedroom window. He was slightly awakened by a tap on the window and by a strange, high-pitched humming sound. He paid no attention and went back to sleep, only to be disturbed again by a more persistent tap on the window. This got more of his attention, but his sleepy mind took over again. A third, more urgent tap finally woke Uncle Cone up. He was mad that something would wake him. He jerked the curtain to the side to look outside.

Startled out of his foul mood, he sees a hideous creature. It resembles a flying pig, hovering steadily in the open air, its wings fluttering vigorously. The grotesque being is less than three feet away from Uncle Cone, with only the window between them. Its menacing eyes pierce through, staring deep into Uncle Cone's. The flying pig demands that Uncle Cone open the window. Uncle Cone is bewildered by the sight of a beast that can talk. Fear grips Uncle Cone's mind! His little heart races as if it might burst. It has never beaten this fast. He doesn't know what to do. He realizes that no one can hear his screams for help or his shouts to the flying pig to go away; at least, he thinks no one can hear him. Uncle Cone understands he's alone; no one can save him. He is now in a state of full panic.

Once again, the pig tells Uncle Cone to let him in. Uncle Cone is so frightened that even if he wishes to let the pig in, he can't; he is frozen with fear. The flying pig asks Uncle Cone, "Do you know why I'm here?" Uncle Cone replies unsteadily, "I don't know why you're here." The flying pig continues, "You don't listen to your parents. You're mean to everyone. You hurt people. You always want your way. You're a brat. There are other bad things about you, too, but I don't have the time to tell you. Anyway, I've come to take you away with me. There's no hope for you. Let's see if you'll listen to me. Open the window and let me in!" A surge of confidence suddenly fills Uncle Cone's mind. Poor Uncle Cone thinks he will be safe if he doesn't let the flying pig in. Quickly, he closes the curtains.

Uncle Cone's confidence begins to return. He feels certain he doesn't have to listen to this evil-looking creature. "I listen to nobody or anything," he growls.

As Uncle Cone celebrates his success in defeating the hideous-looking flying pig, he spots a dark shadow on the other side of the bedroom and hears something hovering in the air. The flying pig is in the bedroom! The 200-pound pig looks almost comical as it flies with its little wings, which resemble petite fairy wings. How can those tiny wings support such a fat pig? Uncle Cone soon finds out that the petite wings can even carry the extra weight of an abducted child.

Swiftly, the flying pig darts toward Uncle Cone, swoops down, and seizes him before he can escape. With all four legs, the flying pig clutches Uncle Cone tightly. Meanwhile, Uncle Cone screams and cries at the top of his lungs. The flying pig flies around the bedroom, laughing and mocking Uncle Cone. "Silly little boy. You'll see who the boss is now!" Uncle Cone's pride and arrogance have evaporated; his confidence has melted away. He is in the midst of a nightmare. Uncle Cone inhales the sickening scent of the pig and nearly passes out.

Dad is four years old and is sleeping in the same bedroom. He has seen and heard everything since the attention-getting third knock on the window. With blurry eyes and a sleepy mind, Dad can't grasp what's happening. Uncle Cone's nervous and trembling voice sends chills down Dad's spine. His heartbeat kicks into high gear. The flying pig's words to Uncle Cone echo in his mind, "You don't listen to and mind your parents." Dad is frozen with fear and can't move or speak. He's unable to assist his older brother, Uncle Cone, in any way. He feels like a bystander with a front-row seat to a horror movie. He reflects on how he, too, has trouble listening and being kind to others. Little Dad begins to cry and prays that no pig will come for his older brother, Uncle Cone, or for him!

With Uncle Cone clutched in its hooves, the flying pig takes off into the sky. They pass through the wall and into the open air. Uncle Cone feels bewildered by everything that is going on. He realizes the flying pig doesn't need him to open the window. Uncle Cone understands that the monster is testing him. They soar away over neighborhood houses, yards, cars, trucks, streets, trees, canals, stores, telephone poles, and wires. He wonders how all of this is happening. Uncle Cone now fears for his life.

He changes his heart and mind like never before. He begins to pray sincerely and is sorry for not obeying his parents, being mean, and always wanting his way. As soon as the flying pig hears Uncle Cone's heartfelt prayers, it stops its course and hovers over a tree in the neighborhood. The flying pig is furious that Uncle Cone is changing his ways. The pig realizes it no longer has any evil power over Uncle Cone. It shows its fury through menacing growls and fits of rage. Uncle Cone continues to pray with all conviction. Suddenly, the flying pig alters its course and returns to Uncle Cone's house. The pig flies through one of the house walls and abruptly drops Uncle Cone into his parents' bed before flying away.

Grandpa and Grandma are jolted awake by Uncle Cone's small body crashing onto their bed, his trembling voice, and the sound of his sobs. Again and again, Uncle Cone cries, "I'll never be bad again; I'll always listen to you." Grandpa and Grandma are astonished by what they are witnessing and hearing. Once they calm their son, Uncle Cone tells them the unbelievable story. As soon as Dad hears Uncle Cone share the entire nightmare with Grandpa and Grandma, he finds his voice and strength returning to him. He rushes to their bed in tears, telling Grandma, Grandpa, and Uncle Cone that he, too, has seen and heard everything. Like Uncle Cone, Dad promises Grandma and Grandpa that he will be a better boy and listen to them.

The guys enjoyed the story. Decky mentioned that he had never heard of the flying pig. I still believe in the flying pig; all my siblings do, too. Even now, when it's dark outside and nobody is around, I wonder if the flying pig will come to me. So far, it hasn't. Once again, the guys tell me they liked the story but have doubts about a flying pig. Jaime shares that he has a story for us.

Jaime begins to share the chilling story of La Llorona, the Weeping Woman. "I've never seen her, but my aunt has. She saw a tall, slim, beautiful woman with long, silky black hair wearing a flowing white gown. My aunt was walking on the sidewalk at night in McAllen, Texas, near one of the canals in the city. She said the woman in the white gown was less than the length of a football field away from her, ahead on the sidewalk. Suddenly, the elegant lady stepped off the sidewalk, effortlessly walked down to the canal, and began to walk across the stream of water. The lady now appeared more like a spirit. With a high-pitched scream, she started calling out for her children, the ones she drowned, the ones she deeply regrets losing, the ones that haunt her with sorrow. My friend's father also saw La Llorona once when returning from Padre Island. La Llorona was on the beach, screaming and wailing at the top of her lungs, calling out the names of her drowned children. He didn't return to the beach at night for a long time."

I ask Jaime about La Llorona. Jaime replies, "She was a poor Mexican woman who lived in a village near a grand hacienda owned by a Spaniard. They fell in love, got married, and later had two children. After they had been married for a time, she was walking along the road when a carriage passed by. Inside the carriage sat her husband with a beautiful Spanish woman from his social class. The wife became enraged. She hurried to the hacienda and took the children to the river, where, in a fit of rage, she drowned them. A few minutes later, she began to feel deep regret and tried to bring them back to life, but couldn't. She realized the terrible mistake she had made and attempted to drown herself. She was unable to die. She is doomed to wander the earth searching for her two beloved and innocent children. I've also heard that La Llorona can enter your room at night while you're sleeping and take you away. I've also heard that if you call her name several times, she will come to you." Jaime finishes his story. I start to feel the heebie-jeebies.

Decky tells us he has a terrifying story about El Cucuy. He describes it as a small, hairy monster with large bat-like ears, sharp teeth, and red eyes that glow in the dark. Everybody in Mexico knows about El Cucuy. El Cucuy looks for misbehaving children. It often hides in a closet or under the bed of the bad child. It waits patiently until the child has fallen fast asleep. Once the child is sleeping, El Cucuy grabs it and eats it.

We keep talking about El Cucuy. None of us has seen El Cucuy. Jaime says he knows people who have. Moi also claims to know people who have talked about seeing it. I've heard Aunt Chacha often threaten her children by saying that El Cucuy will get them if they keep acting as they are. Mom never mentions El Cucuy to us kids, but will bring up the stories of The Bad Girl from Maple Rapids and the Flying Pig. Dad has his successful way of grabbing our attention; he doesn't need El Cucuy. Instead, he says to us, "Where's the belt?" I've had my share of spankings from Dad. After several of those spankings, my butt felt like it was on fire for half an hour.

Although I'm not usually afraid of the dark or of seeing scary creatures, hearing these stories leaves me feeling a little uneasy. It's getting dark outside, and there are many shadowy areas around the farm, orchards, and surrounding locations, including the walk to our tent and the bathroom where El Cucuy or the Boogeyman might be waiting for me. The small cemetery, where something could be hiding, isn't far away. After hearing these stories, I don't feel like walking near the cemetery. The question in my mind is, what if these tales are true? Why do some people we know claim they've seen or heard a friend or neighbor state they've witnessed El Cucuy or La Llorona? And what about the Flying Pig? Why would family and friends lie to us? A big part of me believes these creatures can't exist, but a sliver of my mind wonders whether they might. What would I do if I encountered El Cucuy? I'm enjoying this thrill. Back home, Jim, Junior, and I sometimes share scary stories while camping in the little woods between our houses.

Someone mentioned the Boogeyman. All of us have heard of him. When I think of the Boogeyman, I envision a tall, slim, shadowy figure dressed in all black and wearing a wide-brimmed black felt hat. To me, the Boogeyman has a face with deep scars from knife wounds and cold, piercing eyes that show no mercy. He is a figure intent on harming and potentially killing someone. The Boogeyman targets anyone who misbehaves: the child who ignores their parents and the teenager who disrespects them. He seeks out those going down the wrong path. Everyone back home is familiar with the Boogeyman. Jim and I delight in scaring Tito and Chuck with stories about him. We've made them cry by threatening that the Boogeyman was after them.

No one wants the night to end. We still have more stories to share.

After clubhouse time, I go to the restroom before slipping into the tent for a good night's sleep. I have a mild case of the heebie-jeebies, and of course, it's because of the hour or so we spent sharing scary stories. My senses are more attuned to my surroundings. My eyes scan the pathway to the restroom, frequently looking left, right, and behind me. I keep a wide berth from the living quarters, towering trees, and parked cars and trucks. Several bats fly in their usual erratic manner, swiftly descending and ascending as they hunt for flying insects. I'm walking faster than I usually do. No one is in the bathroom, and I don't hear anyone coming. I've got this. I'm in control of my fear. This place is safe. El Cucuy will not get me.

The slight anxiety I feel from the scary stories doesn't prevent me from having my usual reflection on the road. I begin my reflection only after conducting several 360-degree visual scans to ensure that I am safe and no one or any creature is nearby.

So many things happened today. The cherry fight with Junior was fun; I'm glad I have an older brother like him. He's more than just a brother; he's always been my friend. We've always gotten along well. The memories we are creating here will stay with us forever. I think about the chewing gum wrapper necklace that Ana and Marti made for Lety and me. I have some cute and cool cousins. I don't want to leave this place, at least not until the harvest is over. I remember Dad falling off the ladder after dozing off while picking cherries. I'm glad he's okay. I wish I'd seen it, though, like Sandy did. It would have been funny. I think of Ana bursting my big bubble gum bubble. It annoyed me, but I did my best not to show it, and it took a long time to get the sticky mess out of my hair. I think of the note Lety wrote me today. I wish she lived in Alma. She says she loves to ride bikes. I would take her all over Alma and the surrounding country roads. I remember what Lety said in the note: I'd better see her if I ever visit my relatives in McAllen, Texas. I wonder if we'll go down to Texas as a family. It's a dream of mine. If we go, it would be during winter break, around Christmas, to early January. How cool would it be to see Lety this December! I think about the possibility of us staying longer. If we stay, that means more time with Lety. I want more time to be around her. It's hard to do anything with her alone; the cousins are always with her. I'm sure Lety's parents want it this way, too; it's frustrating. I think about the drag race that took place where I'm standing now. What a show! What excitement! The roaring of engines, the peel outs of the screaming back tires, the awesome cars, and the car talk. I think about the clubhouse, the guys, and all the fun I'm having with them. I wish Moi and Jaime lived in Alma. We get along so well. I think of the scary stories and how we all created a thrilling atmosphere.

FRIDAY, 1 AUGUST 1969

Soon, it will be time to get up. Mom is already bustling about, preparing to make coffee. I didn't get a good night's sleep last night. The stone at my ankles has been bothering me all week. The only way to get rid of it is to take down the tent, move the ground tarp aside, and remove the stone. I know Dad wouldn't be keen on doing that. Lying in my sleeping bag, I think about how nice it will be to sleep in my bed. It's chilly inside the tent; it must be around 65 degrees outside. I don't like getting up when it's so chilly.

I slip into my work clothes beneath my sleeping bag and get up. I unzip the long tent zipper and promptly put on my boots outside the tent. As usual, everything is damp from the night dew.

The small gravel stones beneath me in the driveway crackle as I slowly make my way to the camp bathroom. There's a line, so I head to the water pump and splash some water on my face. A few people exit the bathroom. I get in line before anyone else arrives. It's a busy place.

The camp is vibrant and bustling with activity. I hear the farm dog barking, a child crying, a mother scolding her little one, car and truck engines starting up, excited calls from parents urging their children to hurry, the sound of the Waterman tractor, crickets chirping, grasshoppers, and birds singing their melodies. This continues while I gulp down my bowl of Cheerios with banana slices. I brush my teeth in our tent area and rinse my mouth with water from our Igloo container. Mom anxiously tells us to hurry because we're heading to another orchard to pick cherries. Dad sips his coffee, assuring Mom not to worry; we'll make it in time. Mom rushes to gather the last-minute things needed for her, Timmy, and Tito.

We all pile into the pickup truck to head to our new picking spot. As usual, Tito, Sandy, Junior, and I sit on the tailgate, even though we'll only be on the road heading up the hill to our new site for a short time. Dad joins the caravan of cars and trucks, turning left into the orchard at the northwest corner of Eagle Highway and Esch Road. Anne Waterman directs the workers on where to start picking. Up the sandy two-track, we go to our designated site. My pants and boots get slightly wet from the dew on the weeds that brush against my legs as they dangle from the tailgate.

Since we changed orchards, it takes us a few extra minutes to get ready for picking. We all apply mosquito repellent. The kids and I head to the pile of empty lugs and bring back as many as we can for everyone to use. Junior and I go back for more. Then we visit the ladder drop-off site and select a couple of the tallest ladders they have, as the trees we will be picking are taller. These ladders are heavy and awkward, so I drag them to our picking spot. After that, I put on my support straps and pail. I clean out the small twigs and leaves from the bottom of my pail as I walk to the tree I'll pick. My body shivers as I reluctantly get wet from the dew on the tall weeds I walk through. I still feel groggy, and fun time seems far away.

This is our first time picking tart cherries this year. These are Montmorency cherries. I'm not sure whether I prefer sweets or tarts. I select a handful of the plumpest, juiciest cherries I can find and rinse them with the dew I gather from some nearby leaves. In they go, and they taste so good! While I love the flavor of tart cherries, I can't say that I enjoy picking them as much as I do the sweets.

I need to wake up, and I think a good way to do that is to have some fun with Junior. I walk over to where Junior is picking. He can read my face and knows that I'm up to mischief. He warns me not to do something I might regret. I don't care. I assure him I'm only coming over to see how he's doing. He's still on alert, though not scared of whatever I might do. As soon as I'm close enough to him, I firmly grab a branch near him and shake it furiously. He gets soaked. I get wet. He's on the offensive. I can't stop laughing. Junior charges at me, puts me in a headlock, and drags me to another big branch full of dew. He wears a triumphant grin as he sees my head and face completely drenched. We both laugh; we're now fully awake.

Picking tart cherries differs slightly from picking sweet cherries; it can be messier work. Because the skin of tart cherries is thinner, there's a chance some juice will come out, and your hands begin to get sticky. A tart cherry tree typically has fewer cherries than a sweet cherry tree, like the ones we are picking now. It takes longer to fill a lug due to the time spent moving around the tree while trying to fill your pail. I prefer picking sweet cherries.

I tune in to the sounds around me. I hear the gentle cooing of a mourning dove and several crows communicating loudly with one another. One sound I dislike is the buzzing of mosquitoes near my head. They don't land on me because of the repellent I applied, but it isn't very pleasant to hear their high-pitched buzzing so close to my ears.

It's now about 10 am. The orchard buzzes with movement and sound. A farmworker a few rows away from me is playing an eight-track tape of Tejano music from his car, and he has it turned up loud. I love the accordion and its lively, festive sound. I can hear a young child crying, but the music muffles the cry. In the background, I hear two hawny trucks on Esch Road and Eagle Highway.

I'm always humming or singing throughout the day. I hum the church song, En La Viña del Señor (In the Vineyard of the Lord). I wish there were an English version of the song so we could sing it at church back home. It's one of my favorite Spanish church songs. I look forward to singing it at Grandpa's church in Wauseon, Ohio. Occasionally, I hum it while working with Dad, cleaning the places, foraging for wild fruit, mowing the lawn, or doing other work. It feels so fitting to hum it while I'm picking cherries. I can hear Dad and the other musicians playing in the background as I hum.

En La Viña del Señor (In the Vineyard of the Lord)

Yo quiero trabajar por el Señor. Confiando en su palabra y en su amor. Quiero yo cantar y orar, y ocupando siempre estar en la viña del Señor. Trabajar y orar, en la viña, en la viña del Señor. Si mi anhelo es orar, y ocupado siempre estar, en la viña del Señor.

I want to work for the Lord, trusting in His word and His love; I want to sing and pray and always be busy in the vineyard of the Lord. To work and pray in the vineyard, in the vineyard of the Lord. If my longing is to pray and always be busy in the vineyard of the Lord.

I'm happy to have my fifth lug filled. I place it with the other 15 or so neatly stacked crisscrossed lugs. Several bees walk on top of the filled lugs. They fly off and circle me as I stack my lug on top. Before long, they land again.

I head to the truck to wash my hands and drink some water. I see Mom and say hi. Sandy is helping her pick. Tito and Timmy aren't far away, playing with some empty lugs. I spot Dad, but he doesn't notice me. A smile spreads as I recall how he fell off the ladder yesterday while picking.

Anne is driving the tractor and stops at our stack of filled lugs. Junior and I help her by placing our lugs on the trailer, making sure they fit tightly with the others already loaded. Dad and Anne chat while she hands Dad the tickets for our lugs. The smell of gasoline exhaust from the tractor fills my nostrils as she slowly drives to the next stack of lugs from another farmworker family. I get excited looking at all the filled lugs on the trailer.

I'm daydreaming big time and letting my mind flow freely. I wonder how amazing it would be to know the origins of my ancestors. What would it be like to live in the countries of their origin? What's it like to live in Mexico or Spain? Images of Mexico City from my social studies class come to mind. I see pictures of Aztec temples and warriors, along with the Spanish invader, Captain Hernan Cortes, and his soldiers dressed in armor, armed with rifles, cannons, pistols, swords, and lances, ready for war against the Aztecs and other Native American groups in Mexico.

My social studies classes have always sparked my interest in learning about the Spanish conquerors who arrived in North America, South America, Central America, and the Caribbean islands beginning at the end of the fifteenth century. The Spanish called these lands "The New World" and claimed them as their own. They pillaged the lands of much of their gold and silver and treated the natives as second-class citizens. The past cannot be changed. I cannot deny that this shameful part of history is part of my Spanish heritage.

I think about my Spanish and Mexican Native American ancestors. How did my first male relative from Spain meet my first Native American female relative? Which tribe did she belong to? What language did she speak? Where did her tribe live? What was her life like? It would be fascinating to trace back to that time.

I wonder when the first of my relatives from Spain came to Mexico. I think not only of my Fuentes family but also of my Herrera lineage (my Grandma Fuentes' Side). I wonder about Grandpa Ramon and the Canales family lineages (Grandma Ramon's family). What were their reasons for coming? What were their lives like? Where did they live in Spain? What did they do? When did they leave? Who lives in Spain? Why did they choose to come to Mexico? Where did they settle in Mexico? Were any of my relatives Spanish soldiers or sailors? Did any arrive with Captain Cortés or other Spanish conquistadors? I know Spain claimed Mexico for 300 years, so there are many times when my distant relatives could have arrived.

Do I have any distant relatives in other Latin American countries? I must have some. It could have happened when a brother or cousin left Spain for the New World and went to Mexico, while another brother or cousin went to a different part of the New World. Perhaps to present-day Colombia or, instead, to Chile, Argentina, Paraguay, Uruguay, Bolivia, Ecuador, Venezuela, Puerto Rico, Cuba, the Dominican Republic, Guatemala, Honduras, El Salvador, Nicaragua, Panama, or Costa Rica. Did any go to Peru with the Spanish conqueror Francisco Pizarro or with Juan Ponce de León to Puerto Rico and Florida?

It's almost lunchtime, my stomach growls, and I'm hungry. A bowl of cereal for breakfast doesn't seem to provide enough energy for picking cherries. I often feel quite hungry before lunch in the orchard. Soon, Mom will arrive with the food. I'm also thirsty; I don't think I drink enough water as I should. The tractor is back in the orchard to pick up more lugs.

The sudden realization that we only have a few days left until we go home makes me a little sad. Even though the work is tedious, I will miss this place.

I grab my lunch and sit on a cherry lug under the shade of a cherry tree. Carefully, I place my paper plate filled with food on top of another lug I use for my table. I look forward to eating these flour tortilla meat and fried potato burritos. I feel the heat radiating from the aluminum as I slowly rip open the burrito. The aroma hits my nose. I'm in heaven! Decky offers me some Tabasco sauce. I add some to my burrito, adding more flavor to the delicious meal. I never get tired of these. Nobody talks while we eat. The cherry-flavored Kool-Aid tastes pretty good, too. After eating, I throw my sheet under the shade and take a ten-minute nap. It feels so good.

Back to work we go to start the afternoon picking. The sky is cloudy, as it has been for most of the week. I heard earlier today that the temperature is expected to reach 77 degrees Fahrenheit. There's a mild and inviting breeze that caresses my sweaty skin. During lunch, Decky was humming the hit song "Crimson and Clover" by the Shondells, and now it's stuck in my mind. In the background, I hear cars and hawny trucks driving on both roads. Dad whistles a church song, and his whistle is calming and enjoyable to listen to. Birds fly in all directions in the orchard, some so close that I can hear their wings flapping. There's the ever-present chirping of crickets and grasshoppers. Are they ever quiet? We hear them all day and night. Several cicadas have started their ear-piercing and annoying sound, drowning out Dad's melodious whistle. The cicadas' sounds change tempo, building to a crescendo. Louder and louder, they go, then abruptly stop and start over again.

I think about Lety. I'll go home in a few days, and we haven't spent time alone. I want time to slow down for me. I don't think we'll ever be by ourselves. I'm sure her parents always know where she is. I would love to kiss her, though. If it doesn't happen, which I hope it does, I will always know we have an electrifying chemistry. The song "Can't Get Next to You" by the Temptations plays in my mind. The song has just been released and is one of my favorite current hits.

I shift my picking position and startle a monarch butterfly resting on the branch I'll be picking. Monarch butterflies come from central Mexico and migrate yearly to Michigan and Canada. I love watching them gently flutter their wings. I feel that something magical will happen whenever I'm near one. Away, it flies, disappearing from my sight.

Two yellowish-green butterflies chase each other. They seem to be having fun. Do they get dizzy while flying? I only wonder because of their unpredictable flight paths. I doubt they get dizzy. What silly thoughts I'm having as I pick cherries.

After filling another lug, I spot Junior and ask him what he wants to buy with his cherry money. "If Dad does pay us, which I doubt, I want to get a couple of models and some drag racing magazines," he replies. I ask him what he's looking forward to doing when we get home. "My bed," he answers without hesitation.

After hearing what he wants to buy, I update my wish list and add two or three 45 rpm hit song records. I'm planning to get "Sweet Caroline" by Neil Diamond, "Baby I Love You" by Andy Kim, and "Sugar Sugar" by the Archies.

The afternoon continues as usual: sticky, sweaty, dirty, tedious, achy, and dull for most of the workday. I entertain the hundreds of thoughts, feelings, hopes, joys, fears, and dreams that travel down the stream in my mind.

A tan-colored, shiny cicada skin is a few feet from me on a nearby branch. Actually, it's not a skin but an exoskeleton. I'm delighted to examine it. Carefully, I detach the fragile exoskeleton from the branch. At the top of the exoskeleton is a cross-shaped opening where the cicada slowly emerged from its exoskeleton. I marvel at the two bulbous areas that protrude from the exoskeleton where the eyes once were. Below the bulbous areas are two short antennae and transparent wings. The back four legs have tiny hooks at the ends, perfect for attaching to objects like my skin. The front two legs also have hooks, but are much larger and resemble claws like a lobster. It has a menacing look, although cicadas are harmless. The exoskeleton is a perfect replica of a live cicada. I spend a few minutes observing the exoskeleton and then return to work.

Is Dad going to give us money for picking cherries? I wonder. He said he would. Junior still doesn't think so, but I believe he will. How much is he going to give us? I think about other things I'd like to buy. Maybe I'll get a big headlamp for my bike, which takes four D-size batteries, or maybe a new pair of bike tires. The tread on my bike is getting low. Maybe I should buy new handlebars. I can buy all these things back home at the Tempo Department Store.

Thinking about getting paid makes me wonder how much money I will have made. I calculate that I will have picked 113 lugs at 80 cents per lug, which equals $90.40. This is for 42.5 hours of work. For the same amount of time, at the federal minimum wage, I would make $68.00. I'm earning $2.00 an hour, which is 40 cents more per hour than the federal minimum wage of $1.60.

If I calculate the approximate number of lugs our family will have picked, it will be around 432 lugs. The total wages for the cherries picked by everyone in the family will be around $345.60. Dad will also receive hourly pay for his other job, but I'm unsure of his hourly rate.

I finish my tree and nearly fill my twentieth lug for the day when I start thinking about the two cultures I belong to. I love mainstream American culture and feel blessed and grateful for my rich Mexican culture and heritage. Back home, Mom prepares both Mexican food and traditional American meals. Occasionally, she makes chocolate (Mexican hot cocoa), leche quemada (burnt milk candy), buñuelos (fried flour tortillas with sugar and cinnamon sprinkled on top), burritos, quesadillas, tacos, homemade flour and corn tortillas, salsa, fideo (Mexican angel hair pasta), tamales, and other delightful Mexican dishes. Why wouldn't I want to continue embracing my Mexican culture? I enjoy both cultures. It makes life more interesting.

I love visiting Luis' house, where Tejano, Ranchero, Mariachi, and Norteño music frequently plays on their small record player. They have a tall stack of Mexican music on 45 rpm records. Everyone speaks Spanish and is friendly to me. I enjoy seeing the Catholic items on the walls and tables, as well as the St. Christopher and Jesus on the cross necklaces. I enjoy looking at the Mexican calendar on the wall, with its iconic paintings and images of Mexico.

I enjoy visiting relatives in Ohio, where everyone speaks Spanish. This is why I like attending Grandpa's Spanish-speaking church services. I love hearing Mom and Dad at the kitchen table in Grandma and Grandpa Fuentes' house, talking with Grandma, Grandpa, and other relatives after a meal, enjoying coffee and pan dulce (Mexican sweet bread). I love the homey atmosphere. Although I don't understand much of the conversation, it always fills me with pride for my Mexican heritage.

I love it when the Mexican ladies from church or my relatives gather to make tamales while chatting in Spanish.

I enjoy it when Dad tunes into the Spanish radio program, Variedades en Español, on Saturday mornings on WKAR 870 AM in East Lansing, Michigan. DJs Rogelio Roy Garza and Ramon "Titas" Gonzalez host a varied program that features Tejano and Mexican music, alongside announcements of different festive events like quinceñeras, birthdays, wedding anniversaries, and other Mexican community celebrations. They also always interview someone notable. For the most part, I don't know what they are saying, but I appreciate it because it's part of my culture.

I enjoy sharing my Mexican culture. I love it when my White friends come over and eat refried beans with fresh homemade tortillas that Mom made. Usually, they ask for another tortilla. When Jim visits, he eats two or three tortillas and would eat more, but he doesn't want to be a pig. Jim also loves Mom's tamales, Spanish rice, fideo and buñuelos.

I think it's great when people take pride in their family's cultural roots and heritage. Last year, Alma hosted its first Highland Festival, celebrating Alma's Scottish heritage. The event featured Scottish bagpipe bands, kilts, and traditional athletic competitions like the Caber Toss. Thousands of people attended, primarily from the Midwest states, Ontario, Canada, and Scotland.

Unlike my White friends back home, who have all lost their connections to their ancestral homes, I'm grateful and excited that I still have a link to my family's cultural past and heritage. Many of my friends say they have Irish, German, French, Scottish, English, or Polish ancestry. They know little about their culture, heritage, and roots. Jim mentions that his relatives are from Czechoslovakia, and one was a priest around the Alma area. Jim takes pride in his Czechoslovakian heritage, yet he knows little about it. None of my friends have shown any interest in visiting their homelands to learn more about their origins or potentially meet any long-lost relatives. Being close to Mexico allows me to connect with family from the "old country."

Although we have no relatives in Spain that we know of and are in contact with, we still have family in Mexico. It will be exciting to meet the relatives who live there. Some of our relatives live in Reynosa, Mexico, which is across the border from McAllen.

I hear they are within walking distance of the mercado (the central market), where you can buy all kinds of fruits and vegetables, pan dulce, dulce de calabaza, and camote (Mexican candies), as well as clothes, boots, handmade leather items like belts, purses, and wallets, souvenirs, and more. I look forward to visiting the mercado to buy a handcrafted leather belt, dulce de calabaza candies, and some souvenirs that feature the Mexican flag or other symbols of

Mexico. This is where Grandpa bought his leather Bible cover that has "Mexico" with an Aztec warrior carved into it.

I also hear that Reynosa is famous for cabrito (baby goat meat), where you can see them slowly rotating on a rotisserie over red-hot embers in storefront windows. Downtown Reynosa fills the air with the aroma of this succulent meat.

Uncle Abran and Aunt Elizabet live in Pharr, Texas, in the Valley, just a few miles from McAllen and Reynosa, Mexico. Uncle Abran visits our relatives in Reynosa. He told Dad he would be our guide if we choose to go to Mexico.

Another connection we have with our Mexican relatives is Blanca Almanza, Dad's first cousin. Mom and Blanca often write to each other. Although Blanca lives in the Valley, she frequently visits relatives in Reynosa and Cruz y Carmen, Mexico. She helps keep us connected with our Mexican relatives.

Grandpa Fuentes was born and raised in the small ejido (hamlet) called Cruz y Carmen, in the Mexican state of Tamaulipas. Cruz y Carmen sits off Highway 85, with a dusty two-track road leading into the ejido. No city limit signs or "Welcome to Cruz y Carmen" signs exist. The streets have no names or lights, and they aren't paved. It's a small neighborhood of houses, some with dirt floors, bamboo walls, and thatch roofs made from palm branches. Many plots of land in Cruz y Carmen have chickens, pigs, goats, and trees bearing lemons, oranges, and papayas. Palm trees dot the countryside everywhere.

Cruz y Carmen is located 180 miles south of the border town of Reynosa. The drive from Reynosa to Cruz y Carmen takes approximately 3 hours and 20 minutes. It's a 45-minute drive on Highway 85 north of the capital of Tamaulipas, Ciudad Victoria. Cruz y Carmen lies less than 20 miles east of the beautiful Sierra Madre Oriental Mountains. The Purificación River carries fresh, clean water from the mountains to the banks of Cruz y Carmen and beyond.

We have numerous relatives in Cruz y Carmen, most of whom are Catholic. Fewer than 300 people live there today, and probably fewer when Grandpa lived there. Everyone knows each other. Our relatives in Cruz y Carmen include Uncle Vicente and Aunt Paula Vasquez. Aunt Paula owns a small store situated in front of her house in Cruz y Carmen. Uncle Felipe Vasquez also lives in Cruz y Carmen. Blanca's brother, Ernesto Rodriguez, lives there as well. He's a fuel truck driver for PEMEX (the Mexican state-owned petroleum company), driving a semi-truck tanker across Mexico. I hope to meet him one day to learn about the cities and regions in Mexico where he has traveled. Ernesto owns an orange grove with over 2,000 trees, several miles from Cruz y Carmen. Another relative operates a store in El Barretal, seven miles southeast of Cruz y Carmen. Relatives Margarita Ortiz Vasquez and her husband, Vicente Perales Velasquez, also live in Cruz y Carmen. They live atop a 50-foot cliff on the bank of the river where it bends in Cruz y Carmen. You can see giant turtles gracefully swimming in the clear, clean water below from their house.

People come to the river to wash clothes, bathe, swim, have picnics, enjoy the view of the mountains and river, and enjoy life.

I recall a few more details Blanca shared with us about the Fuentes family history. A couple of miles from Cruz y Carmen and just off Highway 85, a two-track dirt trail leads to a cemetery called El Panteon, where many Fuentes relatives are laid to rest. Blanca also says family records are kept at the Catholic Church outside El Barretal. One day, I'd like to look into our Fuentes family history and connect with our relatives.

Blanca mentions that we have relatives in Ciudad Victoria, the capital of Tamaulipas. Others live in Padilla, El Barretal, and Monterrey, Mexico. Monterrey is the second-largest city in Mexico and is just a two-and-a-half-hour bus ride from McAllen. Certainly, there must be some relatives around my age who enjoy having fun, and I'm sure there are some pretty cousins as well. I wonder what their lives are like and what they do for fun.

From the Fuentes family history, I've learned that in the early 1900s, an American man named Jim Miller owned and operated a large sugar cane plantation near Cruz y Carmen. Some of my grandpa's relatives worked there. I imagine this is why Cruz y Carmen became a hamlet, situated along a main highway and near the sugar plantation. Jim Miller was known to be kind and generous. Grandpa Fuentes was born in 1911, just a year after the Mexican Revolution began. At some point during the revolution, the plantation was destroyed by the ravages of war. Only the chimney from the sugar cane processing boiler and a few concrete foundations remain today.

Dad used to go down to Cruz y Carmen when he was very young, and he hasn't been back since. One of his earliest memories of Cruz y Carmen is seeing his Uncle Lupito, blind from birth, always sitting on a short wooden stool. Uncle Lupito is Grandpa Fuentes' brother. Dad has mentioned several times that Uncle Lupito would get up around five in the morning and head down the road with his stool. Dad was very curious about where he went and what he did. One day, Dad decided to follow him and learned that Uncle Lupito would bathe in the canal every morning, rain or shine, cold or hot. Uncle Lupito would sit on his stool in the canal as he enjoyed the refreshing water.

The orchard is quiet. I'm feeling drowsy and could use a good nap. Everyone is lost in their thoughts while they pick. Suddenly, BOOM! I'm jolted out of my drowsiness by a sonic boom from the plane flying overhead. How frightening! I'm not the only one who was startled; I hear some conversations among the other workers, excitedly discussing the sound we all heard.

Soon, it will be quitting time. This is our last full day of work. At the top of the ladder, as I pick and eat a few plump cherries, I can see the distinctive rusty brown iron ore ships passing by. I never tire of watching them. I fill my pail, get off the ladder, and walk to my half-filled lug.

As usual, bees swarm around the filled lugs. It feels great to unload these ten pounds of cherries. I grab a few cherries I just placed in the lug and pop them into my mouth. The juice is irresistible. My body aches; I'm dirty, sweaty, and feel grimy. How nice it will be to take off these boots. How wonderful it will be to jump into the lake.

Mom yells that it's quitting time. I have half a bucket full and give the cherries to Junior so he can fill his lug. Off come my straps and pail. What a relief! Now it's time to have some fun!

I see Ana from a distance taking off her pail and harness. Revenge is on my mind. She doesn't notice me, which works in my Favor. Between us and close to me are some dandelions that have lost their flowers and are full of seeds ready to be blown through the air. I quietly run up to several dandelions and snip off the tops. I run toward Ana from behind, pressing the dandelions firmly into her beautiful, silky, long, dark-brown hair. Dandelion seeds are attached to parachute-like, fuzzy, lightweight devices and begin to float everywhere. Some of them remain tangled in her messy hair. She is startled and annoyed by my prank. "Paybacks are so sweet!" I call out as I quickly scurry away, laughing. A slight grin spreads across her face as she realizes I just got her back for the bubble gum bubble she popped on my face yesterday.

The farm is bustling with movement and activity, just as it usually is at this time. It's clean-up time, meal time, and relaxation time! Although we'll pick a few hours tomorrow morning, the weekend and free time have already arrived.

I dash to the bathroom, but three guys are already ahead of me. Fortunately, the line moves relatively quickly. Afterward, I hurry to the tent to pack my shampoo, bar soap, washcloth, clean clothes, towel, and tennis shoes. I place everything in my backpack and wait for the others. "Too Busy Thinking About My Baby" by Marvin Gaye plays in my mind.

All piled in and off we go to the beach. It will be our last time before we go home unless Mom and Dad decide we will stay longer. Two hawny trucks loaded with cherries are heading in the opposite direction. Passing by cherry orchards, I can't help but think how the trees look like soldiers, all standing in formation and at attention. We pass the Esch Farm. I see Aunt Chacha's parked car. The farm is as lively as our camp and any other cherry farm camp around Michigan.

I'm looking forward to the lake. I feel so dirty. I snip off a fern leaf from a tree and smell its essence before leaving my wash items on the shore beside the pier.

Lake Leelanau, here I come! I gather my courage to jump into the chilly lake water as I walk to the end of the pier. Without hesitation, I jump in and fully immerse myself. Instantly, I feel revived. I feel so alive! The only way to stay comfortable in the cold water is to move my body vigorously. Before long, the toil and drudgery of the workday fade away as if they never happened. I feel young again. I practice my dog paddling, jumping off the dock, and swimming underwater with my eyes open. The glare on the water makes me squint, but I don't care. Junior and I are having a blast water fighting. I love this place. I don't want to get out of the water. In the distance, several sailboats and a couple of Sea-Doo jet skis can be seen. The jet skis just came out last year, and I would love to ride one. They look like a lot of fun and are incredibly fast. Several seagulls fly overhead toward the trash barrel where someone recently dumped their food scraps.

After leaving the lake, I gather my washing items and walk away from the pier and its surroundings for more privacy. Once I finish my quick wash-up, I pick up a small stick I find on the beach and scratch in the sand: BF + LG = Love (Bob Fuentes plus Lety Gamboa equals love).

It's dinner time at the park. The hot dogs, potato chips, and pork and beans are so delicious. It's quiet as everyone enjoys their meal. I'm eyeing the plate of sliced watermelon and can't wait to have a piece. It's been in the cooler for a long time, and I love chilled watermelon, one of my favorite fruits.

While we eat, a man in a pickup truck towing a small motorboat backs up to the dock to launch his boat. He ties the boat to the pier and moves his truck and trailer to the other side of the parking lot. He gathers his fishing gear and heads to the boat. A few minutes later, he's in the center of the lake fishing. A family of farmworkers with a Texas-plated pickup is having a picnic at a table on the other side of the parking lot.

The air is starting to cool as we head back to the camp. As we pass the Esch Farm, I see several workers stacking lugs onto the Esch flatbed hawny truck. It looks like they're almost finished loading. I see the orchard where Polaco and Abel stoned the porcupine to death. I will never forget this place.

Back at the farm, the activity continues. A couple of guys are washing their muscle cars, the farm dog is barking and chasing a squirrel, some girls are jump roping, a boy is kicking a ball, and a little girl is riding a tricycle. Women are hanging clothes on the line. Abel sits outside with his girlfriend Regina, listening to a Tigers baseball game. The game against the Chicago White Sox clearly comes through on his car radio. It is tuned to WJR Detroit. I hear the familiar voice of Howard Cosell, the Tigers' sportscaster. A lady is dumping used dishwasher outside her quarters. Faintly, I hear what I think is the Esch hawny truck coming up the road toward us. The driver shifts through the gears slowly as he picks up speed up the hill. I alert Junior that a hawny truck is coming. We want the driver to honk his horn when he passes by. We walk to the road and wait for the truck. It's the Esch hawny truck. The driver acknowledges our request. The truck's air horn is much louder than we expected. It gives us a slight scare. With big grins, we keep moving our arms up and down. The driver honks twice, and off he goes to Sutton's Bay to drop off his last load.

Word spreads that we're playing "Loteria" (Mexican bingo) tonight, starting in ten minutes. I head over to Decky's quarters with Junior, where the game will take place. Everyone is there: Mom, Dad, Aunt Maruca, Uncle Joe, my siblings, Decky's siblings, and cousins Rebeca, Tonina, and Raquel. The place is crowded, but no one minds. Everyone is excited to play. Loteria is similar to Bingo, but there are colorful images of various things instead of numbers on a card. Each card has four columns and four rows filled with different images. The name of each image, in Spanish, is at the bottom. A player selects one of the ten Loteria player cards. The images on these cards correspond with a deck of 54 image cards. The announcer shuffles the cards and places them face down. Then, the announcer picks the top card, flips it over, and calls out the image. If a player has that image on their card, they place something on top to cover it. We're using pinto beans for this. The first person to fill a row, column, or diagonal wins the game and shouts, "Loteria." Since only ten player cards come with Loteria, not everyone can play at the same time. We've agreed to play for money, each player putting in five cents. The winner takes the pot. Mom hands us the coins we need to play.

Loteria is about to begin as Cousin Raquel agrees to be the first announcer. She's excited to take on this role and quickly prepares everyone to play. With a big smile on her face and a commanding voice, she reads off the cards: La Escalera (The Ladder), La Botella (The Bottle), La Pera (The Pear), El Corazón (The Heart), La Estrella (The Star), and others. The room is filled with laughter, giggles, chatter, and excitement. Dad and Uncle Joe are enjoying a cup of coffee. After three rounds, I finally get to play Loteria. Following my first game, which I lost, Raquel asks if anyone wants to take over announcing. I offer to do it.

Everyone knows how limited my Spanish is, but it's good practice. I call out El Cotorro (The Parrot). I hear a lot of laughter. Raquel tells me to roll my Rs more. I keep repeating El Cotorro until she approves. I don't mind the laughter; we're all just having fun. After a few more rounds, I'm done playing. I didn't win. However, it was all good, just being with family and relatives.

Before clubhouse time, we toss a couple of Frisbees around. Moi, Jaime, Decky, Junior, and I pass by Tito, who is talking to his imaginary friend, Suitcase, as we make our way to Esch Road to throw the Frisbees. We begin with a few easy throws. Then, we start aiming our throws so that the Frisbee bounces off the road, making throwing and catching them more challenging. It's a beautiful evening, and it feels great to be outside, moving around, and having fun with the guys. After about 20 minutes of this, we head to the chicken coop.

Decky and I tell the boys that we'll be right back. Decky goes to his quarters to get comic books and magazines. I go to the barn to get more newspapers I haven't seen yet. Decky returns with a stack of *Archie* comic books, Superhero comics, and *Mad* magazines. I come back with an armload of old Record-Eagle newspapers.

It's clubhouse time! A mild scent of chicken manure wafts toward me as I walk in. After a few minutes, I adjust to the smell, just like all the other times. Jaime, Junior, and Decky are making armpit farts. Everyone is in a great mood. By now, I feel very comfortable with all the guys and will miss them when I go home. My body has a pleasant ache from all the activities I put it through this week.

Everyone grabs a comic book or *Mad* magazine to look over. I pick several Archie comic books. My favorite character is Betty. She's beautiful and has a much friendlier personality than Veronica. Reggie is a mean brat. Jughead is too silly. Archie is cool. We all engage in small talk as our minds and thoughts linger on the comics and magazines we peruse. After ten minutes, I start looking over the newspapers.

The Monday, July 28, 1969, newspaper headline reads, "EMU Coed Latest Victim in Series of Unsolved Slayings." The subtitle states, "Body Found in Ditch Near Ann Arbor." Karen Sue Beineman was found dead and naked alongside a well-traveled road in Ann Arbor. My heart goes out to the slain women and their grieving families and friends. The female students at Eastern Michigan University must be terrified. This killer needs to be caught before he strikes again. I share the article with the guys, and we discuss it for a few minutes while I continue browsing through the papers. One article is titled, "Wives Meet Moon Men." The astronauts of Apollo 11 were reunited with their wives yesterday, marking the first time they had seen them since returning from the moon. Another piece, "Damage to Docks and Boats – Winds, Waves Batter Areas Along Bayshore," catches my attention. Powerful winds and heavy rains battered the Traverse City area last night. Clinch Park personnel estimate the lake level is 18 inches above normal. Immediately, I think about the severe thunderstorm we had Sunday night and early Monday morning while trying to sleep in our tent. After reading this, I am struck by the intensity of the storm. I'm thankful that no lightning hit us and that our tent withstood the forces of the wind and rain. I'm saddened to see the headline, "Bomb-Laden B52 Explodes." A B-52 loaded with bombs, heading for a bombing run in South Vietnam, exploded on takeoff, killing all eight crew members. A brief article notes, "Geologists Find First Moon Rock Igneous."

I can't believe what I'm reading. I read it three times. It's an ad for a tractor-mounted cherry shaker, Homelite catching frame, and trays, along with a phone number to call. I didn't know such a thing existed. If cherry farmers start using these, I wonder what will happen to all the migrant farmworkers. I share this information with the guys. Decky replies that starting next year, Ted Esch will be using mechanized harvesting for cherries and won't need many farmworkers for future cherry harvests. He's surprised I didn't know this. I'm amazed to hear it. Actually, I'm in shock. I push this sad thought from my mind and continue reading the newspaper.

There's an ad for cherry hauling tanks for sale. Another ad states, "Cherry pickers needed; must bring their own harness, be over 16, or be accompanied by a parent. Incochee Farm, Ramsdell Road." Another ad for cherries reads, "The Big Cherry is open for Big Black Sweets, Schmidts, Tartarians, and Queen Annes at Benjamin Twiggs Cherry Products, 3 ½ miles Center Road, Peninsula." Under sports, there are articles about the Detroit Tigers: "McAuliffe Undergoes Surgery on Monday." Tigers second baseman Dick McAuliffe is having surgery for torn cartilage in his right knee. The Tigers are second in the American League East, trailing the Baltimore Orioles. There are numerous articles about fishing around Traverse City.

In the Tuesday, July 29 paper, the headline reads, "Search Continues: Man Eludes Police Trap in Efforts to Catch Coed Killer." There's another article with photos of damage to boats and marina structures from Sunday night's storm in the Traverse City area, which caused significant destruction. A Vietnam War article states: "Fighting in the Saigon Area Erupts Again." In sports, the American League East shows the Tigers in second place with 55 wins and 42 losses, while the Baltimore Orioles hold the top position with 69 wins and 31 losses. I tell the guys about this, leading to a brief discussion. There's a Kroger ad for Michigan Fresh Blueberries—a 10-pound box for $2.99. In the cinema section of the newspaper, Paul Newman stars at the Lona Theatre in *Cool Hand Luke*." Also showing is *Bonnie and Clyde,*" featuring Faye Dunaway and Warren Beatty. I read the article "Angry Hurkos Quits Search for Killer." The mystic, Peter Hurkos, who had been assisting the police with the serial killer cases, was upset that the police did not inform him of the last murder immediately and chose to return home to Los Angeles.

I take a break from hanging out with the guys and walk outside for some fresh air. The sun has already set, and it's now dusk. What a gorgeous view! The purple-pink sky to the west casts a blue hue over the islands. I will miss the natural beauty of this place. A few minutes later, I'm back with the guys.

I can't believe how quickly the evening slipped away. I don't want to leave the clubhouse, but it's time to go.

I'm standing on the road, having my nightly thought time. I look at what's around me. Down below, I see the islands and Lake Michigan. I can see a white intermittent light on North Manitou Island and a blue intermittent light further north. I wonder what they are used for. I look at the farm and our tent. The sky is clear, and the 71-degree temperature is pleasant for this time of night. Not much more time here. Today was the last full day of picking. I hope we can stay longer. I think about the tasty fried potato burritos I had for lunch, whether Dad will pay us, and about kissing Lety. I think about the cicada exoskeleton I saw today, how today's swim was probably the last time I'll be in a lake until next summer, and how invigorating the lake water feels. The thought of school starting soon, along with the nervousness I feel about beginning high school, flashes through my mind. I reflect on the water fights Junior and I had today. I think of the hawny truck drivers who blasted their horns at Junior and me. Thoughts of playing Loteria and tossing Frisbees with the guys pass through my head. I can't shake the idea of the serial killer on the loose. I can't imagine the fear people must be experiencing in the Ann Arbor and Ypsilanti area. Learning about the arrival of mechanized cherry harvesting is unsettling. I worry about what will happen to Aunt Chacha, her family, and my other relatives who depend on farm work jobs to make a living. I'll probably never return here again to work another cherry harvest. I don't want to dwell on these sad thoughts. I don't want it to affect the quality of my sleep. I think of Lety again. I remember the B-52 bomber loaded with bombs that exploded on takeoff. I empathize with the crew and their families. I wonder how Luis, Tony, and Jim are doing, how Joe and Bruno are getting along back home, and how Quieta Girl is. I'm missing Bruno. He's so much fun to have around and always ready for adventure and hikes. He'll be so excited to see us when we return home.

I head to the tent. I'm ready for my sleeping bag to carry me off to sleepy town. Good night, world! I love life.

SATURDAY, 2 AUGUST 1969

My mind is awake, but I wish it weren't. It must be around six in the morning. The tent is quite chilly. Last night, I put on my jacket and slept with it on. I don't like getting up on these cold mornings. The birds in the bushes near our tent started chirping over an hour ago. I'm so used to them now that they don't disturb my sleep. I can't believe it's our last day of picking, and it's only for a couple of hours in the morning.

It's the usual morning wake-up routine. I put on my work clothes inside my sleeping bag for privacy and warmth, and walk to the tent entrance to slip on my damp work boots. I hurry to the bathroom, hoping to see as few people as possible, especially Lety. I don't want her to see me in this sleepy state.

I have a bowl of Wheaties cereal for breakfast and gulp it down as quickly as possible. I wonder if eating Wheaties will make me as strong as the box claims. Dad sips his coffee, looking ready and eager to start the day. I want to ask Dad for my money, but I am too nervous to bring it up. I'll put it off for now; I'm not fully awake yet.

As we eat, Mom shares the day's plan: we will pick cherries until 10:30, have a picnic at Clinch Park in Traverse City, and shop for school clothes. She informs us we won't be extending our time picking cherries. I've expected this for the past couple of days. I wish I could stay until the end of the harvest.

It's time to head to the orchard. I'll miss these little rides to the orchard while sitting on the tailgate. Dad drives to the same tart cherry orchard and the same trees where we left off yesterday. The mosquitoes are everywhere, so I immediately give myself a good spray of repellent. Lastly, I put on my harness and pail; I won't miss these.

I'm ready to start picking. It's the coolest morning temperature since arriving here, and I'm shivering. I need to warm up. I must move my body to combat the chill from the cold morning dew that will soon soak my arms and legs. I figure I might as well get it over with. I walk to my tree and grasp a branch weighed down by cherries and morning dew. I shake the branch to wet my sleeves and pants. The initial shock of the cold dew makes my senses come alive. I begin to pick and move my body. It doesn't take long for my teeth to stop chattering. Now, I'm motivated to work and start the day.

It's now 9:30, and I've picked four lugs so far. It's starting to warm up. Junior is waking up and seems to be in a good mood. I'm sure it's because we only have an hour left to pick. Decky passes by carrying four empty lugs. I'm sure he's also excited to wrap up the work week.

As I pick, I wonder if I will share what I did this summer when the teacher asks us to talk about our experiences. Like before, some classmates will talk about going to national parks, the Grand Canyon, Disneyland, or Europe. I want to tell my story, but how does picking cherries compare to all the amazing places some classmates visited? I always get extremely nervous when I have to speak in front of a group. My heart races rapidly. It's an adrenaline rush that I don't like.

I let my mind wander freely, thinking about Lety, going to Traverse City, getting paid, heading home soon, how sad and happy I feel, and the hangout times at the chicken coop. I reflect on the smell of pesticide that I will no longer smell, how I will miss eating all the cherries I want, and how nice it has been being around a lot of my relatives. I ponder how wonderful it has been to be immersed in my Mexican culture and the lovely Traverse City area. It would be nice for the little Spanish Pentecostal Church at La Curva to be our church. I consider how the summer is winding down, and school is just around the corner, which makes me sad because I love summertime. I think about how I will miss the hawny trucks hauling cherries, the sound of tractors, and the voices of pickers in the orchard. I will miss the music in the orchard from car eight-track tapes, local radio stations, and the pickers singing as they work. I will miss the Spanish church services at the Esch barn, the starry nights, and hearing Spanish spoken wherever I go. I will miss enjoying delicious Mexican food as often as I did this week, and the aromas wafting through the work camps - nothing compares to the scent of freshly made flour or corn tortillas. I'll miss the beauty of Lake Leelanau and Lake Michigan, swimming in the lakes, and how the chilly water makes me feel so alive. I'll miss watching the ships sail by on Lake Michigan, having picnics, and listening to Spanish church songs. I will miss Lety - her sparkly brown eyes, soft hands, silky hair, radiant smile, and cute little butt. I think about sleeping in my bed, hanging out with Jim and Luis, and sharing all my stories with them. I think about hot showers.

It won't be long before we're done picking. Mom says we have fifteen minutes left, so we should work quickly to finish strong. The motivational speech doesn't motivate Junior to speed up. I've heard the tractor for a while, and it'll be here soon to pick up our lugs.

When the tractor gets about 100 yards away, I finish picking, head to where our lugs are, and fill the last one. I picked seven lugs today. I have a few cherries left over, which I give to Junior. A minute later, Mr. Waterman stops for our lugs and greets Dad. Junior and I load all the family lugs onto the trailer. Mr. Waterman writes down the number of lugs in his pocket notebook and gives Dad the correct token amount and color. He also tells Dad to meet him at his house at noon to get paid. We're finally finished picking!

Before we get into the truck, Mom tells us to hurry, clean up when we return to the farm, and get ready to go to Traverse City.

Once we arrive at the farm, Dad drives us to the barn so we can return our pails and harnesses. It's a bittersweet feeling.

Quickly, I head to the tent to grab what I need to freshen up and then walk to the bathroom. I wait just a few minutes before a shower becomes available. Even though the water is cold, rinsing off the sweat feels amazing. I shower as quickly as I can, being considerate of the other guys waiting for their turn.

I feel anxious because I want to write a note to Lety before we head to Traverse City. I need time to think it through and then find her to give it to her.

It's around 11:45. Being clean and ready to head to Traverse City feels good. We're all going to Mr. Waterman's house with Dad to get paid. After Dad gets paid, we'll be heading to Traverse City.

Dad pulls onto the immaculate asphalt driveway lined with white pines and parks close to the house. The scent of the pines along the drive is delightful. The harmless farm dog barks at Dad as he walks to the front door. Anne answers the door, greets Dad, and invites him in. Junior opens the back of the pickup to let in some air. I join him, and we discuss our plan to ask Dad for our money.

Meanwhile, Dad enjoys the coolness of the air-conditioned house and the stunning view of Lake Leelanau and Lake Michigan from the spacious living room window. He hands all the tokens to Anne, who cross-checks the record in the pocket notebook she and Mr. Waterman used throughout the week. The numbers match up. Dad is paid in cash.

Soon, we see Dad walking out with a big smile. Another farmworker has already arrived and is ready to see Anne to get paid.

We ask Dad for our money. Dad replies, "What do you mean your money? Who feeds you? Who buys your clothes? Who pays for your rent?" Junior and I feel upset but try not to show it to Dad. I'm shaking inside and filled with anger. Dad shouldn't have told us we would get paid. I don't know what to say.

Off we go to Traverse City. I don't want to talk to anyone. I want to be left alone. Judging by the look on Junior's face, he wants some solitude, too. As we pass through Suttons Bay, I'm still in a bad mood, and even seeing the cute girls in line at the ice cream shop doesn't interest me. The M-22 traffic is slow and heavy. We're behind a pickup truck hauling a travel trailer with many cars trailing us. It's hard to pass on this stretch of highway due to all the oncoming traffic. Many vehicles are towing boats. There are numerous pickup campers and other cars. Mixed in with all the traffic are a few vehicles carrying migrant farmworkers like us.

As we approach Greilickville, leisure activities start to pick up. If I don't shake off my bad mood, I'll ruin my day and miss all the fun I could have. Tito and Sandy are thrilled as we pass the yacht club and see the huge yachts. My eyes are glued to the yachts, too. I notice some of their names: *Simmy Jimmy*, *Rose's Delight*, and *Living It*. We're driving by too quickly for me to read any more names. There are various types of watercraft in Grand Traverse Bay, including sailboats, jet skis, yachts (one cruising toward the yacht club), and speedboats. This is Michigan – the Water Wonderland! Seeing these amazing sights lifts the last traces of my bad mood. We're stopped at the Greilickville traffic light. To our left is a 1968 maroon Z28 Camaro, its radio blasting "My Cherie Amour" by Stevie Wonder. The beat makes me feel vibrant and alive.

We arrive in Traverse City. The traffic is heavy in downtown Traverse on US-31. There's so much to see. I can't keep up with all the great things around me: pretty girls, cool muscle cars, fabulous boats, and jet skis—so awesome! With caution, and after two traffic light changes, Dad turns left into Clinch Park. Thank goodness there's a traffic light here; entering the park would take forever due to all the oncoming traffic.

Dad parks in the Clinch Park parking lot. Tejano music plays from the speakers of a 1957 reddish-orange Chevy Bel Air with Texas plates parked in the lot. In the driver's seat, with the windows down, is a young Mexican man in his mid-twenties wearing Ray-Ban glasses. We all carry something to the picnic table. Junior and I bring the heavy cooler filled with ice, food, watermelon, and pop.

Clinch Park is filled with activity. Families are enjoying picnics. A middle-aged man and woman sit in lawn chairs reading. A pretty girl strolls by, listening to "Aquarius" by the 5th Dimension on her transistor radio—the pleasant scent of Coppertone tanning lotion wafts into my nose. Several women are pushing baby strollers. A few teenage boys and girls lie on the grass on their towels, getting suntans. On the beach, a group of people plays beach volleyball.

Fun in Traverse City

Since Dad is away, Junior and I take our time admiring all the attractive girls around us who are wearing pretty summer dresses, skirts, jeans, shorts, bathing suits, and culottes. Junior and I whistle the hit song "Music to Watch Girls By," sung by Andy Williams, as we glance at each other and smile.

A group of guys toss a football to each other. They seem skilled, judging by their crisp, quick, and precise throws. Some children near the sandy beach's shallow, cool lake water build sandcastles and dig in the sand with plastic hand shovels. Four teens spread out, throwing a Frisbee at one another. Several men are playing horseshoes. Many bike riders cruise on the sidewalk that runs parallel to the shore. Seagulls drift around, drawn to where the food is. A couple of seagulls squabble over bread scraps that children toss at them. A little boy, about three years old, is crying, frightened by how close a seagull flew to him. Several speedboats in the bay have their respective water skiers behind them. To our delight, we see a US Coast Guard helicopter, colored orange, white, and black, flying low over the bay, loud and impressive. What a sight to see! I have to tell Luis and Jim about this when I get home.

It's time for Junior and me to explore the park. The wishing well is our first stop. We run to the stone masonry circular well, and a few people are gathered around, tossing in coins. The well has a small roof and a wooden bucket attached to a rope and pulley. The artificial well is filled with shiny and dull coins at the bottom of the clear water. I wonder how much money is in the well. A sign above reads, "Coins dropped will bring luck and improve our zoo, too." I pull a dime and a nickel from my pocket, make a wish for Lety and me, and toss the coins in.

On the other side of the well is a miniature replica of Traverse City. Over the years, we've seen it every time we visit Clinch Park. I've never seen anything like it. We walk over for a better view—Junior points out our location on the replica. Every detail is precisely in place: the streets, stores, schools, hotels, beaches, parks—everything.

We only have a few minutes before returning to the picnic table for lunch. Junior and I head to the zoo. As we walk freely around the zoo, several peacocks cross our path, showing minimal interest in us. We quickly look at the zebras, giraffes, lions, bobcats, black bears, mountain lions, coyotes, elk, deer, and reindeer. It's a fantastic free chance to see the animals up close. The lion appears sleepy and lethargic but remains impressive. I imagine the damage those enormous claws could inflict. My favorite animals and birds at the zoo are the elk, bobcats, owls, and hawks. I wish we had more time, but we need to leave now.

It's time to eat. It's past our regular lunchtime, so everyone is hungry. Dad is grilling hamburgers and is almost done. I walk over to the stream of smoke from the grill to inhale the inviting aroma of grilled hamburgers before washing my hands and getting ready for the meal. Mom leads us in a prayer. In an orderly fashion, we grab a plate, plastic utensils, and a napkin, then head to the grill to get our hamburgers. Afterward, we return to the table to line up for the pork and beans, a bun, ketchup, mustard, sliced cheese, and chips. Finally, we go to the cooler to grab a cold 16-ounce bottle of Nehi Orange, Red, or Cream Soda pop, or RC Cola. Occasionally, the wind shifts, bringing the smoke from the grill our way for a moment. The sound of a low-flying airplane catches my attention; the airport is a few miles from the park. I go back for seconds and wonder if Luis is somewhere in Traverse City right now. Everything is good. Dad mentioned we would be having picnics during our vacation. I finish everything on my plate. Now it's time for a slice of cool, juicy watermelon!

After our picnic, Junior and I walk to the harbor to check out the boats and yachts. The harbor, located within the park, has a breakwater that provides a haven for boats. There are four rows of piers with slips. Some areas show signs of storm damage. It must be from the storm we had last Sunday night. Almost every slip is occupied by a boat or a yacht.

We stroll along the sidewalk that connects all the piers. I feel like I'm trespassing, but I don't see a sign indicating that the area is off-limits. We pass two men and two women lounging at the back of their luxurious yacht, *Skippin Skipper,* from Sheboygan, Wisconsin, enjoying drinks. They pay no attention to us and continue their conversation. All the boats gently rock in the water, appearing squeaky clean. Everything seems well-maintained. Most boats are at least 25 feet long, mostly white, and made of fiberglass, though some are constructed from wood. One of my favorite yachts is white, featuring expensive-looking red hardwood on the deck. Everything looks new and shiny. We can see spacious areas inside some yachts with thick vinyl cushions for seating. One of Junior's favorites is a three-level white yacht. The top level is a covered bridge where the captain commands the boat. The mid-level has an enclosed area, while the spacious stern is open. It's called *Heaven II* and is from Chicago, Illinois. Another yacht that catches my eye *is You Betcha!,* from Key West, Florida! All the boats and yachts are equipped with expensive-looking navigation and communication gear on top. I wonder how much these vessels cost and what kind of jobs their owners have—they must be millionaires to own one of these. Although I'm impressed by the boats and yachts, I never want to own one because I quickly get motion sickness. Occasionally, I experience it while sitting in the back seat of a car on the road.

I enjoy reading the names of the boats: *Groovin'* from Peoria, Illinois; *Sally III* from Kenosha, Wisconsin; *Dreamer Sail* from Traverse City; *Dude II* from Milwaukee, Wisconsin; and *Diggin' It* from Myrtle Beach, South Carolina. Most watercraft are from the Great Lakes, such as Chicago, Milwaukee, Wisconsin, Duluth, Minnesota, and Toronto, Ontario.

We walk down a pier, checking out the boats. Most of them are empty. The crew and passengers probably walked downtown to shop, have lunch, grab a drink, or catch a movie at the cinema. It's all very close by, just across US-31.

Many men wear black and gold-trimmed sea captain hats, which I would like to have. Some women wear sunglasses and the latest fashions, while others are pretty casual, wearing swimsuits. Almost everyone on the boats wears deck or tennis shoes; some are barefoot.

I lose myself in thoughts about what it would be like to be on the Great Lakes in one of these yachts. How big are the waves? It must get chilly in the middle of the lakes, even during a hot summer. What would it feel like to sail to Chicago, under the Mackinac Bridge, or to pass through the Soo Locks on my way to Duluth, Minnesota? What would it be like to glide by Detroit and Windsor, Ontario, on my way to the Canadian locks, and then to pass Quebec City and travel through the St. Lawrence Seaway to the Atlantic Ocean as some of these yachts do? How much time does it take? How much money does it cost? My thoughts continue to wander about this. What an adventure it would be!

Before we leave the park, Dad surprises us by giving Junior and me each a twenty-dollar bill. We thank him. It's nothing like what I expected, but at least it's something. Now, I have enough for bike parts and a couple of 45 rpm records!

After the park, Dad pulls into the parking lot of the Giantway Family Discount Center. It's located east of Clinch Park on US-31. The lot is nearly full. The sun is blazing down on us, and it's even hotter standing on this asphalt lot. A migrant farmworker stake truck with army green canvas on the back and Texas plates is parked in the lot. People are climbing down from the back of the truck using a ladder.

It's time to shop. Giantway, like all other department stores, is having its back-to-school sales. We're mainly here to buy clothes for school. The very thought of returning to school saddens me. It's not that I don't like school; it's just that summer is ending. Junior and I walk inside together. The interior is as bustling as the parking lot outside. The cool, air-conditioned air offers a welcome relief from the heat I've endured all week. However, it's almost too cold for me. Mom says not to stray too far because she will pick clothes for me to try on. Before she's ready for me, she'll be busy selecting clothes for Timmy, Tito, and Sandy.

Meanwhile, Junior and I do our shopping. We go to the record section to browse the albums and 45 rpm pop songs for sale. The store layout is similar to the one in Alma, so we easily find what we're looking for. I spot two 45s I'd like to buy: "Baby I Love You" by Andy Kim and "Sugar Sugar" by the Archies. I dedicate this song to Lety. However, I decide against buying them here. The sun could easily warp them, they might break on the journey home, or Dad could see them and smash them since he considers this devil's music. I'll wait and purchase them at the Giantway in Alma. Before finding Mom, I head to the sports department to check prices for bike tires, handle grips, and headlamps. The Giantway in Alma will have these items at the same prices.

I see Mom and make eye contact so she knows I'm around. She acknowledges my presence with a nod and continues talking in Spanish with a young Mexican woman with a toddler. I stroll to the boys' department to check out pants and shirts. I'm not too excited about the selection. There are many double-knit pants that I absolutely dislike. I'm looking for something made from a polyester-cotton blend.

Mom is ready to help me look at clothes. She meets me in front of the boys' pants section of the store. She has a pair of navy-blue polyester/cotton pants and a light blue long-sleeve button-down collar shirt for me to try on. When I come out of the dressing room, she tells me to walk so that she can better assess whether to buy them. She approves. I approve. Before I take them off, she gives me a dark blue polyester sweater to try on. We like it. I'm glad it didn't take too long to decide what to buy for school.

Mom is always there to help others. As I leave the store, I notice her at the checkout, assisting a Mexican woman by interpreting for her and the cashier. Both the woman and the cashier express their gratitude to Mom. I remember going with Mom several times while she volunteered for the Church Women United Organization in Ithaca. She actively participated in their clothing and food drives for migrant farmworker families. This organization includes women from Presbyterian, United Methodist, Episcopalian, and Lutheran churches. Mom also served as an interpreter for the migrant families who came by for food and clothing. She worked alongside her friend Pauline Souchek, a member of the United Methodist Church in Alma and part of Church Women United. I remember how articulate the ladies were in English; they reminded me of my teachers.

I always felt a bit insecure and shy around them, and I rarely spoke because I didn't want them to judge my English skills. I remember how easy and natural it was for Mom to be with these ladies and chat with them. Many of them were wives of doctors, dentists, and other professionals. I want to be like Mom.

As I wait, I wonder how White people perceive migrant farmworkers here. My mind and eyes act as a kind of radar, constantly scanning for any signs of potential racism. I wonder how comfortable White individuals feel being around so many Mexicans. I notice nothing that appears racist. I hear no racial remarks. However, I also don't see any White person greeting a Mexican, or vice versa. There is minimal eye contact. I remind myself that people are here to shop and have other things on their minds, and that not everyone is as friendly as Mom.

I imagine how challenging it must be for farmworkers who don't speak much English, particularly those from Mexico, who know little about American mainstream culture. I know quite a few Mexican American adults from Texas who have a limited grasp of the English language.

Back home, Mexican Americans my age all speak English. Many are bilingual, speaking both Spanish and English. Others, like me, understand more Spanish than they can speak. A number of younger Mexican American kids I know barely know any Spanish at all.

I notice a beautiful 1968 cherry red Mercedes-Benz 280SL parked beside a large flatbed migrant truck. What a fantastic car! It makes me think of society's haves and have-nots. I think of the person who owns this car and the individual sitting in the back of the flatbed truck for migrant farmworkers; they lead such different lives. I think about what a good education can do for a person versus having a limited education.

I start thinking about what I want to do in life. Do I want to make a lot of money? Do I want to be well-off? Or do I want to find a balance between being poor and rich? Indeed, I don't want to be poor; I know what that's like. I remember having mustard and ketchup sandwiches on white bread because there was nothing else to eat. Teachers always emphasize how important it is to get a good education. I want a better life. I aim to go to college. I don't want to be super rich; I want a life where I can live comfortably. I think about Grandpa Ramon and all my uncles on my mom's side. They all have jobs with General Motors in Lansing or Saginaw, Michigan, and live comfortably. My goal is to go to college, find a job that I enjoy, and live a comfortable life.

We return to the farm around 4 pm. The camp is buzzing with life. Most people have returned from shopping or their other activities this afternoon. Some women are outside washing and drying the week's dirty clothes. Like last Saturday, they wash clothes outdoors using a washing machine and washboards. I notice several pairs of silky panties and bras on the clothesline near Lety's quarters, and I immediately assume they belong to her since she's the only female of that size in that part of the living quarters. They look so pretty. Some guys are busy washing and waxing their muscle cars, taking great pride in their vehicles. Children are playing outside as usual. The farm dog is chasing a chipmunk in the yard and barking.

Before I meet up with Decky and Junior, I write a note to Lety. Fortunately, I spot Lety shortly after writing the note and hand it to her. She is with Ana and Marti.

They show each other the charms they bought in Traverse City, which they plan to add to their charm bracelets.

Dear Lety, I hope you're doing well. Did you have fun shopping today? Did you make it to Traverse City? We visited the park in Traverse City, which has a zoo, saw the big boats at the marina, and enjoyed a picnic there. After that, we went shopping. I'm sad that we're going home tomorrow afternoon. I'm so glad I met you and would love to keep in touch if that's okay. Please share your address in Texas. I really like you; you're so pretty and so much fun to be with. I know we didn't spend much time together, but I hope we can in the future. Are you coming back to pick cherries next year? Could I get a picture of you? I'd love to have one to keep in my wallet. I hope I can see you before I leave.

Robert

We aren't going to the beach. It's been a long and busy day. Mom is going to make some Mexican food.

Dinner is at Decky's place. Junior, Decky, and I enjoy refried pinto beans and rice with chicken. The tortillas are warm and fresh. The sweet lemon iced tea disappears quickly; it's so delicious. I'm in heaven as I savor this food and drink this tea. The aromas of the food fill the air. My belly is quite full. How many tortillas did I have? As I leave the table, I nibble on the lemon rind from my glass of tea and enjoy the tart and tangy flavor.

It's time to hang out with the guys. We grab a few softballs and gloves and play catch in the open area near the water pump. Everyone had a great and fun day. Moi and his family went shopping in Traverse City. I throw the ball more often to Jaime and Moi. They don't throw as fast or as hard as Junior and Decky. They are more laid back, which I appreciate.

Before heading to the chicken coop, I dash to the barn to find recent newspapers. I'm captivated by the serial killer case. Luckily, I find yesterday's paper and a few others. On my way to the chicken coop, I see Abel. He's listening to the Detroit Tigers game against the Chicago White Sox on his car radio. He invites me to sit down with him. He tells me that the Tigers won yesterday against the White Sox, 8 to 0. He's pleased. They are playing the White Sox again on Sunday. Abel says the Tigers haven't scored a hit yet and that the White Sox look good tonight.

We exchange what we did today. Abel tells me he had some mouth-watering homemade cherry pie from his favorite downtown restaurant in Traverse City. I'd like to have some with vanilla ice cream. Abel asks me if I heard the drunk guy last night and continues saying that every Friday, the farmworker wanders around the farm very drunk, mumbling in Spanish, "Where am I? Where am I?" He asks me if I like Lety and says he can tell I do. I gently laugh. I'm surprised when he confides in me and tells me in a softer voice that he and Regina had their first kiss last week behind the mulberry tree. It takes me a few seconds to place where the mulberry tree is and then remember that it's behind Decky's living quarters. A few minutes later, I see Regina walking toward us and say goodbye to Abel. Regina and I smile at each other and exchange hellos. A smile comes to my face as I hope to have a mulberry experience with Lety.

This is the last night at the chicken coop. I feel a bit downhearted about it, but I know I'll be uplifted by spending time with the guys. Everyone is here. The aroma of smoked fish fills the air. Decky offers us some healthy chunks of freshly caught white fish from Lake Michigan. So succulent! I take small bites and eat slowly to savor the flavor. I thank Decky for the fish and ask him how his afternoon was. He says he enjoyed taking out the trash and driving the four-by-four Dodge Power Wagon pickup. Afterward, he picked up his fish in Leland, saw the pretty young blonde teenager who works at NJ's, and got himself ice cream and the latest edition of Mad magazine. The evening is filled with discussions about cars, girls, food, favorite movies, and more.

We start talking about cars. Most of us like Mopar cars. Although Mopar is the brand name for Chrysler's authentic vehicle parts, the name has become synonymous with Chrysler's "muscle" car line, which we love. They make the Dodge Charger with a 426 cubic inch Hemi engine with 425 horsepower! Plymouth makes the Roadrunner with the standard 383 cubic inch engine. It also comes with a 440 cubic inch or a 426 Hemi engine.

Although I like Mopar, I appreciate any car that catches my eye. I like the sexy look of the 1966 and 1967 Pontiac GTOs with a Hurst four-on-the-floor shifter. My preference is a dark burgundy GTO with a white interior. Johnny Mojica, who attends our church, has a similar one. Decky likes Pontiacs as well. His parents have owned a few over the years.

Once Junior starts talking about cars, you can't stop him. He hands out the drag and race magazines he brought so we can browse them while he talks. He always buys the latest editions of drag and stock racing car magazines. He learns a lot about cars and engines by reading those magazines from cover to cover.

Jaime asks Junior how he got into cars. Junior tells us, "A few years ago, Bob and I were helping our dad clean one of his commercial cleaning accounts, Greening Buick auto dealership in Alma, Michigan. Dad, Bob, and I were at the front of the building cleaning the showroom when suddenly, we heard a loud engine roaring and revving from the maintenance and repair shop at the back of the showroom. Bob and I quickly went to the shop and saw an impressive black 1965 Chevy Malibu. Standing by the car was John Greening, the son of the Buick dealership. I know him from school, and we get along just fine. I approached John to see what was happening. He introduced me to the owner of the souped-up car, Jim Ure. I'd never met Jim, but he's well-known in drag racing circles, at least around Gratiot County, where we live. I asked Jim if we could take a look at his car. He's a friendly guy who was happy to let us take a look. Bob and I started by examining the engine. The car features a 427 cubic inch Chevy big block engine, dual four-barrel carburetors, and a tunnel ram manifold for quicker fuel flow to the combustion chambers. The engine compartment is filled with cool racing equipment. The car also has a 4-speed Hurst racing shifter and Mickey Thompson slick tires in the rear. Jim and I had a long conversation about his car. He races it at the Stanton Drag Strip near our house and wins many races. We could have talked longer, but I had to get back to cleaning. He gave me an old copy of *National Dragster* Magazine, which I read cover to cover. That's what got me into cars. Now, I buy every new issue of *National Dragster*."

Junior's story sparks a lot of discussion about cars. He loves to ignite conversations about who makes the best muscle cars. He often stirs debates when he tells people that Mopar is king and everything else follows. This usually brings out the pride that others feel for their preferred car brands. Junior dives deep into car knowledge, but I understand little of what he's saying.

The conversation shifts to professional car racers. We all respect Richard Petty a lot. However, Junior is upset that Richard Petty stopped driving Mopar Plymouth racing cars and decided to switch to Ford. I'm upset, too; it seems unbelievable. This year, he's racing a Ford Torino Talladega. Seeing his number 43 on a Ford feels so strange. He's been racing blue Plymouths for years. Decky points out that Richard Petty, the King of NASCAR, won the Daytona 500 in 1966 and 1964. He has claimed many other victories as well. Richard Petty's name always comes up when talking about racing. We talk about other racers, like Leroy Yarbrough, who won this year's February Daytona 500 Grand National Series race. We all admire the world-famous racer Mario Andretti, who won at Daytona in 1967. Cale Yarborough won Daytona last year. Whenever we watch a race on television, these racers are sure to be in it.

I take a break from the conversations and begin looking at the newspapers. The Wednesday, July 30 edition features the headline, "FBI Help Asked as Governor Milliken Places State Police in Charge of Sex Murder Probe." The governor is now involved in the effort to catch the serial killer. Another article is titled "Push Search for Sadistic Sex Killer." A different headline reads, "Second Day of Fighting

Near Saigon." Under the classified ads, there is a listing for a "1957 Chevy 2-door hardtop, mint condition." Dad had one a few years back: a light brown four-door with a three-speed column shift. There's also an ad that states, "Cherry Pickers, Frank Rousch, Rousch Rd. Traverse City." Another ad reads, "CHERRY PICKERS WANTED. Good bonus, 946-5488. LADIES 16 YEARS OR OLDER for sorting cherries at Traverse City Canning Company, day and night shifts."

I'm saddened to see another cherry shaker ad for the "Homelite Portable Fruit Harvester" at DeWayne's Power Equipment in Traverse City. The ad claims, "The harvester will pay for itself many times during harvest season." There's a number to call for an "In-Your-Orchard" demonstration. The ad features a man holding the machine as he harvests cherries. My cherry world is coming to an end. I'm upset that we probably won't return to pick cherries again.

The article's heading reads, "US Dept of Agriculture Urges Help for Machine-Idled Hands." It states that due to the mechanization of agriculture, the US government needs to develop programs to train farmworkers for new jobs. There's an ad for cherry pie filling: "Thank you, Cherry Pie Filling, for perfect cherry pies every time. One pound, five-ounce can for 29 cents." Giantway is holding several summer clothes sales.

The newspaper's main headline from Friday, August 1, 1969, blows my mind. I immediately tell the guys and read it to them: "Ex-Student Charged With Slaying EMU Coed." The subtitle states, "Officers Say Ypsilanti Home Murder Site." John Norman Collins, a former Eastern Michigan University student, age 23, was arrested and charged with the killing of 18-year-old Karen Sue Beineman. She was the seventh victim of a sexual murder in the past two years. We discuss the serial killer case for about 15 minutes and feeling relieved that they have a suspect.

Since no one is looking at the new *Mad* magazine from July 1969, I decide to pick it up and take a look. I've never been interested in satire, so I've never been a fan of this magazine. I quickly flip through it, return it to Decky's stack of Mad magazines, and chat with the guys a bit longer before getting ready for bed.

Once again, clubhouse time was over before I knew it. The night slipped by too quickly. A farewell to everyone, and I head out to get ready for bed.

I reflect on the day on the road. What a day this has been. What a week it has been. I think of Lety and feel sad that tomorrow is the last day I will see her. I think about Dad paying us, the animals I saw at the zoo, and the storm damage at the marina. Thoughts of all the fun things people were doing in Traverse City run through my mind. I think about the records I will buy when I get home, the excellent smoked white fish I had, and the game of catch we played today. I think of our chicken coop clubhouse and how much fun it's been hanging out with the guys. I am grateful for everything I experienced today.

Images pass through my mind's eye as I lie in my sleeping bag. I see so many cherries on the trees, in lugs, on the trailer, in the orchards, and in my pail. I see the John Deere tractor and trailer making its way through the orchard, loaded with lugs of cherries. Images of Lety recur frequently. I see people enjoying themselves in Traverse City. Random thoughts pass through my mind. Slowly, I drift off to sleep.

SUNDAY, 3 AUGUST 1969

I still have at least another hour to sleep, yet my mind begins to stir with uneasy thoughts. The reality is setting in that it's our last day here, and this beautiful experience I'm having will soon end. I feel a sense of melancholy because Lety and I never had any time alone together. I never had the chance to hold her hand for an extended period or the opportunity to kiss her. These thoughts are making me anxious. I try to push them to the back of my mind so I can continue sleeping.

The morning chill and the dew on the grass urge me to hurry to the bathroom. The farm is waking up as people begin their day. Only a few people are ahead of me, waiting to use the bathroom. Standing in line, I notice the dew-covered cherries in the orchard near the farm sparkling in the sunlight. I'm really going to miss being around cherries.

At breakfast, Mom tells us the day's plans and information, which include church, a meal afterward, packing up our things, taking down the tent, picking three lugs of cherries to take home, and not to stray too far in case we are needed for something else.

After we eat, Mom tells Junior and me to pick the three lugs of cherries she wants to take home. Junior doesn't mind doing this because he enjoys driving the pickup. We hop into the pickup and head to the barn to grab a couple of pails and several lugs from the big pile of unused cherry lugs just outside. One says Waterman, another one Esch, and the third one says Red Path. We drive north of the farm on the two-track path that leads through the orchard. One last time out in the orchard we go. Junior has the pickup's five-speed manual transmission in "creeper gear." The gear is so slow that it's not used for driving on roads. It's made for slow work on a farm or a work site. We pass a lot of cherry trees that we can pick from, but Junior enjoys driving the pickup and goes deeper into the orchard. I don't mind; I'm enjoying this cheap thrill.

I hesitate for several seconds, wondering which tree I should choose. I push this thought aside and begin selecting only the largest clusters of cherries nearby. I will miss the sound of cherries hitting the bottom of a galvanized pail. I know I'm quirky, but I enjoy it. As usual, the biggest ones go into my mouth while I pick. I will miss being in the middle of a cherry orchard and eating all the cherries I desire. These big black cherries will be a treat to savor at home for the next week and a half. We pick only one lug of sweet cherries because Mom wants more tart ones for canning. Junior drives us to the tart cherry orchard, which isn't far from where we are now. We fill two lugs with tart cherries.

Mom will can these to make cherry pies and other treats throughout the year. She typically cans about 18 Mason jars of tart cherries each season. She stores them in our basement, which has its fair share of creepy spiders and webs. Some canned cherries will be used as a fruit topping for desserts. I love eating the canned cherries on their own. I'll sneak down to the basement in winter to grab a Mason jar full of delicious tart cherries. There's always plenty of juice in the jar, so I pour it into a tumbler and drink it. We all look forward to Mom's cherry pies.

After 30 minutes in the orchard, we head back to the farm to finish the tasks we need to complete before church. Then we return to the barn, drop off the pails, and make our way to the campsite to start packing and prepare for church.

Junior, Decky, and I walk to the Esch Farm for the church service. I have my small New Testament Bible in one pocket and my gum and black clip-on tie in the other. We leave much earlier to have some fun before the service. Like last Sunday, I find a beer can on the side of the road to use for "kick the can." Off we go, kicking it to each other as we walk downhill by the Mitchel Farm. After passing the Mitchel Farm, we encounter another hill at the cemetery. Kick the can becomes a bit more challenging when heading uphill. As we get closer to the Esch Farm, we hear Dad and the other musicians practicing. Dad doesn't mind practices; he can play for hours if he's jamming with other great players. We pass the Esch stake truck, Aunt Chacha's car, and several farmworkers' vehicles. Further into the farm camp is a parked Case Orchard tractor with the trailer hooked up. The farm is alive with activity. Many farmworkers and families are outside doing their thing.

Just before entering the barn, I notice a large, oddly shaped, clumsy-looking farm implement parked further down toward the orchards. I ask Decky what it is. He tells me it's a cherry shaker machine and reminds me that Ted Esch will start mechanized cherry harvesting next year. I feel sad that this machine will end our coming back to pick cherries.

After entering the barn, we start swinging on the tire swing. Because I'm wearing polished shoes, I can't enjoy swinging and moving around as freely as I wish. I'm going to miss the smell of this old barn.

After a few minutes of swinging, our attention turns to the hay loft. Junior and Decky want to head up. The climb scares me because the wooden ladder nailed to the wall goes straight up. I worry about losing my footing and messing up the polish on my shoes. From what I can see, it also has several spider webs with spiders lurking between the wall and the ladder. I get the heebie-jeebies just thinking about being inches away from the spiders.

Decky is the first to go, followed by Junior. Peer pressure sets in. If Decky and Junior can do it, I can, too. I'm determined to climb up. I won't let my fear rob me of this hay loft adventure. They seem to have no problem passing by the spiders, which makes me feel more at ease about climbing up. Up I go. My stomach feels the same sensation I get when I'm in a speeding vehicle going up a hill and quickly descending on the other side. My adrenaline surges as I approach the spiders while climbing the ladder. What will I do if a spider tries to bite one of my hands that are firmly gripping the ladder? Will I freak out and lose my grip? Just concentrate and do it, I tell myself. Decky grabs my forearm as I reach the top. I feel a sense of accomplishment for overcoming my fears once again.

The dusty wooden floor of the loft covers half of the big barn. There are a couple of pallets with cherry pesticide bags and large farm equipment parts. Plenty of cobwebs, spiders, and several bird nests are in the corners of the loft. The view is lovely from up here. I can hear Dad and the musicians in the other barn playing their instruments.

The church service is about to start. Down the ladder we go, passing the creepy spiders once again. Outside the barn, I button up my top shirt and put on my clip-on tie. There are already people seated inside the barn for the church service. Others, like Mom, are greeting each other at the entrance. Mom is pleased to see that we are on time. The musicians have stopped practicing and are finely tuned for the morning service. Most people I see have big smiles and are glad to be here. Almost every teenager and adult has a Bible in hand. It's part of the culture of Pentecostal churches to bring your Bible so you can follow along with the sermon or class.

Grandpa warmly welcomes everyone and begins the service with a prayer. We all stand as he prays. Like last Sunday's service, we sing some songs and then attend our Sunday school class.

Junior, Decky, and I wander toward the large tree in front of the farm where our teen class took place last week. I pass a cedar tree, snap off a piece of fern, pinch it between my thumb and index finger to capture its scent, and then quickly rejoin Decky and Junior.

The teen Sunday school class begins, and the teacher leads us in prayer. A few cars on the road make it hard for me to hear. The day is starting to warm up. In the background, various birds chirp, competing with a cicada in a tree near the orchard on the other side of the big barn. Our teacher, Aurora Tijerina, is around 18 years old and has a friendly personality. Aurora asks us to introduce ourselves by stating our names and where we're from. Since I did this last Sunday with a different teacher, I'm not as shy about introducing myself again. Most of the teens in the class already know I don't speak Spanish. I'm one of the last to introduce myself. Even though I feel more comfortable than last Sunday, my heart is still pounding fiercely. With my limited Spanish, I briefly introduce myself. The teacher asks me in Spanish how many years I've lived in Michigan. Decky translates for me, telling the teacher that I don't know much Spanish and have lived in Michigan all my life. You can tell she has taught before; she makes the class interactive and exciting.

Just like last Sunday, the Perez girls from Archbold are in class: Gloria, Regina, Rosy, Mary, and Estella. Estella seems to be around my age. I see them at the

Waterman Farm. Abel and Cousin Ester (Decky's older sister) are here too. There are other teens I don't know.

The teacher announces that it's time to play Bible Swords. It's a game where you look up a specific verse in the Bible called out by the facilitator. The facilitator says the verse, then gives a "ready, set, go" command. All participants have their Bibles ready to look up the scripture. The first person to find the verse quickly stands up and reads it aloud. The facilitator verifies the correct verse. If the verse is incorrect, the next person to stand up and read the right verse wins. One of the Perez girls finds the first verse. I'm discovering that cousin Esther is good at this; she wins three times. I feel motivated to play. There's a lot of energy in the air, and everybody is having a good time. Because of the small pages and print in my Gideon New Testament, it's hard to find the verses. Since I don't have the Old Testament, I'm limited in what I can look up.

Aurora transitions to the class lesson on God's desire for us to be strong and courageous. We're instructed to turn our Bibles to Joshua 1:9. I follow along in Decky's Spanish Holy Bible. Once everyone has located the verse, we all read it together.

As the Bible lesson continues, the sadness I've felt all morning deepens. I battle it and succeed. I don't want to feel down; I want to enjoy every moment here.

Sunday school has ended, and the main service will begin shortly. The musicians start playing as people return to the barn for the main service. There's a lot of excitement in the air, and everyone is feeling joyful.

Grandpa welcomes everyone returning from their Sunday school class and begins the main service. I choose to sit with Moi instead of Junior and Decky. We sit in the middle of the congregation. From my observations during last Sunday's service and my conversations with Moi at the chicken coop, I notice he is much more attentive to spiritual matters than Decky and Junior. Decky and Junior are at the back. We all stand as Grandpa offers a word of prayer to start the service and to help us enter a spiritual frame of mind.

After a few announcements from Grandpa, the song leader steps forward and directs us to sing "Cristo la Roca" (I've Anchored in Jesus), "Una Mirada de Fe" (A Look of Faith), and "Las Promesas de Dios" (Standing on the Promises). Moi and I sing as he holds the *Himnos de Gloria y Triunfo* songbook. I feel so alive singing as much as I can in Spanish and clapping my hands to each song we sing. Most of the congregation sings from their hearts, and I hear many lovely voices and a few that are not as harmonious. Several ladies and teenage girls are playing tambourines. I'll miss the sound of the tambourines, as we don't have anyone who plays one regularly at our church back home, though sometimes Mom does. I wish someone would. After the singing, the song leader invites us to greet those around us, and I enjoy doing this.

The song leader transitions and invites anyone to share their testimony about what God has done for them. Mom is one of three people who speak. She's talking in Spanish, so I don't know exactly what she's saying, but the people seem to appreciate her words. As usual, Mom is crying while giving her testimony. Her tears are of joy and gratitude, not sadness. She has a tender heart.

After the testimonies, Grandpa takes charge of the service. He asks if there are any prayer requests from the congregation, and many are shared. Once gathered, he leads us in prayer. Numerous people raise their hands and pray earnestly to God for answers to these requests.

Grandpa's message is about faith in God. Moi and I share his Spanish Bible as we follow the scriptures Grandpa has chosen. I make a strong effort to recall every Spanish word I know to understand better what Grandpa is preaching.

As the sermon continues, I find myself lost in the specifics of what Grandpa is preaching. I begin to think about the shocking news Decky shared regarding Ted Esch and many other cherry farmers turning to mechanized harvesting in the coming years. It feels as if my heart has been wrenched out of my body. The future opportunities to immerse myself in my Mexican culture during cherry harvests have now been taken from me. Now that I'm older, I look forward to going to Lake Leelanau with Decky and his family to pick strawberries and cherries all season long. These possibilities are now gone. The thought of never returning to the Esch and Waterman farms saddens my heart. This place is a historic marker for the Fuentes family, as cherries played a big part in bringing the family to Michigan. I love history. To think that I'll never be able to return to these farm camps, the places that hold so many fond memories for me, is difficult to bear right now. How can my hope come to a halt so swiftly? Will I never again hear Grandpa preach from the barn at Esch's? Will Dad never play his accordion or guitar here? Will I never work another cherry harvest and enjoy the freedom to eat as many cherries as I want? Will I never return to Lake Leelanau to swim and have picnics with my family? Will I never be close to Lake Michigan and Lake Leelanau with the family again? I will miss these lakes. I'll miss the beauty of the orchards, the majestic view of the Manitou Islands, watching the big ships sail by, and experiencing vibrant Traverse City and all its attractions. I will miss Sleeping Bear Dunes, the quaint village of Lake Leelanau, and the picturesque, winding, narrow roads surrounding this area.

The thought that Lety and I will likely never see each other again dampens my heart. I hope we write letters to each other often and that I'll see her this December if we go to Texas during the winter school break. Sadness tries to invade my mind and ruin my day, but hope, as a strong force, overcomes me and keeps me tied to the belief that this year will not be the last time I pick cherries and that I will see Lety again.

I thank God for the wonderful experiences I had this past week. I wish I could make this time last three times longer. I don't want to go home yet. This

226

morning, I asked Mom again if I could stay until the end of the harvest. Her response that I couldn't was not surprising.

Every time Grandpa shares a new verse, I snap out of my inner thoughts and try again to follow his words. As usual, I'm lost again within a few minutes, and my mind starts wandering. I glance around the room and notice several ladies fanning themselves; I wish I had one. There isn't much air circulation here. Everyone has a slight sheen of moisture on their faces from the heat and humidity. Several kids are fidgeting, grabbing their parents' attention. The Perez girls look so angelic and pretty. I'd love to remove my tie and unbutton my top shirt button; it feels so restricting and makes it hard to breathe and turn my head from side to side. The thought of school starting next month zooms through my mind, but I push it aside. The anticipation of seeing Jim today and meeting Bruno excites me. Grandpa snaps me out of my mental wandering as he directs us to turn our Bibles to another verse.

Moi looks up the verse in his Bible and points it out to me. I then look it up in my English version. After reading it in English, I can anticipate what Grandpa will preach in Spanish.

In a few minutes, I find myself lost again. I start thinking about what to write in my note to Lety, if we will get any private time together, what I must pack, and what I must do before we leave. I can't forget to give Ana the gum wrappers I've saved.

Grandpa concludes the sermon and asks us to stand, close our eyes, and bow our heads. The musicians begin to play "Pecador, Ven al Dulce Jesus" (I Believe Jesus Saves) as Grandpa invites anyone who wishes to become a Christian to show this by raising their hand while no one is looking. He patiently waits for someone to raise their hand. I assume no one did since Grandpa gave no further instructions for those wishing to become Christians.

Grandpa then asks us to sing as the musicians play "Todo a Cristo Yo Me Rindo" (I Surrender All) and invites those in the congregation who wish to come up to the altar to pray for a deeper walk of faith with God. Many people come forward. He then encourages others to come forward with any special prayer requests they may have. He invites the church elders to join him in praying for those who desire prayer. The altar becomes quite crowded since half of the congregation has gone forward. Moi and I continue singing, following the lyrics from the songbook. I'm feeling very emotional, as I usually do when I'm at a Pentecostal Spanish church service. I let my tears flow down my face. Moi raises his hands and prays. I close my eyes and raise my arms as well. I feel much more comfortable doing this around Moi.

After everyone is finished at the altar, Grandpa concludes with a prayer. The musicians start playing the song "Hay Poder" (There is Power in the Blood) as people shuffle out of the cramped church and into the open air. No one seems to be in a hurry to leave. Conversations and laughter fill the space. Dad doesn't want to stop playing; he keeps extending the songs. I take off my tie, tuck it in my pocket, and unbutton my top button. I feel so much better.

Mom takes a break from talking with people and informs Junior and me that we will eat at Decky's at 2 pm, that Grandpa and Grandma will eat with us, that we will leave around 3:30 pm, and that we must have everything packed.

I'm feeling nostalgic because I know I'll probably never return to this place to pick cherries. I want to sit on the orchard tractor one more time. I want to walk on the trailer used to haul the cherry lugs from the orchard. I want to take one more stroll through the barn and swing on the tire swing again. I want to sit in the Esch's hawny stake truck cab and climb back onto the flatbed.

Decky and Junior agree to join me. We start by heading to the tractor with the trailer still attached. It feels so good sitting on the cushioned seat. I then jump onto the trailer and avoid stepping on the cherries scattered on the floor. Several flies and a couple of bees are drawn to the juices of the crushed cherries. Beside the tractor is a large pile of empty cherry lugs, all stained with dried cherry juice. In the background is the sandy two-track path leading to the orchards. The orchard slopes upward at the end, meeting the woods. I have childhood memories of this place. I must have been 4 years old when Mom and Dad were picking cherries in this area. They told me to stay in the car while they picked cherries. It was so boring. I recall how difficult it was to open the car doors due to the steep incline where our car was parked.

We pass the cherry shaker, and I feel nothing but contempt for it. I want nothing to do with it. I don't even want to look at it; it will only sour my mood. Our next stop is the barn. We pass by the cinder-block dwelling where the Chapa family stays. They always stay here. At the barn, we each take a quick swing on the tire swing. Since we were here before church, we don't spend much time at the barn. The Esch stake truck is our next stop. This is the truck from my early childhood memories. When will be the next time I can sit in the cab of a big hawny truck like this one? I spend a few moments enjoying the feel of the driver's seat. I feel a sense of power sitting so high up. I love the view. The only thing I don't like about the truck is the force needed to press down the clutch.

Before walking back to Waterman's, I rush to one of the cedar trees, snap off a small fern, and breathe in the sweet resin. I believe the mental images of this place will last for the rest of my life; only time will tell. Goodbye, Esch Farm.

Back at the Waterman Farm, Decky tells us that he just found out his dad needs his help for a few days with a masonry job back in Archbold, and that he will be leaving this afternoon with his dad. Junior and I are excited about possibly riding home with Decky and Uncle Joe. Since they pass through Alma, it wouldn't be much trouble for them to drop us off. Decky likes the idea and quickly goes to ask his dad. A minute later, Decky comes back with the answer that we can go with them! Junior and I are thrilled to spend more time with our favorite cousin.

It's time to pack my things and get ready for the trip home, but first, I'll change from my dress clothes to my favorite blue jeans and T-shirt. It feels great to be in comfortable clothes.

I feel compelled to take another walk around the farm. As I did at the Esch Farm, I go to the tractor and trailer parked next to the barn where they usually are. I sit on the seat and feel the smooth surface of the John Deere tractor. The yellow, cushioned seat still has its protective plastic covering in place. Next to the tractor is a pile of empty cherry lugs. A few minutes later, I'm at the barn, walking on the main floor, taking in the smells. After the barn, I head to the chicken coop clubhouse. It's so empty. The smell of chicken poop seems stronger. I start to reminisce about the highlights of our time here. I can almost faintly hear our voices and laughter from the days and nights we spent here. Before I know it, five minutes have passed by.

After the chicken coop, I walk to the road for a more panoramic view of my surroundings. How beautiful the lakes and orchards look! I will miss this view. I cross the road to examine the stones scattered around the dirt barrier separating the road from the orchard. I pick one up for a closer look and am amazed to discover it's filled with fossils. Nostalgia gives way to curiosity.

My attention is now focused on the chalk-colored stones, ranging from six to twelve inches. Many of these contain fossils. I begin searching for the best stones to take home. I select one and rub off the dirt, cobwebs, leaves, and pine needles clinging to it. Jim will think this stone is cool. I discover another stone, six inches long and fractured in the middle, revealing the cross-section. It's filled with seashell fossils and other prehistoric creatures; how fascinating! There are small fossils that look like barnacles. Other fossils have a honeycomb shape. More common are the fan-shaped seashell fossils. All of them are amazing.

I wonder if it's common to find fossils around here or if I've discovered something interesting for geologists and rock enthusiasts. I walk along the barrier for about thirty feet in both directions and notice many more fossil stones. How did they end up here? This land is so much higher than Lake Michigan below. In my science class, we briefly discussed how Michigan and the surrounding Great Lakes were formed by glaciers thousands of years ago.

I'm not supposed to believe in the theory of evolution since our church is against it. They say it is a sin to accept this idea. Our church believes that God made the heavens and the earth in six days and rested on the seventh. Again, I wonder how these fossils ended up here. I'm feeling a bit confused. Holding the stone, I step off the dirt barrier onto the road, look down the long hill, and see Lake Michigan in the distance. We must be at least a couple of hundred feet higher than the lake.

As I hold the rock in my hand and gaze at Lake Michigan far below, I, for a moment, question my beliefs about how the world was created. For now, I revert to what I was taught. I believe God is omnipotent; if that's true, then why couldn't God create diverse rock formations just for fun or beauty? I want to spend more time pondering this later when I have more time. There's so much about life that I don't understand.

I choose three of the best stones to bring home: one for Mom, one for Jim, and one for myself.

The time has come for us to eat lunch. Everyone is gathered around the tables and standing. Grandpa says a prayer of thanksgiving for the food that Grandma, Aunt Maruca, and Mom made. I can't believe how tall the covered stack of homemade flour tortillas is, but it must be that way since fifteen of us are hungry and ready to eat. I make room for two tortillas, refried beans, Spanish rice, and carne guisada (stewed meat) on my plate. I fill my plastic tumbler with the sun-kissed, sweetened lemon iced tea and ensure a few ice cubes fall into my tumbler. I sit with Decky and Junior at the end of the picnic table. Everything tastes incredible. By the looks of it, everyone is as hungry as I am.

As I sit and eat, I take in the view surrounding me. To our east, atop the hill, I can see the ultra-modern hexagon-shaped new Waterman home with its large deck overlooking the farm, Lake Leelanau, Lake Michigan, and the Manitou Islands. To the north, there are some of the Waterman Orchards. Half the orchards have been harvested, but many more delicious cherries remain. About 30 yards away, in the same direction, is the Mulberry tree where Abel and Regina had their first kiss. The tree is near the dwelling of the guy who, when drunk, babbles loudly over and over, "Where am I?" in Spanish as he stumbles around the work camp. There are farmworkers' vehicles with license plates from Ohio and Texas. Although I want to eat slowly, there's no time to waste.

Grandma and Grandpa stand by their Buick Le Sabre, ready to leave. Although Grandpa has never owned a brand-new car, his vehicles are always clean, well-maintained, and rust-free. Grandpa's hand-tooled leather briefcase rests in the back seat, which he bought at the mercado (marketplace) in Reynosa, Mexico. It features a large image of the Aztec sun calendar and an Aztec warrior. Grandpa's Bible is also in the back seat. A bumper sticker on the rear bumper reads "Pastor." Grandpa has had a "Pastor" bumper sticker on all his cars for as long as I can remember. On the rear window is a decal of a cross. One by one, we kids approach Grandma and Grandpa to shake their hands and say our goodbyes. They give each of us coins and pieces of Mexican candy, "dulce de calabaza" (pumpkin candy). This is one of my favorite Mexican treats. The older we get, the more money we receive. Junior gets three quarters and a dime. I receive three shiny quarters. Sandy gets two shiny dimes and a nickel. Tito gets a nickel and five shiny new pennies. Timmy receives five pennies. We wave at them as Grandpa slowly drives out of the driveway. With a honk from Grandpa, he accelerates up Esch Road, beginning his five-and-a-half-hour ride home to Ohio.

CHAPTER FOUR

GOING HOME

SUNDAY, 3 AUGUST 1969

It's time to get ready to leave. While Mom helps clean up after lunch, Junior and I assist Dad in taking down the tent and other things. Junior and I remove everything from inside the tent. I grab the broom and start sweeping the interior. Once the inside is done, we each take a corner and flip the tent over so I can clean it thoroughly. The bottom of the tent is damp. We make sure the entire tent is dry before folding it and putting it in the box. The grass beneath the tent is yellow due to the lack of sunlight. It will take a few days to regain its normal green color.

Dad is in the back of the pickup, calling out items for us to hand him. There's so much stuff that needs to go in. Dad is an excellent packer; he'll make everything fit and organized. I find a spot in the pickup that's out of the way to place my stones. Since Junior and I are going home with Uncle Joe and Decky, we set our bags by the bushes and later put them in the back of Decky's pickup.

There's only a little time left before we leave. Uncle Joe wants to leave precisely at 3:30 pm. Lety, Ana, and Marti are here; so are Jaime and Moi. Lety looks gorgeous in her jean skirt, white puffy shoulder short-sleeve top, a white ribbon in the back of her hair, and leather sandals. Her skinny legs look so silky. I give Ana the rest of the gum wrappers I have. I'm wearing the necklace Ana made for me out of gum wrappers. Lety is wearing her necklace too!

This is it. The time has finally come for us to leave. My heart is racing. It doesn't feel real. Ana and Marti give Lety and me some space to be close to each other. We hug one another. Parting with the person who made my vacation magical is hard for me. As we embrace, I run my fingers through her dark brown hair. It

233

feels silkier than I imagined and smells terrific. I take a deep breath to savor the fragrance she's wearing. I wish I could capture her scent and breathe it in whenever I wanted. I'd love to have a few strands of her hair for memory's sake. It's too late to ask for them now; too many people are around. I have so much to learn about romantic relationships. After we hug, I take her hand. She repeatedly tells me that I had better write to her and send her a school picture of me as soon as I get it. I can feel the electricity flowing through our linked hands. We exchange gentle squeezes. Oh, how I wish we had privacy so I could give her the goodbye I'd like to give her: a big, long hug while we kiss. I want to whisper in her ear how much I care for her. I want to hear something from her in my ear. Lety then hands me a perfume-scented envelope with a letter inside. She drew pretty flowers on the envelope, and I love the girly touch. Lety tells me not to read it until I get home. She seems firm about this. I promise her I will do as she wishes.

I say my farewells to Moi and Jaime. I've found a new friend in Moi and look forward to seeing him again when we visit relatives in Ohio. It's been a pleasure hanging out with Jaime, and I hope to see him again, maybe when we visit Texas during Christmas break, as Dad has been talking about it.

Uncle Joe is ready to leave. Mom and Dad are ready, too. Decky, Junior, and I climb into the back of Uncle Joe's pickup. The cap is on the back. Junior is thrilled that the day has finally come to go home. Lety and I keep our eyes locked on one another. Our big smiles frame our faces. Uncle Joe starts the pickup.

Off we go! Slowly, he leaves the driveway. Ana, Marti, and Lety follow the truck to the road. They wave goodbye until we are out of sight on the other side of the steep hill. I never want to forget this mental image of Lety with Lake Leelanau and Lake Michigan in the background. Uncle Joe stops at the stop sign at the top of the hill, at the Eagle Highway intersection.

On our trip home, I want to observe anything related to cherries, and I'm starting now. There are cherry orchards, as far as I can see. I don't know of any other place in Cherryland with so many cherry trees. What a spectacular sight! I look at both orchards in the northwest (where we picked the tart cherries) and the southwest corners.

Across Eagle Highway, Esch Road becomes Horn Road. Uncle Joe continues on Horn Road. The winding road takes us through fields of oats and cherry orchards. We pass a farm camp featuring a few vehicles with Texas plates, including a hawny truck covered in green canvas at the back. Several minutes later, we reach the intersection of M204, which links Lake Leelanau village to Suttons Bay. Uncle Joe makes a left turn toward Suttons Bay. Quickly, we descend the steep hill. I'm reminded that this is where Dad nearly had a terrible accident while hauling a full load of cherries to Traverse City.

I'm quickly learning that Uncle Joe is on a mission to get home as soon as possible. There's nothing slow about his driving; he's a fast accelerator, too. He makes full stops but only for a microsecond at stop signs. When he turns, we have to hold onto something fixed in the back of the pickup or be tossed around by the force of the vehicle's changing direction.

I'm working hard to get comfortable for the long trip ahead of us. Where is the best place to sit? What's the best way to sit? How can we eliminate the annoying exhaust fumes coming into the back of the pickup? How can I hear Junior or Decky better when they're trying to talk to me over the competing sounds of the truck engine, the wind hitting the truck, and the traffic around us? Decky tries different methods to block the exhaust from coming in, but nothing seems to work. I search for a spot with some fresh air coming into the back. I find a place; it's not ideal, but it will have to do.

Uncle Joe stops at the M-22 intersection and makes a right turn. On the other side of West Grand Traverse Bay, I admire the sight of the cherry orchards dotting the peninsula's hills. As we near downtown Suttons Bay, I position myself for the best view of people-watching. Uncle Joe is driving slowly due to the traffic ahead. Decky, Junior, and I don't mind; we now have a few extra moments to observe the pretty girls at the ice cream shop. We spot several girls enjoying their ice cream. They are cute, but my thoughts are on Lety. Some vehicles passing through town have Texas plates; I suspect they belong to other farmworkers.

Decky and Junior want to play the "Slug Bug" game. The first person to spot a Volkswagen Beetle in this game yells, "Slug Bug." That person then punches all the other players on their arms. The only way you don't get slugged is if you say "Slug Bug Detour" before the person who sees the Volkswagen can finish saying "Slug Bug." Decky is the first to see one and shouts, "Slug Bug." Immediately, he punches us in the upper arm. It hurts. Decky never holds back on the force of his punches. I had better stay focused on spotting any Volkswagen Beetles.

As we travel through Suttons Bay to Traverse City, we pass the last cherry orchards until we reach Acme, heading toward Kalkaska. Some orchards have been harvested, while others are filled with sweet and tart cherries. We spot a farm camp with several children playing outside. A few young men sit in lawn chairs in front of the farmworker dwellings. Nearby, cars and trucks with Texas license plates are parked. Just beyond the farm camp is the Suttons Bay Processing Plant, where all local cherry growers send their cherries to market. Cherries spill on the road, having fallen off trucks turning into the processing plant. Cherry spills are often seen at road intersections where trucks loaded with cherries make turns. Mile by mile, the signs of cherry-related activity diminish, although I notice several vehicles with Texas plates parked at small roadside parks along M-22.

As we approach the section of M-22, where numerous houses along the bay block the view, I try to catch as many glimpses of the bay as possible. I see sailboats and skiers riding behind motorboats and people on jet skis savoring their Sunday afternoons. Junior spots a Beetle, shouts, "Slug Bug," and punches Decky and me in the arm.

As expected, traffic is heavy and slowing us down at Greilickville. We don't mind, though, because it gives us more time to admire the yachts and other boats at the harbor. We're busy pointing out which ones we think are cool to each other. There's an increase in farmworker traffic at the intersection leading to Empire. Thousands of cherry orchards stretch west of Greilickville and beyond.

Beyond the intersection of Empire and Sleeping Bear Dunes, we enter Traverse City. The beach at the bottom of the bay is bustling with people and activity. Some are sunbathing, some are in the lake, some are lounging in lawn chairs, others are tossing Frisbees, and many are walking, running, or biking along the sidewalk. A guy on a jet ski, wearing sunglasses, is checking out the beach, likely admiring all the pretty girls in their bikinis. Goodbye, beaches.

Downtown Traverse City is bustling with people walking around and enjoying the restaurants, shops, and bars. We have a red light near Clinch Park. Beside us is a new red Corvette with its top down, occupied by a handsome young couple. From the car's radio, we hear loud and clear, "Sweet Caroline" by Neil Diamond.

How many cool cars are we spotting in Traverse City? Firebirds and Camaros are everywhere, along with Road Runners, Chargers, GTOs, 442s, Corvettes, and Malibus, to name a few. Seeing these awesome cars around me distracts me from my deeper thoughts.

On we go, inching through the chaotic Traverse City traffic. The congestion comes to a complete stop at the intersection leading to Old Mission Peninsula. Many vehicles with Texas plates are here, either arriving from or heading to Old Mission Peninsula. Luis is somewhere up there. I wonder how he's doing. I can't wait to share my experience with him. Decky spots another 'Bug, and I get another bruise from him.

The state park is coming up soon. We all know this is another spot to see pretty girls. Decky points out a few cute girls he notices walking in the park. While he's pointing them out, I spot my first Volkswagen Beetle parked inside the state park and take pleasure in punching Decky and Junior in the arm. After giving Decky and Junior a smack and relishing the moment, I tell them I'm done playing the game; my mind is focused on other things.

Before we get to Acme, I can see the East Grand Traverse Bay, with no houses or hotels blocking my view. This is the last view of Lake Michigan.

At the Acme traffic light, we turn right onto M-72, heading toward Kalkaska. A few vehicles with Texas license plates head in the opposite direction, including a two-axle hawny truck with a green tarp in the back. On the roadside, there's a stand with a small sign that says, "Cherries." Several cars and people are at the stand buying cherries.

Piece by piece, my cherry world is coming to an end. I have to accept that there is a season for everything, as it says in Ecclesiastes in the Bible. Even the rock group The Byrds has a song about the turning of the seasons. The season for hand-picked cherry harvesting is giving way to mechanized methods. Farmworkers are losing jobs, while farmers are seeing higher profits. That's just how business works.

I'm becoming very concerned about these fumes. They're starting to give me a slight headache. What worries me most is what I can't smell: carbon monoxide. Breathing in carbon monoxide can be deadly. I've heard of deer hunters who have died in their sleep, unknowingly overcome by carbon monoxide from their cabin heaters. Knowing this makes me anxious to nap, even though I feel like I need one. Isn't feeling drowsy a symptom of carbon monoxide poisoning?

We find little interest in the scenery as we drive through the forest-covered terrain on our way to Kalkaska. Eventually, we withdraw and become absorbed in our mental worlds.

I begin to think about what Jim told me, and it hurt. Back in sixth grade, Jim and I were walking home from school. I was lost in the warmth and beauty of the day. When I looked at Jim, I noticed a strange grin as he abruptly asked me why there were no stories in the school books about "your kind of people." The grin on his face seemed to imply that people like me aren't important in the USA. The hurt felt like colliding head-on with a hawny truck. Anger ran through my veins, and I was in disbelief. Although Jim is one of my best friends, he occasionally reveals a mean streak, almost like Doctor Jekyll and Mr. Hyde. I don't know if he meant to hurt me, but it sure felt like it at the time. I was speechless and didn't know how to respond. His provocative question about why Americans of Mexican descent are not represented in school books settled deep in my mind. I've often wondered the same myself. I never showed him how much his remark hurt me. In the long run, Jim's comment only strengthened my determination to attend college.

I then think of my early childhood. The reading classes used the Dick and Jane series. I enjoyed reading the stories and looking at the colorful pictures. Still, I felt a certain sadness that Americans like me, who are not White, were neglected in the storylines of the different Dick and Jane books and in the other story books we read. One of the first things I would do when the new school year started was check the books assigned to me to see if there was anything about Mexican Americans. I never found anything in elementary school.

I think back to when I talked with Cousin Rebeca Acevedo about my desire to attend college. She laughed and said that college was only for White people. I was amazed that she could think such a thing.

I think of the changes that are happening. In my government class, I studied Martin Luther King Jr. and his "I Have a Dream" speech. I learned more about segregation, what happened in Selma, Alabama, and the Civil Rights movement across the USA. Two years ago, Detroit experienced many riots due to poor race relations. Cesar Chavez is leading farmworkers to unite under the United Farm

Workers Union of America to fight for better wages, working conditions, and living conditions.

People are getting organized. I'm learning about the Black, Brown, and Chicano Power movements. These groups fight for respect and dignity for minority groups in the United States.

Many younger Mexican Americans are beginning to identify as Chicano or Chicana. I like the term and use it with my Mexican American peers, but not with older Mexican Americans. Mom and Dad don't want to be called Chicanos, and neither do many other older Mexican Americans.

It makes me feel good that America is waking up to the fact that there are many different types of Americans, not just White ones. We are neither better nor worse than any other American. I know I am valuable. I know God made me. I have a brain and manage just fine. I recognize my worth. I see the worth in my people. I'm hearing about college opportunities for low-income students, and I want to seize this chance. Learning about this fills me with hope for a better future for myself and my family. I want my people represented in American history and other books. I want to see my people achieve their own American Dreams.

We enter Kalkaska, and I set my thoughts aside for a while. I haven't seen much in Kalkaska that catches my interest. I spot a cherry stand at the other end of town, where the road turns for Grayling. As expected, the price for cherries displayed on the sign is higher than what I saw in Acme.

When we approach Grayling, we come to life. We see army trucks and jeeps on the road and in town. Junior, Decky, and I have played army countless times. The town's ice cream shop has numerous customers, including several groups of cute girls. We pass by the fighter jet displayed at the side of the American Legion post. Decky, Junior, and I have talked about this jet for years but have never seen it together. Experiencing it together is a highlight for all of us.

South of Clare, the green forests turn into healthy corn, bean, and sugar beet fields. The hills become flat land. We're almost home.

I can't wait to get out of this truck. How many brain cells have I lost from inhaling these awful fumes? I need to pee, and this headache is such a pain!

Joe Hernandez must have been in the living room because as soon as Uncle Joe parked in front of the house, he was out the door, standing on the porch to see who had just pulled up. He doesn't know Uncle Joe, so he is confused when he sees him get out of the truck. When Joe sees Junior and me get out of the back, he immediately greets us all. Bruno is still in the house, barking. He knows something exciting is happening. Joe opens the door, and Bruno instantly runs to Junior, who is already on his knees, ready to receive Bruno's slobbery kisses on his face. I introduce Joe to Uncle Joe and Decky. Decky and I then rush inside to use the bathrooms. I'm about to explode. As soon as we finish using the bathrooms, Uncle Joe and Junior take their turns. To save time, Joe unloads Junior's things while I unload mine, and we chat. I take all my stuff to the boys' bedroom and rejoin everyone outside.

It feels great to stretch my legs and body while breathing in fresh air. However, I feel groggy, and my brain feels like it's filled with cobwebs. I'm sure it's due to the toxic fumes I've been breathing for the past two and a half hours.

Uncle Joe and Decky are ready to leave. I notice Quieta Girl on the west side of the tall, stocky spruce tree beside our house as Junior and I say our hearty farewells to Decky and Uncle Joe. I'm confident we'll see Decky within three months when we go to Ohio. We wave at Uncle Joe and Decky until they are out of sight, driving away on their three-hour trip home. I had such a fantastic time with Decky. Upon seeing Decky leave, I feel that my vacation has now come to an end.

I can now read Lety's letter. I go upstairs to the boy's bedroom and sit on my bed for privacy. As usual, the room is hot and there is no air movement. I take a whiff of the scented letter and open it.

Dear Robert, I'm sad to see you go. Yes, we will be here for another week or until the cherry season ends, and then we'll head back home to McAllen. I'm glad we met and got to do some things together. I know your cousins Marti and Ana would always tease you, but they told me you're a really nice guy. My parents, as you know, are a bit protective of me. I'm happy that I met you. I like you a lot, too! You're a lot of fun, handsome, and cool. You made my time in Michigan picking cherries fun. You have pretty eyes and eyelashes. If you ever get a chance, come and visit me in McAllen. You said you have relatives in the Valley, right? Come and visit them, and when you do, you'd better see me too. I can't wait to tell my girlfriends back home about you. I want a picture of you, too. So, when you take your school pictures, please send me one as soon as possible.

Lety,
PS: I will never forget you!
Leticia Gamboa, 1207 N 19 ½ Street, McAllen, Texas 78501

My heart jumps for joy as I read Lety's letter. All the heartache of leaving Lake Leelanau fades away. A huge, warm smile spreads across my face. I feel as if a princess has spoken to me. My heart and spirit are joyful and full of delight. She likes me a lot! She thinks I'm handsome, fun, and cool. I knew she had feelings for me. I'll always treasure this letter.

Joe and I chat while we wait for Mom and Dad to arrive. Jim hasn't shown up yet. Joe mentions that nothing exciting happened while we were away, but he's eager to hear about our experiences. I take Lety's letter from my back pocket and inhale its scent as I share some highlights from the trip with Joe.

Mom and Dad arrive half an hour later. It took them longer to get home because they stopped at a rest stop to use the bathroom and for Dad to take a short coffee break at one of the picnic tables. Timmy gets out of the truck with sleepy eyes, while Sandy and Tito are fully awake and jump out of the back of the pickup. I'm glad they made it home safely. Mom says it's too late to attend the evening church service because of the time. We very rarely miss the evening service.

Junior and I help Dad unload the pickup and bring things into the house and garage. Jim rides his bike to our place, and we smile at each other. I tell him I won't be free for a while and will come to his house when I finish my chores. I carry three lugs of cherries to the back room, located between the garage and the house, and set them on the workbench. Above the bench, on the wooden shelf, sits an empty cherry lug that once held cherries we brought home from another year. Back and forth I go, carrying lugs to the back room and snacking on a few as I move. We transport a couple of boxes and the ice chest to the kitchen, take Mom and Dad's bags of clothes to their room, bring the tent to the garage, and carry all the sleeping gear to the bedrooms and other heavy items. I take all my things upstairs to the bedroom and sit on the bed for a few seconds; it feels so soft and inviting.

I take all my dirty clothes to the hamper by the washing machine, except for the shirt and pants I last wore when picking. They smell of pesticide, and that scent takes me back to the orchards. I want to enjoy this smell for as long as I can. I wrap them in a plastic bag that is as airtight as possible and place it on the floor of the boy's bedroom closet. Every day, I will open the bag and take a deep breath to get a whiff of Cherryland.

It's time to relax. All the chores are finished. We had a quick and easy dinner of bologna sandwiches and chips from NJ's in Lake Leelanau. Joe and Dad are sitting in the kitchen, drinking coffee and enjoying a coffee cake purchased from NJ's. Mom and Sandy are busy cleaning the kitchen and putting away things from the trip.

We can now hang out with Jim. I run to Jim's house to let him know we're free. When we return to the house, I show Jim the cherries in the back room. He's amazed to see three lugs of cherries. I also show him the fossil rocks I brought back and give him one of them. A big smile spreads across his face. Jim joins Junior, sitting in one of the lawn chairs in the backyard under the willow tree, while I go inside. From the kitchen, I grab a bowl and some cherries from the back room. After washing them, I meet up with Jim and Junior. Jim's eyes light up when he sees the plump, dark purple sweet cherries in the bowl. His eyes widen after tasting the first ones. As we enjoy the cherries, Jim tells us that nothing happened while we were gone.

Jim is interested in hearing about our trip. Junior and I excitedly share all the cool things we did and saw with Jim. He listens patiently to our stories, asking questions while enjoying the sweet black cherries. He's always been a great listener. As I share my stories, Bruno climbs the willow tree at Junior's command. The tree's trunk is huge, about six feet in diameter. It splits into two large trunks around four feet up. In the background, the crickets and katydids in the little woods play their instruments at a high volume as we share our stories with Jim.

I tell him about the guy on the motorcycle with long hair and a Nicaraguan license plate, all the army jeeps, trucks, soldiers, and the jet in Grayling.

Junior and I share stories about the pretty girls and cool cars we saw during our trip. We tell him about our clubhouse and the fun we had there. We talk about Jaime, Moi, and Decky, and swimming in Lake Leelanau. We share stories about the picnics, Lake Leelanau, Traverse City, the cherry orchards, the tedious work of picking cherries, the orchard tractors, the hawny trucks, the cool farms, barns, the tire swing, and the church services held in the barn. Jim is amazed to learn that church services were held in a barn.

We talk about the creepy woods, the military chest, the fossils, the drag race, the cold showers, and sleeping in the tent. Junior brings up that I had a girlfriend, too. Jim's eyes light up, eager to hear more about that. It's around 10 pm, and it's too late to share everything I'd like to tell him about Lety. We could talk and hang out all night, but I'm exhausted and feel like I'll sleep well in my cozy bed. We say goodnight to Jim and head inside.

It's time to get to bed. Before I do, I walk to the closet to smell the pesticide on my work pants. The scent immediately takes me to Cherryland. Junior is already in bed. We exchange our good nights. Bruno is on the floor next to Junior. Tito is fast asleep. Even though the rotating fan is on, the air is still hot and muggy. I don't mind. It feels so good to be in my soft and comfortable bed.

Within seconds of getting into bed and closing my eyes, my mind's eye brings up hundreds of images. Thoughts and sounds race through my head; some linger longer than others. I see trucks loaded with cherries—hawny trucks with green canvas and Texas plates, the view of Lake Leelanau, Lake Michigan, and cherry orchards from the top of a ladder, along with Decky, Moi, Jaime, and Junior in the clubhouse, sitting on cherry lugs and having a good time. Images of the poor porcupine killed by my cousins and the cherry shaker machine flash across my mind. I try to avoid sorrowful thoughts. Lety's image appears and immediately brings me peace. I see cherries up close, in large clusters, cherry trees heavy with fruit, and countless cherry orchards. I picture Lety and me hugging, Sunday school class, and church services in the barn. I recall moments with the guys at the chicken coop clubhouse, the tractor moving through the orchard, picking up cherry lugs, images of Lake Leelanau beach, the chilly refreshing water, and back to images of Lety.

Thoughts of the delicious Mexican food I enjoyed and the coins Grandpa and Grandma gave me come to mind. The unsettling thought of possibly never returning to pick cherries crosses my mind, followed by pleasant memories of Lety and me gazing at the stars and sharing ice cream outside NJ's Store. An image flashes by of the first time I saw Lety, and the beautiful eyes and lovely smile she gave me when our eyes first locked. This memory is so vivid. She wears well-fitting blue jeans, a flowing white top, and a lovely white ribbon tied around her ponytail. The notes she sent me quickly flash on my mental screen. I want to keep seeing these vivid images. I never want them to fade from my memory, but I must go to sleep. Thank you, God, for bringing us home safely. Thank you for everything I learned, the people I met, the fun I had, and the experiences I had. Amen.

MONDAY, 4 AUGUST 1969

As soon as I wake up, I open the bag in the closet and catch the scent of cherry pesticide from my soiled work clothes. Instantly, my mind takes me back to Cherryland. I wonder how Moi and Jaime are doing. I wonder how Lety is doing. How I wish I were there.

As we savor a bowl of clean, chilled black cherries, I share more stories with Jim about our experiences and Lety. I'm unsure if Jim enjoys the cherries he's eating more than the stories I tell, but it doesn't matter; I'm happy to share my stories.

After spending time with Jim, I help Mom wash the three lugs of cherries. I then put many sweet cherries in the bottom drawer of the refrigerator for everyone to enjoy—there's nothing like the flavor of ripe, fresh, and chilled cherries.

TUESDAY, 5 AUGUST 1969

Sandy and I help Mom pit the tart cherries she will use to make two pies. One pie is for Dad, and the other is for us kids. The rest of the tart cherries will be canned and used throughout the year.

SATURDAY, 9 AUGUST 1969

Mom got the pictures from our vacation back from the store. Only a few turned out, while the rest were overexposed. I feel sad because we have very few photographic memories of our time in Lake Leelanau this year.

SUNDAY, 10 AUGUST 1969

Luis is back from picking cherries. I visit his house to see how he's doing and to share our cherry-picking experiences. Luis tells me that his living conditions were nothing like ours. Due to a lack of space, his parents and the young twins, Barbara and Valerie, had to sleep in the car. The rest of the large family slept on the floor of an old, dilapidated house with large holes and boards missing on the walls that offered views of the outside world. While staying in the run-down house, Luis and his family had to put up with mosquitoes at night while trying to sleep. Only when the nighttime temperature dropped did the mosquitoes go away.

TUESDAY, 12 AUGUST 1969

Aunt Chacha and her family make an unannounced stop at our house before heading to Archbold. I see their 1957 Pontiac Star Chief coming down our street. I love it when they visit. They usually bring us a lug of cherries. Aunt Chacha steps out of the car and greets me warmly. Raquel, Rebecca, Abel, Tonina, and Cheque also climb out. Aunt Chacha tells me she has a lug of tart cherries in the back seat and asks me to bring them into the house.

Aunt Chacha's car is packed to the brim with everything they brought from the Esch Farm. It's amazing how it all fits. When I open the car door, I'm pleasantly overwhelmed by the scent of cherry pesticide, which instantly takes me to Cherryland! A flood of vacation memories rushes through my mind: Lety, the orchards, the clubhouse, the beach, and more. In a flash, I recall how Aunt Chacha and her family sometimes stayed overnight with us before heading up north to pick cherries. We kids would end up sleeping on the floor, giving up our beds for the adults. Our cousins would join us, sprawled out on the kitchen, living room, dining room, and bedroom floors. I loved all the chaos and frantic activity that occurred whenever they visited us.

To the kitchen I go, a big grin on my face as I bring in the lug of cherries. I'm the first to eat some of the lovely, fresh cherries. Yum! The cherries arrive at the perfect time because the ones in the refrigerator are almost gone. Mom, Aunt Chacha, and Cousin Raquel are in the kitchen. Aunt Chacha and Mom are preparing dinner for all of us. They're making flour tortillas, refried beans, fideo, and salsa. Cousin Raquel spreads a ripe, soft avocado onto a freshly made tortilla and then rolls it up like a burrito. She wants me to try it. It looks disgusting, but she insists I give it a chance, saying I will like it. Slowly, I chew the tortilla and soft avocado, letting the small pieces linger in my mouth as I savor the taste of something new. I love it! She tells me to finish the burrito, which I do without hesitation.

SATURDAY, 16 AUGUST 1969

It's time to take my dirty pants and shirt to the washer. They no longer smell of cherry pesticide. They no longer remind me of Cherryland.

SUNDAY, 5 OCTOBER 1969

It's now October. A lot has happened since our vacation. The daylily and black-eyed Susan flowers no longer bloom, and the leaves fall from the trees. Unlike the warm summer days, the temperature is now much cooler. I'm back to the sounds of the neighborhood, with frequent trains passing by, their horns blasting a warning to everyone that a train is approaching the intersection. I'm back to the trains switching boxcars for Lobdell Emery, who fills them with Ford pickup truck front metal grilles. I'm back to the sounds from the enormous presses making the grilles, the hissing white noise of the petroleum refinery, and the bright light the refinery produces through the east window in the boy's bedroom. With the curtain open, the room is never dark.

I'm back in my old routine of school, helping Dad clean, going to Royal Rangers on Saturday mornings, and hanging out with Junior, Jim, and Luis. I'm realizing that being in ninth grade (my first year of high school) isn't as dreadful as I once thought it would be. Just as I did when I started Junior High School, I feared the unknown. I'm making new friends and enjoying school.

I've had many thoughts about the vacation and everything that happened during it. As for Lety, I often think about her throughout the day. I've written and received two letters from her. She sent me her school picture, which I keep in my wallet and show all my friends. Everyone says she's so pretty. Her photo helps me remember this wonderful person and gives me hope that we'll see each other again.

On the first day of class, the teacher asked us to share what we had done over the summer. Some students mentioned visiting Yellowstone National Park, Grand Teton National Park, or the Grand Canyon. Another student shared that she went to France. Others discussed camping up north, and some students talked about attending various summer camps. Some participated in cheerleading, sports, church, or music camps like Interlochen and Blue Lakes Music Camp.

As they spoke, sharing what I had done took root. My heart pounded furiously. The fear of wondering if they would laugh at me when they heard what I had done and of speaking in front of the entire class gripped me. I decided that I would not let fear stop me from sharing an experience that is deeply meaningful to me. The desire to share my story grew stronger as more students shared theirs.

I raised my hand to let the teacher know I wanted to share my summer experience. As I spoke, I trembled inside. My heart felt as if it were on the verge of exploding. After talking for two or three minutes, I experienced a strong sense of accomplishment for overcoming my fears. The teacher was impressed, and so were many of the students. They even asked me questions. After class, several students wanted to know more about what I had done. Many told me that my experience sounded cool. Some of them, I am now closer to since telling the class what I did.

Mom and Dad are talking about going to Texas during our Christmas break from school. I'm excited about the possibility. It would be awesome to visit my relatives in the Valley and in Mexico and to see Lety and Jaime.

I reflect on the "Vacation" experience. Everything Dad said came true: we went to the beach, swam, had picnics, camped, and enjoyed the beautiful Michigan outdoors. But how could it be a vacation if we had to work picking cherries for 42 hours? It doesn't matter to me. Our vacation was much more fun, exciting, and memorable than I expected. I also learned a lot and set new goals.

One thing I learned on this vacation surprised me. I didn't think I would explore and participate in the world of romantic relationships. There's so much to learn, but also so much interest.

The vacation inspired me to learn Spanish and explore more of my Mexican heritage, culture, and family history. Recently, Mom has given me several Spanish lessons on the alphabet and the pronunciation of the letters. She plans to use the Spanish Bible to teach me how to read and speak Spanish.

I've set a goal to be less shy. I'm tired of being timid. I'm tired of not expressing my thoughts in group settings or doing what I want in front of others. I'm tired of worrying about what others might think of me. I want to be confident. Even though I dislike the discomfort that comes with adrenaline rushing through my body whenever I'm afraid to take action, I realize that if I push aside that feeling and act on what I want, great rewards await me. I'm spending time with some guys and girls at school who are helping me overcome my shyness. They constantly challenge me to do things that make me uncomfortable.

During this vacation, I've become more confident. I've learned confidence grows by taking chances and stepping outside my comfort zone. Lety is an excellent example. If I hadn't overcome the butterflies in my stomach and the uncomfortable feeling of my heart about to explode with fear of the unknown, I never would have had the confidence to meet her. I've realized that with confidence, I can attract beautiful girls with kind hearts. Also, by being confident, I conquered my fear of opening my eyes underwater, making swimming much more enjoyable and safer.

I've learned that even though I love coming up north to pick cherries, I wouldn't want to make a living as a migrant farmworker. My past short-term experiences picking strawberries and cherries, and this week-long experience, don't even come close to what it's like to do this for a living. I wouldn't want to follow the crops that are harvested throughout the year. I wouldn't want to be away from the comfort of a permanent home like we have now. I wouldn't want to change schools several times during the year. I wouldn't want to be away from my friends. I have a lot of respect for those who do this for a living.

Aunt Chacha, Uncle Ruben, and their family work on farms all year round. They pick fruits and vegetables in the Valley, cotton in northern Texas, strawberries, cherries, apples in Michigan, and tomatoes in northern Ohio.

This vacation has made me want to focus more on getting a good education and going to college. Throughout my life, I've heard teachers emphasize the importance of education and doing well in school for better opportunities in the future, and I believe them. Mom had to leave school at thirteen to help Grandpa care for the family after Grandma passed away, and Dad only completed tenth grade. I'm unsure what to be when I grow up, but I know I need a good education. It seems to me that Mom and Dad constantly struggle to make ends meet. I've experienced living in a cold house during winter because we can't afford to pay the heating bill. I don't want to deal with the constant worry of paying the mortgage, food expenses, water, electricity, gas, car payments, repairs, and other unexpected bills. Despite our financial struggles, Mom and Dad have worked hard to create a better life for us.

I reflect on how the vacation allowed me to be around thousands and thousands of cherries. It's a bit nutty, but I love cherries. I'm a cherry freak. I ate all the cherries I wanted.

I'm glad I wrote down what I did, thought, heard, felt, tasted, smelled, and saw. I don't have to worry that these precious memories will fade over time. Thank you, Mom and Dad, for the opportunity to take a "vacation" that you provided me. I will never forget the time I had at La Cherry Dulce! It was one of the best experiences of my life!

PHOTOGRAPHS

Napoleon (also named Royal Ann or Queen Anne) sweet cherries

Montmorency tart cherries

Filled cherry lug with sweet cherries

Gold sweet cherries

Ulster sweet cherries

Lake Leelanau area cherry orchard

Lake Leelanau area cherry orchard

Dad's siblings—Aunt Esther (center), Aunt Rebeca (left), and
Uncle Eli (right)—during the hoeing season in Ithaca, Michigan, (circa 1946).

From left to right, Aunt Maruca, Uncle
Abran, and Dad are hoeing a field for
Enrique Vasquez, Ithaca, Michigan,
(circa 1947).

From left to right, Uncle Eli, Aunt Rebeca,
and Aunt Esther, In the cherry orchard,
Ted Esch Farm, Leland, Michigan (1946).

Joe and Sara Fuentes (Mom and Dad)
are ready to pick cherries at the
Ted Esch Farm, Leland, Michigan,
(circa early 1950s).

Mom's cousin Esther Martinez from
Saginaw, Michigan, picking cherries at the
Ted Esch Farm, Leland, Michigan,
(circa mid 1950s).

Picking cherries at the Esch Orchard,
Leland, Michigan. Left to right, Aunt
Rebeca, Aunt Chacha, and an unknown
person (1956).

Dad with his 1948 Chevrolet stake truck,
used for hauling cherries for Ted Esch,
Leland, Michigan, and transporting migrant
farmworkers (circa late 1940s to early
1950s).

Reverend Clemente and Eucaria Fuentes
(Grandpa and Grandma Fuentes), early 1950s

The Leelanau Enterprise-Tribune

THURSDAY, AUGUST 17, 1950   PAGE 9

Sundays They Sing the Gospel Songs In Spanish

Here are the Rev. Clemente Fuentes and his flock, ready for Sunday morning services on the Theodore Esch farm in East Leland. The songs are in Spanish, the ritual is that of the Assemblies of God churches.

Mr. Fuentes, whose home is in McAllen, Texas, shepherds a hundred of his church members while they pick cherries here in the county. They come regularly each season.

Enterprise-Tribune Photo

Article from the Leelanau Enterprise-Tribune, August 17, 1950, about Grandpa Fuentes' church at Esch Farm, Leland, Michigan. Used by permission.

adjunto al grupo a la Escuela Dom. en Suttons Bay, Mich

Grandpa Fuentes and several church members are standing in front of the Esch farmhouse in Leland, Michigan. However, the bottom of the photo indicates that it was taken in Suttons Bay, Michigan, during Sunday School in the early 1950s.

Singing church songs at the tomato farm camp in Archbold, Ohio, (circa 1949).

Dad at Esch Farm, Leland, Michigan, during cherry harvest (circa late 1940s).

Dad playing guitar at Esch Farm Leland, Michigan, (circa 1949).

Dad playing accordion at Esch Farm, Leland, Michigan, during the cherry harvest, (circa late 1940s).

The Leelanau Enterprise
and Tribune

LELAND, MICHIGAN   THURSDAY, JULY 23, 1953

And the Cherry Harvest Rolls Right Along

Miss Martha Ramon, left, is one of an estimated 5,000 itinerant workers . . . including Whites, Mexicans and Negroes . . . in Leelanau County for the cherry harvest. The Michigan Employment Security Commission, which made the estimate, says still more are needed.

The picture below was taken Sunday at the Theodore Esch farm in East Leland as the Rev. Clemente Fuentes of Texas, who doubles as picker boss, conducts Sunday School on the lawn for children whose parents are working in East Leland orchards. Music for Sunday School and Church services comes from the two steel guitars and accordion, left. Church is held twice during the week, in addition to Sunday.

This article from the Leelanau Enterprise and Tribune, dated Thursday, July 23, 1953, discusses Aunt Martha picking cherries (above) and Grandpa with some members of his church holding services on the lawn of the Ted Esch Farm in Leland, Michigan (below). Used by permission.

260

Mom picking cherries at Ted Esch Farm in Leland, Michigan, 1967.

From left to right: young Tito, Sandy, Bobby (author), and Junior at a beach on Lake Michigan near Leland, Michigan, 1960.

Spanish Pentecostal Church near Ithaca, Michigan, 1946. Grandpa Fuentes is third from the right, wearing a suit and tie. This is where Mom and Dad met as young teenagers. Enrique Vasquez (far left, leaning against the car) is the man who brought Grandpa and Grandma Fuentes, along with their family, from McAllen, Texas, to work his sugar beet and cucumber fields. The church was later moved to La Curva, outside Alma, Michigan.

Janice and Larry Esch in front lawn of the Esch Farm, circa 1947.

Lake Leelanau is on the left, while Lake Michigan is on the right, as one looks southward from north of Leland, Michigan (photo by Noel Fuentes).

The beach on Lake Michigan, Leland, Michigan.

In the early 1970s, mechanized cherry harvesting replaced the traditional method of hand-picked cherries. This recent photograph shows a cherry shaker in the orchard, ready to harvest cherries at Kolarik Farm in Suttons Bay, Michigan.

Cherry harvesting at Kolarik Farm in Suttons Bay, Michigan, using a cherry shaker machine that vibrates the tree trunk, causing the cherries to drop onto a conveyor belt, which then transfers them into the cherry tank.

A close-up view of the conveyor belt filled with cherries from Kolarik Farm in Suttons Bay, Michigan.

Cherries are put into a tank that holds 1,000 pounds of cherries and 1,000 pounds of water. The water cools the cherries to enhance their freshness (Kolarik Farm, Suttons Bay, Michigan).

ABOUT THE AUTHOR

Robert "Carlos" Fuentes retired from Michigan State University and the U.S. Army and now resides in Lansing, Michigan. He holds a Bachelor of Science degree from Central Michigan University and a Master of Arts from Michigan State University. *The Vacation: A Teenage Migrant Farmworker's Experience Picking Cherries In Michigan* is the first book he has authored. As a migrant farmworker, Carlos has experience picking cherries, strawberries, blueberries, cucumbers, and tomatoes. He has also worked in mechanized cherry harvesting and apple harvesting.

Carlos is an adventurer with a strong sense of curiosity. His passions include history, international travel (35 countries), and inspiring others to pursue their dreams. He is dedicated to service and has created or facilitated numerous group service projects both in the USA and abroad. He enjoys foraging for wild berries and other fruits, and loves being in the orchards during harvest time. He is a huge fan of cherries. Off the record, Carlos enjoys singing Gospel and Neil Diamond songs. Additionally, Carlos is a devoted dancer and will be the first to arrive and the last to leave the dance floor.